ARCHAEOLOGICAL RESOURCE MANAGEMENT

Archaeological resource management (ARM) is the practice of recording, evaluating, preserving for future research and presenting to the
public the material remains of the past. Almost all countries uphold a
set of principles and laws for the preservation and professional management of archaeological remains. This book offers a critical and comparative perspective on the law and professional practices of managing
archaeological remains. Beginning with a global history of ARM, John
Carman provides an overview of legal and professional regulations
governing ARM today. He then turns to consider the main practices
involved in managing archaeological remains: namely, their identification and recording, their evaluation for 'significance', their preservation
and their presentation to the public. As a whole, the book offers an
overview of what ARM 'does' in the world, with implications for understanding the role of archaeology as a contemporary set of practices
that determine how future generations will access material remains of
the past.

John Carman is Senior Lecturer in Heritage Valuation at Ironbridge
International Institute for Cultural Heritage at the University of
Birmingham. His authored works in the field of archaeological
resource management include *Valuing Ancient Things: Archaeology
and Law* (1996), *Archaeology and Heritage* (2002) and *Against Cultural
Property* (2005). He has co-authored *Archaeological Practice in Great
Britain* (2011) and co-edited *Managing Archaeology* (1995), *World
Heritage: Global Challenges, Local Solutions* (2007), *Heritage
Studies: Methods and Approaches* (2009) and *The Oxford Handbook
of Public Archaeology* (2012).

ARCHAEOLOGICAL RESOURCE MANAGEMENT

An International Perspective

JOHN CARMAN

University of Birmingham

CAMBRIDGE
UNIVERSITY PRESS

CAMBRIDGE
UNIVERSITY PRESS

32 Avenue of the Americas, New York, NY 10013-2473, USA

Cambridge University Press is part of the University of Cambridge.

It furthers the University's mission by disseminating knowledge in the pursuit of education, learning and research at the highest international levels of excellence.

www.cambridge.org
Information on this title: www.cambridge.org/9780521602594

© University of Birmingham 2015

First published 2015

Printed in the United States of America

A catalogue record for this publication is available from the British Library.

Library of Congress Cataloguing in Publication Data
Carman, John, 1952–
Archaeological resource management : an international perspective / John Carman
(Dr. John Carman, senior lecturer in heritage valuation, Ironbridge International
Institute for Cultural Heritage, School of History & Cultures, College of Arts & Law,
University of Birmingham, Birmingham, UK).
    pages cm
Includes bibliographical references and index.
ISBN 978-0-521-84168-9 (hardback)
1. Antiquities – Collection and preservation.   2. Antiquities – Collection and
preservation – Government policy.   3. Historic preservation – Management.
4. Historic preservation – Government policy.   5. Antiquities – Collection and
preservation – Law and legislation.   6. Historic preservation – Law and legislation.
7. Historic buildings – Conservation and restoration.   8. Historic sites – Conservation
and restoration.   9. Cultural property – Protection.   I. Title.
CC135.C33   2015
930.1 – dc23
2015020955

ISBN 978-0-521-84168-9 Hardback
ISBN 978-0-521-60259-4 Paperback

For Patricia, as always

CONTENTS

TABLES

The management of the archaeological resource – that is, the globally applicable practices of recording, evaluating, preserving for future research and presenting to the public the material remains of the past – currently employs more professional archaeologists than any other branch of the field worldwide. It is particularly a field of increasing importance in archaeological education: specialist courses in archaeological resource management (ARM), archaeological heritage management (AHM), cultural resource management (CRM), cultural heritage management (CHM) and public archaeology (all synonyms for the same sub-field of archaeology) proliferate in universities across the globe at both the undergraduate and (especially) postgraduate levels. Almost all countries have a system in place, usually grounded in a body of legislation, for the preservation and professional management of archaeological remains. The principles upon which the management of the archaeological resource is conducted are held to be universally valid; accordingly, the basic practices of its management are also similar the world over, although specific local circumstances make for differences in approach to these common functions. Using this fact as a basis on which to start, this book offers a critical approach to the specific professional practices deriving from those agreed principles to outline how archaeological resource management is done under different conditions in different parts of the world and what these practices may mean.

This book is in some ways a companion to my earlier volume *Archaeology and Heritage* (Carman 2002), and the two can be read and used together. Whereas that book took a more 'theoretical' perspective on issues in ARM, this book addresses the common practices of ARM across the globe. In its approach it is perhaps no less 'abstract' than the earlier text – at least, in that it does not aim to offer advice or prescription on how

ARM should be done – but it differs significantly in its structure, focus and
content. Nevertheless, both books derive from teaching aspects of the
management of archaeological remains over a considerable number of
years, and I am sure former students may recognise in this book much
that they were introduced to in lectures and seminars from 2003 (and
indeed before) to the present. The justification for turning this material
into a book is that there currently exists no single text providing a critical
international overview of the functions of archaeological resource management. This book therefore seeks to provide what students of the field
currently lack and to be a source of comparative and hopefully thought-
provoking material for practitioners.

In terms of content, the book begins with an introductory overview
of how the idea of preserving the remains of the past took hold, and
therefore the purposes of preserving ancient objects, sites and places,
emphasising the lack of intent in creating the system that exists today. It
goes on to discuss the more recent developments in the field which have led
to current international accord on archaeological resource management
practices and the role and structure of systems of regulation – both legal and
professional – to be found today. In considering these matters, the book
begins from the assumption that, far from being a 'normal' or 'inevitable' set
of practices, ARM as we know it has a particular form, with a particular
historical trajectory, and originated from very particular historical and
ideological circumstances: what we may see as ARM in the past was in
fact a very different phenomenon, with very different aims and objectives
sustaining it. The second and main part of the book then examines chapter
by chapter the four main functions involved in managing the resource as
they appear in various parts of the globe today: these are the identification
and collection of remains; the assessment of value, importance and significance; the various forms that preservation and conservation of the
archaeological resource may take; and finally the various issues involved
in presenting the material past to a wider public. The book's concerns are
limited to those directly relevant to the management of the resource, and
accordingly it does not attempt to cover all aspects of archaeological
excavation or prospection. A final chapter considers this 'public' face of
contemporary archaeology in its wider global context.

A noticeable omission – except for occasional passing references – will
be any discussion of museums. Although archaeology and museums are
connected in a number of ways – museums are a common repository of
material retrieved from archaeological work, they often employ archaeologists, and archaeological research is frequently conducted out of and

on behalf of museums – they nevertheless represent quite distinct institutions. Archaeology is concerned with the study of the past through its material remains and in consequence with the processes and practices of ARM. Museums are also concerned with the collection, preservation, research and public presentation of materials, but their interests are not limited to the archaeological: many museums are devoted to other disciplines entirely, such as geology, zoology, botany and history; and for others archaeology and related fields are only one among a diversity of concerns. In terms of their recognition as areas of study, museology has a long and distinguished tradition, which has developed a huge and growing dedicated literature; ARM has a shorter period of currency as an area of study and research in its own right and a growing literature separate from that of museum studies. Treating the two areas as distinct is therefore justifiable and also serves to further promote ARM as a distinct discipline.

An overarching theme of the book – sometimes made explicit, and elsewhere running more as a subtext – is that, like it or not, ARM is as much a branch of political activity as it is anything else. The idea of ARM as a tool of 'governance' is one that has been noted especially by Laurajane Smith (2004), but it is also evident in the work of others (e.g., Firth 1995). Clues to the political nature of archaeology abound in its dependence on national law (Cleere 1989, 10; Carman 1996; Soderland 2012; Chapter 3 herein), the role of state agencies and the authority wielded by archaeologists over sites, monuments and objects in exercising their professional status. I shall aim to demonstrate how the practice of ARM represents the exercise of political authority, and to show the consequences of this for archaeology, for archaeological material and for the wider world. Although this represents a critical approach, it is not intended as an unduly negative one. My view is not that practitioners of ARM necessarily intend to be agents of political authority, but that archaeology (like any academic discipline, or any activity authorised and sanctioned by the state) is inevitably a political process. As Michel Foucault once commented (quoted in Dreyfus and Rabinow 1983, 187, my emphasis), 'People know *what* they do; they frequently know *why* they do what they do; but what they don't know is what what they do *does*.' My aim in this book is to go some way to giving readers an idea of what doing ARM does in the world, continuing a trend in my work to encourage matching our rhetoric to our practice. On this basis we can move forward.

How to use this book

As a narrative text that flows in a particular direction, this book is written to be read from beginning to end. However, in recognition of the fact that books such as this are rarely approached in this way, each chapter has the capacity to stand to a large extent alone. I do, however, urge users to read each chapter in its entirety, rather than merely using it as a source of raw information. The book is designed as a critical text in every sense of the term, and there is therefore also an argument contained in each chapter that must be understood in order to appreciate how relevant information is selected and presented. For specific practices or ways of approaching the archaeological resource that do not appear in these pages but which are addressed in the literature deriving from the experience of particular regions, I ask readers to use this text as a way of understanding them in a wider context. I do not expect readers to agree with me in every respect, or even in any: however, it is in their interest that they comprehend what the book is really about.

ACKNOWLEDGEMENTS

As always, no book is the product entirely of its author alone.

I am especially grateful to staff at Cambridge University Press over the course of the years it has taken to see this book into print. I offer special thanks in particular to Simon Whitmore for advice and help in putting the outline of the book together and arranging for its acceptance for publication. I also owe him and Beatrice Rehl gratitude for being understanding when an extension of the delivery date was needed. Asya Graf finally saw the book into publication, for which yet further thanks. I am also grateful to various others at Cambridge for their important roles in editorial and production and to two sets of anonymous referees for insightful comments and very helpful advice.

The book saw its inception and beginning in one institution and its completion in another. I am grateful to several generations of students – undergraduate and postgraduate and, in the case of a few of them, both – at Cambridge University for listening critically but with keen interest to the initial ideas that form the core of this text. To colleagues at Cambridge – particularly Dr Marie Louise Stig Sørensen – I owe a debt of gratitude for a convivial and stimulating working environment for a number of years. To colleagues at Birmingham – including especially those in fields other than my own – I also owe thanks for critical advice, inspiration and ongoing friendship as the book took shape: naming names can be an invidious practice, but I must name here especially Professor Simon Esmonde-Cleary and Drs Andrew Bayliss, Andy Howard, Niall McKeown and Gareth Sears of the former IAA, as well as (now) Professor Megan Brickley. Colleagues elsewhere also, of course, played a part: their evident eagerness to see it in print provided a valuable spur when ideas and understanding faltered.

In July and August 2012 – a period of rebirth for the project of writing after a hiatus – I was very ably assisted by Natasha Fenston, particularly in collecting materials for Chapters 4–7, which form the core of the volume. Tash was a keen, cheerful and convivial assistant who proved to develop a fascination for the topic of the book and did much to rekindle my own interest. For this I owe her much gratitude. I am also especially grateful to those who took the time and effort to read all or parts of the manuscript as it came hot off the printer, namely Patricia Carman, Natasha Fenston and Anna Woodham.

As always, my wife, Patricia, was at my side to see me through those periods when writing became difficult and was there to provide a valuable sounding board for ideas. She too played a role in keeping me on the straight and narrow writing path, and this book would not exist without her urging. I consider it at least as much hers as mine, and so I dedicate it to her.

PART I

HISTORY AND PRINCIPLES

CHAPTER 1

Historical antecedents to archaeological resource management

A definitive – or indeed reasonably complete – history of archaeological resource management (ARM) that goes beyond the specifics of individual territories has yet to be written. So far as broader histories of archaeology are concerned (e.g., Daniel 1978; Daniel and Renfrew 1988; Trigger 1989; 2006; Schnapp 1996), the management and preservation of remains generally form a minor element in a broadly evolutionary intellectual history. ARM appears more prominently in national stories of archaeological endeavour as well as forming the content of more focused research. Useful – albeit brief – overviews often preface discussions of national ARM practice (see, e.g., papers in Cleere 1984a; papers in Pickard 2001b; Pugh-Smith and Samuels 1996, 3–7) and occasionally form complete contributions in others (e.g., Boulting 1976; papers in Hunter 1996; Fowler 1986; Knudson 1986). Where specific papers are written on aspects of the history of ARM, they either tend to focus on particular moments (e.g., Chippindale 1983; Saunders 1983; Twohig 1987; Chapman 1989; Murray 1990; Evans 1994; Firth 1999) or are designed to support a particular view of archaeology (e.g., Carman 1993; Kristiansen 1996).

This chapter and the two that follow do not claim to offer the definitive global history that the field perhaps requires and deserves, but they do hopefully represent the first outlines of what such a history might look like. The history of ARM is interesting: more interesting, perhaps, than previous attempts at partial history have often made it appear. The aim of this chapter is therefore to provide not only a narrative of key moments within the emergence of the ARM idea but also a rough outline of a Foucauldian 'archaeology' (as in Foucault 1970; 1972; 1977) or a Nietzschean genealogy (as in Nietzsche 1899) of the notions that came together to create the global system of ARM that we see today. This is approached from the perspective that ARM as we know it was not necessarily the intention of those who first created mechanisms to preserve objects from the past; indeed, it proceeds from the idea that this is exactly what they did not intend at all.

In contrast to much of the rest of the book – which will focus inevitably on what is common across territorial boundaries in the practice of ARM – this chapter will celebrate the diverse origins of what is now ARM in different countries, under different regimes and at different times. Although organised roughly chronologically – with the earliest instances of ARM-like practices first – it is, more importantly, organised thematically, to show the different ideologies and contexts within which the idea grew, and some of the historical processes that have contributed to its rise. The culminating section of this chapter is not the emergence of a universal ARM, because the emergence of a large measure of global agreement on how we should preserve our material pasts is more properly the topic of the next chapter, which brings us to our own time, but instead consists of one distinctive contribution to the rise of the idea that we should do so. This in turn has become one of the most influential national 'strands' of ARM – one that has contributed much to the field – but it is doubtful that this was intended at the time. This inherent 'nationalism' of the field is itself an important element in ARM as it has developed, and derives directly from its diverse historical origins, but it is still a potent force in the way ARM is practised, despite the global acceptance of common practices and principles.

Speaking of common principles, it can be noted here that general histories of archaeology (e.g., Trigger 1989, 27–31; 2006, 40–48; Barker 1999; Schnapp 1996, 13) often begin by noting that an interest in and reverence for the past are the hallmark of many cultures. These are often described in modern terms, so that re-dedication of a much older statue in fourteenth-century BC Egypt is described as 'one of the oldest references to archaeological practice' (Schnapp and Kristiansen 1999, 3) collections of ancient objects in ancient Babylonia are identified as 'the first museum' (e.g., Woolley 1950, 152–4) or the reconstructions of ancient temples on the site of the original as an exercise in 'antiquarianism' (e.g., Woolley 1982, 233–59; Schnapp 1996, 13–18, 41–2). Of course, these are nothing of the kind (see, e.g., Thomason 2005, 219–20), nor do they have any real affinity with any interest in the past dating from more recent times in the Western world. The collection of objects – ancient or modern – and the marking of them as somehow special are activities carried out within the cognitive frame of a particular time and place. It is always a cultural practice, with all that that implies in terms of cultural specificity, contingency and contextuality: as Evelyn Welch (2005, 4–5) has said in relation to buying and selling in Renaissance Italy, 'far from pinpointing the start of ourselves[, it] challenges rather than reinforces a sense of the linear transfer from past to present'. Whatever Ka Wab, King Nabonid and Princess Bel-Shalti-Nannar were doing with ancient objects (Schnapp and Kristiansen 1999; Woolley 1950; Trigger 1989, 29; 2006, 44), it was an exercise in neither museology nor ARM as we understand them. In particular, none of these acts represents the idea that preserving things from the past is an expected and normal function of political authority, supported by appropriate laws and the establishment of bureaucratic agencies to oversee it, and responsible to the citizenry as a whole; these are, instead, the hallmarks of modern ARM.

Preserving the objects and structures that come to us from the past and making decisions about how we should treat them as things that matter to us collectively is essentially a very modern idea. It is arguably one of the key characteristics of the culture in which we live: rather than being distinguished from previous and subsequent manifestations of culture by the objects we use and discard (e.g., the idea current a few decades ago that future archaeologists would designate us as 'the Coca-Cola culture' because of the ubiquity of that product and its containers), perhaps we shall instead be remembered as the culture that preserved old things (and see Fairclough 2009; Holtorf 2012). It is therefore one of the aims of this chapter to emphasise the peculiar and distinctive nature of that particular obsession of our time and its diverse origins, providing a valuable jolt to commonly held assumptions, one that will prove a useful starting point for further consideration of the ARM field as it presents itself today in the rest of the book.

The areas chosen for consideration here have been selected with some care to illustrate the origins of the elements of ARM that are covered by this book, although other combinations and sequences both are possible and would no doubt be equally enlightening. The elements of ARM of particular concern here are, especially: the grounding of preservation practice in law; systems of recording and inventory; the various types of and approaches to preservation; and issues of access. The earliest examples – late medieval Italy and early modern Scandinavia – show the emergence of the idea of preservation out of a different framework of thought, of understanding and of legitimate authority from our own. Greece and Italy in the nineteenth century represent early – and, in the case of Greece, the first in Europe – examples of the creation of a state-controlled national heritage. Britain was relatively late in the game, in many ways atypical in the field, and other European states might be more indicative of certain processes; but Britain was an Imperial state at the time of discovery of its national heritage, and the idea was not home-grown: instead it derived from the experience of British colonial administrators elsewhere and was transported into Britain from the territories of subject peoples. Finally, the United States and Australia represent encounters with an Indigenous population whose culture was capable in the thought of the time of being treated as part of 'nature', resulting in a number of interesting, if tragic, consequences. The selection of historical examples is therefore highly Euro- and indeed rather Anglocentric, and leaves out of account large parts of the globe. Together, however, they illustrate what are arguably the main processes involved in the development and spread of the idea of preservation of the past. These did not emerge anywhere in the world as a complete package to be handed down to us; rather, they emerged haphazardly in different contexts. It behoves students of ARM to be aware of this in order that we should not fall prey to the belief that our approach to the past is the only one possible and justifiable.

Predecessors: Papal Italy, Scandinavia

In medieval Europe, the ruined past was generally something to treat with suspicion. It represented a degenerate and pagan world, at odds with established biblical authority. Earthen mounds were thought to contain treasure or demons; ruined buildings were unholy and their material ripe for secular reuse. The medieval world view (neatly summed up by Trigger 1989, 31–5, and expanded upon by Schnapp 1996, 80–118) had no need of a distant past: the people of that time imagined themselves to be locked in a present doomed to imminent replacement by divine intervention (but for a slightly more nuanced view see Trigger 2006, 48–51). There were nevertheless occasional attempts to protect ancient structures: as at Rome from 1162, reaffirmed in 1363 (Schnapp 1996, 94), or in England at Glastonbury Abbey in 1194, when the supposed burial place of King Arthur was found by monks rebuilding the great church after a fire.

Despite a general attitude that was disparaging of material from the past, the 'glorious pasts' of ancient Greece and Rome left abundant traces across the landscapes of Europe. The rediscovery of Classical literature – and increasing literacy among the wealthy laity of Italy – provided ample evidence of the superiority of ancient Republican states such as Athens and pre-Imperial Rome, an idea ripe for application in justifying new city polities and secular, non-royal government. The replacement of Gothic art and architecture, with its feudalist overtones and associations, meant the search for inspiration elsewhere, and this was found in the

forms of Classical ruins. Greek and, especially, Roman forms were therefore copied and emulated in the new building of the merchant-prince
rulers of Italian city-states. The political authority of the popes – founded,
as it was, in the Christianity of the late Roman Empire – also found its
expression in Classical forms and their reuse of ancient statuary and
architectural features.

Part of this process was the promulgation of law to preserve ancient
remains: in particular, a law of 1363 protecting ruins in Rome was reaffirmed by Pope Pius II in 1462 and subsequently reaffirmed and recast by
successors. Such regulations concentrated on banning the reuse of monuments for building purposes, and the administrator of antiquities was
dubbed from 1573 the 'Commissioner of Treasures and other Antiquities,
and of Mines' (Schnapp 1996, 123). For Schnapp (1996, 125) there was clear
purpose in this: 'in putting treasures, antiquities and quarrying on the same
level [of control], the papal administration revealed . . . that the control of
antiquities was an instrument of power . . . because antiquities were one
of Rome's resources.' As such, they were a realisable source of wealth as
pre-formed building material (Welch 2005, 279) but could also be considered as in some sense 'natural' since they lay within the soil. Accordingly,
control over their exploitation served to emphasise the authority of the pope
as a secular ruler: the fact that the rulers of Tuscany in 1571 chose to follow
their lead (Pellati 1932, 31, cited in O'Keefe and Prott 1984, 35) should not
come as a surprise. These laws of the popes can claim to be the first efforts to
legislate the protection of ancient remains anywhere in the world, but they
were not really about preserving antiquities. Instead they control access to
pre-cut stone and material to make lime (Welch 2005, 279).

The same is true of Renaissance Italian collections of antiquities from
exploratory excavations. Digging was frequently carried out for the purpose
of creating wealth from their sale, and a market in Roman antiquities was
well established by the early years of the sixteenth century (Welch 2005,
281–3). On the death of the owner, such collections would normally be
broken up and distributed among heirs or sold to settle debts: accordingly,
they were initially seen as just another household object (Welch 2005,
291–2). However, as the value of these collections grew, the idea of keeping
them intact into the future also grew. As Welch (2005, 292) explains it, in
wills 'the language of family honour would become increasingly popular as
testators urged their heirs to respect the integrity of their collections . . . To
the notion that . . . antiquities were "virtuous riches" that demonstrated the
owner's taste and intellectual standing was attached a strong sense of family
obligation.' Where such calls on family duty failed, or were likely to fail, an

alternative was the donation of the collection to the state. These were not, Welch (2005, 294) notes, donations to the city-state or its citizens but efforts to preserve the memory of the donor in the corridors of power: in at least one case, destined for a room in the Ducal Palace that the Doge of Venice would pass on his way to and from his private apartments, this term can be taken quite literally. These 'proto-museums' (as they have been called: Welch 2005, 295) were not about the material of the past as a public good but about the satisfaction of private concerns as to future memory. Where they presage our future – if indeed they do – is in the establishment of a realm of ownership where the concerns of the market do not penetrate (Carman 2005b). But they were neither public collections nor museums as we know them.

It was, however, also during this period that the first systematic surveys of archaeological remains were being carried out. Trigger's 'first archaeologist' Cyriacus of Ancona was a merchant travelling extensively in the late fifteenth century to make drawings and other records of monuments and inscriptions and, crucially for Schnapp in the development of archaeology, taking a critical attitude to interpretation (Trigger 1989, 36; Schnapp 1996, 110). However, the sixteenth century was the time of the first recognisable attempt to identify and record the monuments of Rome. In 1519 the artist Raphael urged on Pope Leo X the project of making full architectural drawings of monuments, comprising external and internal elevations as well as detailed plans (Schnapp 1996, 126), and such plans were subsequently published by a series of individuals: Ligorio in 1533, Marliano in 1534 and Bufalini in 1551 (Schnapp 1996, 341–3), among others. Such was the influence of these works that the idea of seeking out and recording monuments spread to other lands further north: in France, across Germany and to England, where, in newly founded states or where precarious dynasties had become newly established, the primary concern became one of identifying ancient origins (Trigger 1989, 45–52; Schnapp 1996, 133–53). Beyond the narrow confines of Rome the idea of recording ancient features became combined with that of travelling to seek them out: this is a true beginning of the process of inventory.

Scandinavia – divided between two rival kingdoms, Denmark and Sweden, in the sixteenth and seventeenth centuries – was the laboratory where these trends came together to form the earliest instances of ARM as we might recognise it. Johan Bure and his assistants travelled through Sweden in the early seventeenth century collecting runic inscriptions: as tutor to the heir to the throne, Bure had access to all the conveniences and resources of official royal patronage. The same can be said of Bure's Danish contemporary Ole Worm, who was given similar support. The underlying purpose of these surveys was to provide evidence of the antiquity of the Danes or the Swedes, especially their priority over the people of the other state. Without written evidence from the Classics, they had to rely on runic inscriptions and the investigation of landscape monuments. Although it may be too much to claim for Bure's status, as Schnapp (1996, 159) does, that 'Sweden was thus the first state to endow an archaeological service', since Bure's team was not officially an organ of the state, it is nevertheless true that much subsequent ARM practice has been based on that model. The care that was put into the work and the equal concern for publication of results represent aspects of any modern system of inventory. Out of official recognition came also the precursor to a 'national' identity, although at this stage the nationalist ideology of the nineteenth century lay in the future (Hobsbawm 1990), and the service was owed to the monarch rather than to the citizenry.

By contrast with Italy, in Sweden legislation came after the first steps towards inventory rather than preceding it. An edict concerning the protection of antiquities was issued by the Danish king, and, not to be outdone, in 1630 the Swedish monarch published a statute covering Swedish antiquities (Schnapp 1996, 176). The destruction of ancient monuments and relics was expressly forbidden by a Swedish proclamation of 1666, and in 1684 a further decree declared all ancient objects found in the ground to be the property of the Swedish crown (O'Keefe and Prott 1984, 35; Cleere 1989b, 1; Kristiansen 1989, 25). Although not the first preservation legislation, and although the fact of their regular renewal implies a level of ineffectiveness, these are the first laws that seek to place ancient remains under the control of the government and to deny them to private owners. Combined with the simultaneous creation of an Antiquaries College at Uppsala to continue the work begun by Bure and his associates, these laws also represent the earliest creation of an antiquities service as we would recognise it.

Schnapp (1996, 167–77) charts the development of the ordered collection of objects out of the Renaissance 'cabinet of curiosities', culminating in the publication in 1654 of Ole Worm's *Museum Wormianum*, collections from which would go on to form the basis for the Danish Royal Collection (Trigger 1989, 49). Typical of such assemblages, it was an eclectic mixture of the natural and the fashioned. Less typically, at least as published in book form, it was organised in a hierarchy of progression from the less 'designed' to the more: from mineral samples through vegetable material to animal forms. The major contribution comes in the section devoted to made objects, which for Schnapp (1996, 174) represents 'the first general treatise

on archaeological and ethnographic material': it is divided essentially by
the kind of material the object is made from, thus separating objects out not
by assumed function but by form. In developing his *Museum*, Worm largely
prefigured the synthetic work of the modern archaeological scholar, who
sees a programme of research from its inception through the gathering of
data to its analysis and finally to publication.

By the early eighteenth century in Europe three of the key components
of a modern ARM system had, in various places, been invented: legislation
to preserve and protect ancient remains; a service to carry out inventory and
recording; and the publication and public display of results. At this stage
archaeology was not yet professionalised, had to develop many of its now
'standard' techniques and tools and was the province of a few private
individuals rather than of institutions and nations. Archaeological resource
management as it is understood today was thus still a long way off. These
were, in particular, matters for the latter decades of the next century. But
the question remains: if not ARM, what do these efforts at preserving,
recording and legislating the past represent?

In the case of the northern Lutheran countries, it is an exercise deriving
from international rivalry. The context is the declining influence of
Denmark in northern Europe and the rise of Sweden as a major military
power; a wider context is the ongoing conflict between European
Protestant states and Catholic ones, in which both Sweden and Denmark
were involved against Catholic German states and Spain. At the same time,
'in both [countries], the centralizing authority of the Crown was checked
by an ambitious nobility ... [and both were led by] kings who intended by
the encouragement of the merchant and professional classes to subdue the
aristocracy' (Wedgwood 1957, 30). Royal claims on the past can be read in
this context to be an effort to assert the legitimacy of the crown over
nobility, by making a connection with a deeper past: the similarity in
approach in both states may be an example of 'peer polity interaction'
(Renfrew 1986), driven by identical religious and political ideology and
similarity of circumstance. The end result is an effort to 'outdo' each other
in similar fields of endeavour, and the investigation and control of the past
constitute only one of these.

Understanding late medieval and Renaissance Italy is more problematic
from a modern perspective. The nascent nationalism represented by
Scandinavian activity is recognisable from the perspective of the twenty-
first century as something akin to our own efforts. By contrast, the apparent
confusion by popes of archaeological remains with mineral resources is less
easy for us to identify with. It is clearly an exercise in power and control over

material, as in Scandinavia, but here the relations of authority are less similar to those of our own day. The legal controls placed by the popes on ancient remains represent a very different attitude to the material from that of today, and indeed from that of seventeenth-century Scandinavia: we and the Danes and Swedes recognise this material as something deriving from and able to inform us about the past. For fourteenth- and fifteenth-century popes, however, they represent a resource in a more conventional and economic sense: as exploitable building stone which carries with it an aura of authority derived from a 'noble' past on which the papacy makes a direct claim by line of descent. It is in essence a 'royal' claim like that of Scandinavia, but, unlike the latter, made in an assertion not of monarchical authority but of secular power combined with the spiritual. Whereas the Scandinavian kings asserted a collective past for Denmark and Sweden, thus confirming their status, the Roman past was exclusive to the papacy and asserted the popes' direct lines of succession from the days of the Roman Empire.

The emergence of national heritage: Greece, Italy

The proto-nationalism of Scandinavia and some other territories in seventeenth-century Europe was replaced over the course of the nineteenth century by an outbreak of fully fledged nation-building (see, e.g., Anderson 1983; Gellner 1983; Hobsbawm 1990; Hutchinson and Smith 1994). Archaeology – among other disciplines – was deeply implicated in the process since it could provide material on which to base an understanding of 'the nation' as something with a deep past (see, e.g., Atkinson et al. 1996; Díaz-Andreu and Champion 1996; Kohl and Fawcett 1995; Graves-Brown, Jones and Gamble 1996). It was on this basis that nation-states were able to establish national – rather than local, regional or transnational – agencies for archaeological work and to legislate for control of archaeological remains at the national level. The models for this that emerged during the nineteenth century have persisted to our own time as the 'correct' way to do ARM.

The first country to make the point that ancient remains on its soil were the property of the state and not of foreign powers or individual visitors from overseas was Greece, which, on gaining independence from Ottoman rule, immediately passed a law in 1832 preventing the export of ancient remains. Even before achieving statehood, the provisional Greek government had prevented a French excavation at Olympia (O'Keefe and Prott 1984, 36), thus effectively defying its allies. The Greek self-vision was one founded on the belief of a continuity of Hellenism from the Classical age through the Byzantine period to modernity: the fact that the educated citizenry of other European states chose to explore and to enjoy Greece as the source of Western civilisation and to mould their politics on Classical models (at least, as interpreted by them) gave support to this idea. Accordingly, the Greek past – and especially the ancient Greek past – represented the foundation of the modern Greek state. As Mouliou (1996) has argued, it did so in two ways. First, as 'heirs and guardians' of the Classical heritage, Greeks were granted a special place of honour among European nations and were able to claim equality with the citizens of other European powers in their dealings. Second, it provided an idea of '*ethnos*' that could be used to bind together a diverse and fractured mix of populations (Mouliou 1996, 179–80).

The Greek uprising against Turkey had not begun with a unified model of Greek ethnicity that could be offset against a Turkish one. The Orthodox Christian Church, which acted as the binding agent and basis of support for the uprising, was itself supported by a range of different ethnic groupings: Serbs, Romanians, Bulgarians, Vlachs, Orthodox Albanians and Arabs, as well as a loosely defined Greek population. As Gallant points out, any sense of identity in the Balkans prior to the nineteenth century was based on social status as much as on biological descent: 'it was very common for society at the time to label shepherds as "Vlachs", peasant farmers as "Serbs", and merchants as "Greeks" regardless' of other aspects of identity (Gallant 2001, 3). Accordingly, a sense of Hellenic unity and community needed to be created: it was not an organic force awaiting liberation. Basing such a sense of identity on the Classical and Byzantine pasts had a number of advantages: it was an idea that would appeal to the wider European Romantic imagination, thus attracting overseas support for military intervention (which would turn out to be the final arbiter of Greek independence: Gallant 2001, 26); and it offered the citizens of the new state an identity that was older than and different from that of the rulers of the region since the middle ages (western European states from 1204; Ottoman Turkey from the 1400s). To be Greek was to be distinct and to be special, and the mark of that uniqueness was the ancient culture to which Greeks – and only Greeks – could lay direct claim.

This is not to say that Greeks took complete control of their cultural heritage – or indeed of their country – from the 1820s, for a series of international accords established Greece as a protectorate of Western powers and appointed as its head of state a German prince. It was therefore a matter of several decades before the Classical past was fully incorporated into Greek identity. O'Keefe and Prott (1984, 36–7) chart the role of German scholars in the establishment of Greek control over ancient remains: by an agreement in 1874 finds from German excavations at Olympia were to belong to the Greek state; the principle was enshrined in law from 1899, and the relationship of the Greek state to researchers from overseas has remained on this basis ever since. It is perhaps no accident that the 1870s also saw the official recognition of those figures who had led the Greek revolution by celebrations in Athens: despite the bitter disagreements that had divided them in life, the key figure of the Orthodox Church who led the revolt was to be established as a national martyr alongside the figure who had espoused the Classical past as an appropriate model for the new nation (Gallant 2001, 71). The unity of the Classical and Byzantine pasts was thereby granted official sanction.

Italy achieved its independence and unity some three decades later than Greece – in 1861 – and although the rulers of parts of Italy had been early to place a claim on their material cultural heritage (see above), Italy as a modern nation-state was slower to do so. Here the argument was not between the proponents of an ancient and those of a late antique past, but between a prehistoric and a Classical tradition. Guidi, in his discussion of archaeology and Italian nationality, has summed up the unification of Italy into a single state as 'a true "annexation" of the country to the little kingdom of Piedmont' (Guidi 1996, 109) and 'Rome's conquest, [as] in reality an "annexation" of the central and southern region' by the north (Guidi 1996, 111; see also von Henneborg and Ascoli 2001, 7; Riall 2000, 146–7; and Beales and Biagini 2002, 125–6). The fragmented political structure of Italy before unification – into seven pieces, two of which were ruled by Austria – was reflected in the earliest administrative procedures for governing archaeology, whereby under the influence of Classical archaeologists responsibility was divided among twelve regional inspectorates (d'Agostino 1984, 73). A more unitary approach was reflected in Italian prehistory by the 'teoria pigoriniana', which argued that waves of population movement from north to south in the Bronze Age superimposed themselves on the Neolithic populations: in due time, migration of the descendants of the Bronze-Age colonisers crossed the Apennines to create the Villanovan and Latin cultures which came to dominate the Italian peninsula (Guidi 1996, 111–12). Here was a prehistoric model of unification giving long-term legitimacy to what had been a much more contingent (and negotiated) modern political process.

The regional structure for the administration of ancient remains was not supported by a body of national legislation until 1902. In part this was

due to a series of political and constitutional crises, threats to stable government from radical political positions of both Right and Left, and indeed the
alternation of governments from the Right to Left of the political spectrum,
all of which took priority over other issues (Hearder 1990, 198–207; Clark
1984, 119–35). Nevertheless, a programme of social welfare and compulsory
education was introduced under governments of the Left from 1877
(Hearder 1990, 206–7), and from 1896 a programme of industrialisation
took hold (Clark 1984, 119–35). From 1900 the social welfare and development programme of Prime Minister Giolitti, together with an extension of
the franchise, leading in 1911 to universal male suffrage, aimed to further
unite the Italian people. This was the context within which the law of 1902
protecting monuments, and its more developed successors in 1909 and 1912,
came into being. As Gianighian (2001, 186) puts it: 'It is no coincidence that
the law [of 1902] was passed [now: Giolitti's] was a more democratic
government [than those preceding it], and the economic conditions were
more favourable to reform. Giolitti wanted to strengthen the powers of the
central government, by asserting its right to protect public interests against
private ones.' Accordingly, efforts to assert state control over ancient
remains were part of a more general process of centralising the Italian
state and placing controls on private rights: although at odds with an
apparently 'Liberal' agenda, in the case of a society riven by difference
and economic inequality (as Italy in large measure still was: Clark 1984,
177), placing limits on the rights of the wealthy to exploit both their fellow
citizens and the common patrimony may have seemed reasonable.

Accordingly, by the early part of the twentieth century both Greece and
Italy had established more or less centralised state control over their ancient
heritages, at the service of creating national unity through a sense of
national identity. In Greece this overcame the ethnic diversity of a 'poly-
glot' nation; in Italy it overcame a more regionalised diversity. Both were
constructed on convenient myths that could be mobilised to give time-
depth to these identities: in Greece, that of continuity from the ancient
Classical 'Golden Age' through the medieval to the modern; and in Italy a
'wave of conquest' model for prehistory that mirrored the political realities
of Italian unification in 1861. Both of these myths in turn focused on specific
pasts: in Greece, on Classical and Byzantine pasts that could be claimed as
exclusively 'Greek' in nature and origin; and in Italy – at least initially – on a
prehistoric past that could be seen as leading to the glories of the Roman
Empire. Both chose – perhaps inevitably – to exclude any hint of disunity
and later cultural mixing: as newly independent states, they sought to assert
'Greekness' in the one case and 'Italian-ness' in the other, denying the

influence of the Franks and Turks on Greece and of Norman, French, Spanish or Austrian conquerors on Italy. This is not to say that these influences were not evident or important, or even that they were unrecognised, in terms of Greek and Italian culture and politics, but to argue that the sense of being 'Greek' or 'Italian' was founded on a notion of cultural, and indeed racial, purity asserted by the construction of what was deemed to be the 'national' heritage.

The fact that heritages are essentially 'nationalist' constructions is one of the ongoing criticisms of heritage, and commonly recognised in the literature of the field. It is also a problem that the field needs to address: it is not entirely overcome by notions of 'world' heritage or attempts to create transnational (continental or regional) notions of common heritage. The legacy of the nineteenth-century creation of national heritages has, however, been to establish this as the norm for the way in which we treat the heritage, and – as will be seen in subsequent chapters – it persists.

Bringing the Empire home: India, Ireland, Britain

At the same time as newly independent and unified European states were creating their national pasts, British Imperial administrators were encountering the spectacular remains of conquered alien peoples. Although instances of reverence and endeavours to preserve material from the past were evident in Britain from the medieval period and the first attempt at some form of regulation dates from England in 1560 (Boulting 1976), it was not until the late nineteenth century that attempts to create and maintain an archaeological resource as we know it came into being. Whereas in other states – especially Italy and Greece, as outlined above – the driving force lay in the creation of a sense of nationhood where one had not previously existed, in Britain such a sense of identity had already largely been created (Colley 1992; and see Hobsbawm 1990), leaving no perceived need to actively preserve a specifically British material past. A number of factors conspired, however, to bring about a change of attitude: the specifically domestic circumstances have been outlined elsewhere (Carman 1996, 69–91) and will be revisited below; those relating to British foreign relations are exemplified by the interest in British protective measures for monuments shown by the Austro-Hungarian Ambassador to Britain in 1875 (Boulting 1976, 17), the response to which served to reveal the shortcomings of Britain relative to continental neighbours and rivals. It was nevertheless the influence of Empire empire that had the greatest impact.

India

The interest of British colonial administrators in the physical remains of India's past exhibited itself relatively early, with government-sponsored surveys of the antiquities of Mysore and eastern India from 1800. Throughout the later nineteenth century, however, as Thapar (1984, 63–5) makes clear, attitudes to the cultural heritage depended on the whim of individuals: while one governor would arrange for monuments to be surveyed and would prepare for their care and protection, their immediate successor would prepare other plans for dismantlement of that monument and its shipping to the UK. This alternation of concern for the study of monuments and interest in reaping their material benefits continued through several terms of office, despite the establishment of the Archaeological Survey of India in 1861 (Thapar 1984, 64–5; Trigger 1989, 181). This provided for the accurate description and recording of monuments in northern India. In 1866, however, a new Indian government closed the survey, and it was restored only after a further change of government in 1871.

Throughout this time the task of preservation of monuments was kept separate from their recording, to the extent that the survey was not empowered to undertake any measures to conserve monuments. Preservation was only given recognition in 1873, but was still kept separate from survey by making it the responsibility of local governments rather than of central authority. An attempt to make this a central responsibility was refused by the home authorities in 1878 but was successfully adopted, albeit only temporarily, in 1881. This arrangement was then abolished after a three-year trial, but restored again with the appointment of a new head of the survey in 1885. A further period of local responsibility followed after a few years, until the matter was finally resolved in 1900 with the appointment of Lord Curzon as governor-general. Curzon took matters firmly in hand with the creation of a newly constituted Archaeological Survey, organised around five regions or 'Circles' (Thapar 1984, 64–5). In subsequent years the passing of several pieces of legislation saw responsibility for archaeology become increasingly central to administrative concerns and the responsibility pass from regional and local authority to the centre. The creation of an independent federal India saw a redistribution of responsibilities but no loss of official concern for the material past (Thapar 1984, 65).

The story of the development of ARM in India – inevitably more complex and more interesting than this very brief coverage would suggest – reveals something of the attitudes of Britain's political and administrative class to the material past: that it was something in which individuals were interested, rather than being automatically a matter for government. Nevertheless, the idea that government could and should take an interest in such matters is evident from an early date. Efforts to take government control of monuments pre-date similar efforts in Britain by ten years and are more firmly in place than in the home country by a similar amount (see below). The role of individuals should also not be underestimated, as the place of Lord Curzon in British ARM will indicate (see below). Essentially, in the case of Britain, the idea that the material remains of the past should be preserved, and that this is a matter for government, first took firm root in India.

Ireland

Ireland can claim to be the first part of the British Isles to have put legislation in place relating to its ancient monuments, albeit more by accident than design. The 1869 Irish Church Act was passed specifically to disestablish the Irish Anglican Church, but leading Irish antiquarians – especially Lord Talbot de Malahide, of whom more below – pressed strongly for the new law to make provision for historically important redundant places of worship. It did so by providing for the state Office of Works to maintain such sites as National Monuments, with funds diverted from the church (MacRory and Kirwan 2001). The consequence was to provide a model for the state management of the archaeological resource that would become the system in place across the Irish Sea, in mainland Britain.

The concern for preserving religious monuments reflected in many ways an underlying theme of Irish archaeology and its links to a sense of Irish nationality. As Cooney (1996, 152) puts it, 'the vision of a glorious Christian past [as represented by such monuments] was used by national movements ... in the 1830s and 1840s as the basis of an identity that was separate from and the equal (at least) of Britain.' Over the years from its foundation in 1849 to 1890 the Kilkenny Archaeology Society grew from local to national status as the Royal Society of Antiquaries of Ireland (RSAI), and as it grew in status its membership increasingly comprised members of Ireland's other leading cultural organisations, such as the Royal Irish Academy, founded in 1782 (see, e.g., McEwan 2003, 50–67). The primary interests of the society from its inception were in the medieval period, and especially in ecclesiastical sites, but there was always some interest also in prehistoric monuments, as reflected in the associations between members and Augustus Lane Fox Pitt Rivers, who conducted work on sites while stationed in Ireland between 1862 and 1866 (Twohig 1987).

One function of the Irish antiquarian and archaeological societies was to record sites and objects, a function supported for sites by the Ordnance Survey Place-Names and Antiquities Section, the creation of which in the late 1820s was 'based ... on the assumption of a need to recover the past as a basis for Irish identity and to recreate it as a reality for the present' (Cooney 1996, 151). Arguing for the preservation of remains was also a key task, reflected in Pitt Rivers's concern that approximately half of the sites shown on the 1840s' Ordnance Survey maps had since been destroyed (Twohig 1987, 37). Such concerns underpinned Talbot de Malahide's efforts with regard to ecclesiastical sites under the 1869 legislation and the support that bodies such as the (then) Royal Archaeological and Historical Association of Ireland (the intermediate title of the RSAI) gave to John Lubbock's attempts (see below) at legislating the preservation of prehistoric monuments in 1879 (McEwan 2003, 63). In the 1860s the society also made arrangements for the acquisition of portable antiquities by providing payment to finders who then gave them to the society, and by allowing members to sell their own finds through the society museum for a portion of the sale proceeds, thus giving the museum first choice and adding to its own funds (McEwan 2003, 64–5). These measures, although inadequate by modern standards, nevertheless pre-date those in mainland Britain by a decade.

Cooney (1996, 155–7) charts the 'institutionalisation' of archaeology in Ireland from the first university posts in the 1840s through the legislative measures in the nineteenth century to the creation of a specifically Irish law for the newly independent Republic in 1930. In the north of the island – which remained part of the United Kingdom – specific laws to cover the remains of that part of Ireland were promulgated in 1926 and again in 1937, serving to emphasise the political division between the two areas. In Ireland efforts directed at the preservation of ancient remains – as elsewhere in Europe – were closely connected to ideas of national identity and therefore inevitably served the needs of contemporary politics. This created the conditions under which protection would be afforded to Irish remains years earlier than to British ones, and for Irish influence to be a significant factor in Britain.

Britain

The tradition of antiquarian research had its roots deep in mainland Britain by the time the first legislation was passed: from the interest of the medieval monks of Glastonbury in Arthur, through to Stukeley's researches into Druids in the eighteenth century, and on to the origins of 'scientific' excavation by Cunnington and Hoare, among others, in the late eighteenth and early nineteenth centuries (Trigger 1989, 45–8, 61–4, 66–7). While most surveys of efforts to protect ancient remains in Great Britain focus upon the English and sometimes Scottish personnel involved (e.g., Chapman 1989; Murray 1990; Carman 1997), the influence of other parts of the Empire should not be underestimated. The story as conventionally told is relatively straightforward. Leading figures in British prehistoric archaeology – John Lubbock and Augustus Henry Lane Fox Pitt Rivers, in particular – agitated for the preservation of prehistoric monuments to protect them from damage by private landowners. Despite appeals based upon the public merit of offering such sites for the education of the population at large and as a generalised public good, a series of Parliamentary bills were all defeated by the landed interest until Lubbock was able to force a vote in support of a government measure to achieve this. The subsequent legislation of 1881 – although weak – provided a list of sites so protected, and created the position of Inspector of Ancient Monuments, to which Pitt Rivers was appointed and it was through his efforts and willingness to go beyond the limits of the post that the principle of preservation and state-sponsored investigation took hold. Subsequent laws strengthened the principle, giving rise to the legislation currently in place.

The Irish connection

The relationship of between those, on the one hand, who went on to become the leaders of efforts to provide for the preservation of ancient monuments and the promotion of British archaeology and those, on the other, whose primary interest lay in Ireland has generally been treated as an accidental 'footnote' to the story of ARM in Britain (e.g., Chapman 1989). However, there are good reasons to presume that the relationship was not wholly accidental. The first lies in the personal connections to the Irish peerage of key figures in the emergence of British legislation in this area. Contrary to popular imagining, those generally regarded as the first 'scientific' archaeologists in Britain and largely responsible for the first legislation – John Lubbock, Augustus Henry Lane Fox and A. W. Franks – although closely linked to the intellectual elites of their time, were not also attached to the highest echelons of society until later in their careers. Lubbock, who would rise to become Lord Avebury in particular, is frequently represented as a member of the aristocracy from the outset, and Lane Fox (later Pitt Rivers) always as the country gentleman; and the recognised professional status of Franks at the British Museum is taken for granted. In fact, they represented new and rising but not yet established professions: banking (not yet a field with any status and still classed as a 'trade') in the case of Lubbock; the army (not yet professionalised by the Cardew reforms) in that of Pitt Rivers (who, moreover, as an engineer officer lacked the status of field command); and museology and anthropology (terms not yet invented) in that of Franks. As such, they were not yet attached to the highest echelons of society but could create useful connections elsewhere.

One of these was with Irish peers, excluded from the House of Lords and thus also not members of the upper layers of society, who nevertheless largely dominated the London-based learned societies (Chapman 1989). The close connection that Lubbock and others thus established with James Talbot, Baron de Malahide, allowed them to rise through the ranks of relevant organisations. Talbot had been active in the service of archaeological preservation before he took Lubbock, Pitt Rivers, Franks and John Evans (another associated with the application of science to archaeology) under his wing. Raised to the UK peerage in recognition of his service to government, in the late 1850s he had championed the cause of Treasure Trove as a device whereby those with antiquarian interests could gain access to otherwise privately owned material. His attempts at legislation in the area all failed; but after time, and drawing on precedent in Scotland and Ireland, he nevertheless wrung from the government the key concession to grant rewards to finders of Treasure Trove objects so long as the objects themselves went into public collections (see Hill 1936, 239–41; Carman 1996, 49–55; Bland 1996; 2004, 273). Together, Talbot, Lubbock and others sought to establish the importance of studying and preserving British material within the emerging archaeological establishment and to promote its links with anthropology. In these efforts they had limited success, but the entry of Lubbock in to Parliament provided a new opportunity.

Despite early successes as a legislator, Lubbock's several efforts to create laws for the protection of ancient monuments, as mentioned above, all faltered, largely at the hands of landed interest and the lack of support from government. At the same time as this, however, other concerns were dominant in British politics. Among them were questions about the future of Ireland: was it to be incorporated in a fully United Kingdom or given a measure of home rule? Each argument was supported by a different anthropological theory of the make-up of the British population. For

Prime Minister Gladstone, Britain contained four 'nations': the English, the Welsh, the Scots and the Irish. The separation of the Irish from the others by sea indicated to him a case for Irish home rule. The alternative vision, supported by Lubbock and others, saw instead three 'races' in the British Isles, distributed identically through the two main islands of Britain: the Celtic in the west, the Anglo-Saxon in the south and east, and the Norse in the north and east. This indicated that the Irish people were, to all intents and purposes, identical to the rest of the UK population and therefore deserved full integration with them. Accordingly, Lubbock's draft laws on preservation included Ireland in their coverage. By contrast, the legislation he forced on government specifically excluded Ireland from its provisions, and a separate law provided for Ireland.

The impact of Ireland on preservationist efforts in mainland Britain accordingly took three forms. First, it provided influential connections that allowed entry by newer, younger scholars to influential positions within the emerging linked disciplines of archaeology and anthropology. Second, through figures such as Talbot it established the idea of legislating for control over archaeological material and using political position as a counter in achieving disciplinary authority. Third, Ireland provided a context within which cultural battles – especially about the fate of ancient sites – could be meaningfully fought: because the Irish issue mattered, other issues that related to it would matter also. Whether intended or not, the defeat of efforts to legislate for the preservation of ancient remains in both Ireland and the mainland helped the cause of promoting Ireland as a distinct political entity from Great Britain.

The Indian influence

As covered above, preservation of the monuments of India was achieved nearly ten years prior to that for Britain, although later than the accidental protection given to ancient churches in Ireland. As the most important and largest British Imperial possession, India served as the model for governance and the training ground for many future aspirant leaders of the British state. Among these was George Curzon, who after a career as a Conservative Member of Parliament became viceroy of India in 1898, described as a 'proconsular imperialist, notorious for his pomposity and aristocratic hauteur' (Shannon 1976, 481) and 'a man of enormous energy, intelligence and megalomaniacal belief in his own power to rule' (Cohn 1983). Apart from several efforts to create his own expansionist foreign policy independently of the government (both as a private MP and in India), Curzon is notable for developing an interest in the cultural heritage – especially the architectural heritage – of the subcontinent and finally giving permanent status to the Archaeological Survey (see above). Among other indications of this interest are the arrangements for an Imperial 'Durbar' in 1903, at which the new Emperor of India (also king of Great Britain) would be proclaimed. The style of the event reflected Curzon's own aesthetic choices: 'Indo-Saracenic' rather than 'Victorian Feudal' and 'more "Indian" than the assemblage' (Cohn 1983, 208). This was an influence he brought home with him in the early years of the twentieth century.

The Act of 1881 had become defunct during the 1890s, on first the retirement and then the subsequent demise of Pitt Rivers. An Act of 1900, brought in specifically to protect so-called 'Eleanor Crosses' (medieval monuments raised across England to record the passage of Queen Eleanor of Aquitaine to her burial place in the thirteenth century), which were under threat from damage and destruction, extended the scope of protection beyond the specifically named prehistoric remains of the 1881 Act to anything that could be classed as an 'ancient monument'. Further legislation in 1910 created a public right of access to such monuments held in state or local government care. The crisis, of sorts, came in 1912, with the impending sale and removal to the USA of medieval Tattershall Castle, triggering new legislation which consolidated and extended the coverage of the existing laws. This new law was guided through the process by Curzon as the responsible state minister. In accordance with Curzon's own pre-dilection for religious monuments, reflecting the interests he had devel-oped and demonstrated in India, the Act greatly expanded the coverage of the legislation and placed the management of protected monuments on a sounder footing. The law as originally drafted also sought to include ancient churches, in a manner similar to the legislation of 1869 in Ireland. This was resisted, however, by the Church of England, and instead a compromise was achieved whereby the church would manage its own properties in a manner to meet the conditions required by secular law for other historic structures (Carman 1996, 102–5). This Act of 1913 created the system of monumental protection that remained in place in mainland Britain until 1990 (see Chapter 2).

A parallel not generally drawn in the literature of ARM in Britain is between the creation of the Archaeological Survey of India and the equiva-lent bodies for the recording of historic monuments in Britain. In 1908 the first of these Royal Commissions – bodies appointed theoretically under the authority of the monarch and therefore independent of government – were established to record the monuments of England, Wales and Scotland

and to create a national inventory. In 1910–11 the state Office of Works was made officially responsible for the maintenance and management of monuments in state care. Between them these two organisations undertook the same kind of work as the Archaeological Survey in India and other national bodies elsewhere. The coincidence of form and of date is perhaps indicative of the influence being brought to bear: the model applied in India was the model applied in the United Kingdom, brought home by Curzon, now an influential member of government.

The influence of experience in India on the protection of monuments in Britain was twofold. First, it worked to expand the coverage of protection under law beyond that of certain named prehistoric monuments only, to any monument of any period. This allowed protection to be offered to medieval monuments in particular: only the resistance of the church interest prevented this being extended to church property. Second, through the work of the Archaeological Survey of India, it helped to provide a model for the recording and management of sites in Britain. The system thus put in place would remain so – largely unchanged – for most of the twentieth century.

Claiming the wilderness: United States, Australia

India and other parts of Asia were – and were recognised to be – host to ancient civilisations to which conquering Europeans could claim to be heirs and successors. By contrast, the lands of the American and Australian continents appeared empty and devoid of human interference: where such interference was evident, it could be ascribed to 'lost' peoples or civilisations rather than to the existing non-European population. Such attitudes correspond most closely to what Trigger has referred to as 'colonialist' archaeology, defined as 'that which developed either in countries whose native population was wholly replaced or overwhelmed by European settlement or . . . where Europeans remained politically and economically dominant for a considerable period of time' (Trigger 1984, 360). Trigger's review of such archaeologies (Trigger 1984, 360–63) covers, in particular, North America, Australasia and sub-Saharan Africa, but his concern is more with intellectual developments than with the establishment of systems of ARM.

The earliest legislation specifically on cultural remains in the USA dates from 1906, but this post-dates earlier laws which nevertheless impacted on Native American archaeology. Throughout the nineteenth century the world of the Indigenous population was understood to be a world of unchanging ways with little or no evidence of progress or development from the earliest times (Trigger 1984, 361). Accordingly, ethnographic research in the present was used to interpret the past under the assumption that the past was exactly like the present. Where remains suggesting ways of life different from that of the present were encountered – as in the Mississippi and Ohio river basins – they were ascribed to a lost culture of 'Moundbuilders' (Trigger 1984, 361). The climate of belief was therefore one in which the Indigenous populations of North America had made little or no impact on the land and therefore effectively constituted part of the 'natural' environment. This combined with a growing late nineteenth-century concern for America as an arena of natural wonders, and it was no accident that American 'Indians' were included in the coverage of museums of natural history rather than those concerned with cultural aspects.

Since the pre-European heritage of America was felt at this time to be one of nature rather than culture – a wilderness to be tamed by European colonisers – the earliest efforts at protection were directed towards that natural heritage by the creation of the first National Parks. These included places inhabited by Native Americans, and these protective laws therefore also regulated their ways of life there. In the discussions and debates concerning the passage of the 1906 Act and its unsuccessful precursors, a primary concern of objectors was not the preservation of archaeological material as such (a contrast with Lubbock's difficulties in Britain), but the amount of exploitable land it would remove from private ownership (Soderland 2009; 2012). As Laurajane Smith argues for both the USA and Australia, the designation of the material culture of the Indigenous population as 'relics' under such legislation 'reinforced dominant perceptions that Indigenous peoples had either vanished or that they were no longer "real" Indians ... because cultural practices had changed following the depredations of colonization' (Smith 2004, 18). She points out that the regulation of archaeological activity on public land by the Act served at once to professionalise archaeology as a discipline and to reposition Native American material as property of the federal government in a bid to make it part of a collective American history (Smith 2004, 129–30). She goes on (Smith 2004, 130–43) to outline how subsequent legislation and cultural resource management practice in the USA have perpetuated the privileging of scientific archaeological professionalism over other interests, especially claims of Indigenous knowledge, commercial exploitation of land and amateur artefact-hunting.

Smith's analysis continues with a review of Australian legislation. She identifies certain differences between the USA and Australia – that in the

USA the governance of archaeological material mostly operates at the federal level, while in Australia state law prevails, and that legislation in Australia covers all land, regardless of ownership – but nevertheless points out the fundamental similarity: that Australia exhibits the same underlying attitude towards Indigenous cultural material as the USA (Smith 2004, 143–4). In Australia the idea that the territory was devoid of human occupation was enshrined in the concept of *terra nullius*, which declared that no ownership rights existed in Australian land until the advent of European settlers, implying also a completely empty land devoid of human intervention. Legislation on archaeological remains came relatively late to Australia, in the 1950s, despite a long-standing interest in the study of Aboriginal culture; indeed, the first legislation to concern itself directly with such remains was in New South Wales in 1967. This law was entitled the National Parks and Wildlife Act and was concerned to set aside 'primitive areas' that would be safe from damaging activity such as industrial development and mining: an amended version in 1969 provided for all Aboriginal 'relics' to become state property. The implicit association of concepts such as 'wild', 'primitive' and indeed of Indigenous material as automatically a 'relic' is clear, and reflects common attitudes at the time (Smith 2004, 145). Elsewhere in Australia – such as in the state of Victoria in 1972 – the concept of 'relic' was extended to include Aboriginal human remains, relegating them to the status of objects.

In both North America and Australia the attitudes expressed by cultural resource legislation and the treatment of Indigenous peoples they represented led to significant challenges to archaeological authority (Smith 2004, 136–8, 152–4; and see later chapters). Lobbying by Native Americans led to successive amendments to US federal legislation, granting recognition and authority to Native Americans over archaeological remains on Tribal lands. At the same time Native American groups became more vocal in challenging the rights of archaeologists and others to decide the fate of human remains. One result was the passage in 1990 of the Native American Graves Protection and Repatriation Act, which provides for the return to Native American groups who can establish cultural links with the material, objects and human remains from funerary contexts. In Australia challenges to archaeological control over Aboriginal material took a similar turn and resulted again in significant legislative changes. In 1992 a decision in the Mabo court case overturned the concept of *terra nullius*, and subsequent legislation has confirmed the right of Aboriginal Australians to lay claim to land so long as they can demonstrate cultural affiliation (Smith 2004, 25). The debate concerning issues of control is ongoing, but evidence of a developing measure of accord is evident (see, e.g., Carmichael et al. 1994; Davidson et al. 1995; Swidler et al. 1997; Watkins 2012; Chapter 7).

Two key differences from European concerns appear in relation to the 'new worlds' of North America and Australasia so far as archaeological resource management is concerned. Universally in Europe a concern for the preservation of cultural remains pre-dated any effort to protect areas of natural interest (e.g., for Britain, see the timeline, which emphasises the point, in Carman 1996, 99–100), whereas in North America and Australasia it was the natural wonders that first excited interest and, especially, legislative action. The protection and designation of 'natural' areas inevitably included areas where the Indigenous populations lived and accordingly relegated them too to being part of 'nature'. This ideological difference underpins the distinction shared in the USA and Australia between Indigenous 'prehistoric' material and post-colonisation 'historical' remains, one that finds a place only rarely elsewhere. Nevertheless, the model of ARM represented in the USA and largely exported to Australia has become a model which has been adopted across the globe. This is the story to be told in Chapter 2.

Conclusion

Each of these examples, despite their variation in time and place, has highlighted certain common features of which we should be mindful when considering the history of ARM. The first is the importance of cultural context, which has varied considerably over time and across space. It is this which has determined the view taken of ancient remains, whether as sources of building material in late medieval Rome, or the building blocks of political supremacy in seventeenth-century Scandinavia, as the foundations of national identity in the later nineteenth-century Mediterranean or within the British Empire, or as arguments for the colonisation of territory and the conquest of Indigenous inhabitants by incoming people of European stock in 'new worlds'. Accordingly, while many of the current, highly sanctioned, practices of modern ARM were in place from a relatively early period – certainly by the seventeenth century in Italy and northern Europe – they did not represent a true system of ARM because the idea of managing for a generalised good the material of the past was not yet in place. This would emerge in association with the rise of nationalism in the nineteenth century and is most evident in the efforts in Britain, which in turn derive from experience elsewhere.

Nevertheless, a central similarity exists in all these cases. It is the role of law in creating systems for the preservation of ancient remains. While the next chapter will bring the international history of ARM up to date, Chapter 3 will examine the place of laws in ARM and point out some of the factors it is important to consider in relation to them.

CHAPTER 2

The development of current structures

It is clear from Chapter 1 that archaeological resource management does not cover all activities anywhere at any time related to the retrieval, collection, storage and presentation of material from the past. Instead, these activities – however similar in form to those of modern archaeological resource managers – must be understood and appreciated in their own ideological, social, political and economic context. It will also be evident from that chapter that systems of law and regulation are considered central to any system of ARM and that, indeed, they underpin and in many ways can be considered to define the parameters for any ARM system. However, there is more to ARM than a system of laws, as any practitioner can tell you: as a former employer put it to me once, 'There is the law, and then there is the lore.' This chapter will therefore outline how the key elements of ARM have come together in recent years by focusing on three of the areas of practice central to most modern systems of ARM.

The first of these is the rise of professionalism in archaeology. This in turn relates to the role of archaeologists in dealing with threats to the archaeological resource from more invasive systems of land use, such as industrial development, housing provision for larger and more diverse populations, intensive agriculture and the like. The first section will chart the change from 'reactive' systems of rescue and salvage archaeology to more proactive systems. It will also compare developments in anglophone territories with those elsewhere, where the consequences of the ideological differences seen in legal regimes outlined in the next chapter will become evident. A consequence of increasing professionalisation is a concomitant diversity in archaeological specialisms. This is evident in academic archaeology as the differences between 'cultural' archaeologists and archaeological scientists of various kinds (palaeoethnobotanists, archaeozoologists, geoarchaeologists, etc.). It can also be seen in the realm of ARM at the 'gross scale' as a perceived division between 'academics' based primarily in universities and 'field archaeologists' who ply their trade at the service of others, either as agents of government or as private contractors. More particularly in ARM it can be seen in the divisions recognised in the UK between 'contractors', 'consultants' and 'curators' (Schofield et al. 2011, 100–5) – all of whom are largely concerned with mitigating the effects of activities on the archaeological resource – and further in the separation from all of these of 'public' or 'community' archaeologists, known by various names, whose primary interest is in engaging with the wider community they serve (Dalglish 2013; Skeates et al. 2012; Waterton and Watson 2011). These in turn reflect the wider division between 'mainstream' archaeology – concerned with research into the past as a worthwhile endeavour in its own right – and ARM, where decisions about those remains are made. Some of the implications of this divide will also be evident.

The third area for this chapter is also connected to the theme of increasing professionalism in archaeology and largely prefigures the material for Chapters 4 and 5. While these two chapters will examine current practices in the areas of inventory and valuation, the third section of this chapter will outline the developments in thinking about issues of how we value the resource that led us to those practices. An important factor was a recognition of the increasing need to be systematically selective in the way the archaeological resource is managed. A reliance on individual professionals to make appropriate decisions was increasingly replaced by systems of valuation based on particular sets of criteria, promoting and allowing more standardised practices and greater comparability between decisions.

A final section will specifically address one of the central themes of the book: archaeology – and especially ARM – as a political activity. There has been growing recognition over the past two decades that archaeology and politics are inevitably related. Studies of archaeology and nationalism (e.g., Kohl and Fawcett 1995) inevitably focused on ARM as the most politicised sector of archaeology (and see Carman 1993), although studies of archaeological theory have also noted the impact of political concerns (e.g., Ucko 1995). More recent literature has identified the presence of political factors in all aspects of the practice of archaeology (e.g., Hamilakis and Duke 2007) and indeed the role of archaeology in international politics (Luke and Kersel 2013). The relationship between politics and archaeology is inescapable.

It will be clear throughout this chapter that there are clear differences between some parts of the world and others. Anglophone archaeologies (especially in the UK, USA and Australasia) have seen similar – if not identical – developments since the mid-twentieth century. These include the rise of a partially 'privatised' system of archaeological investigation, creating a perceived distinction between longer-term 'academic' research and shorter-term 'commercial' work which is evident in a number of ways. Where the state has more direct control over archaeological work, such distinctions are far less evident. Nevertheless, all parts of the world have seen a shift of focus from responses to threats to a more managed approach which is evident across the globe, albeit at different scales and with take-up rates dependent on local circumstances.

From 'rescue' and 'salvage' to 'management'

> During the mid-1970s . . . archaeologists suddenly awoke to the realization that the discipline had changed dramatically. No longer were granting agencies and universities archaeology's major sources of financial support. Instead, federal agencies . . . state and local governments, and even private industries were funding the lion's share of American archaeology (Schiffer and Gumerman 1977, 1).

This statement of the situation in the USA in the mid-1970s reflects the situation there today and in other parts of the English-speaking world. From the gentlemanly pursuit of the nineteenth century, archaeology had by the later years of the twentieth century been transformed to a profes-sional activity largely funded either by the state or by private industry under systems of development control. For Schiffer and Gumerman (1977, 3) the process in the USA was led by legislation: an Act of 1935 – passed in the context of the Great Depression – authorised the federal government to take steps to preserve 'cultural resources' and led to a series of government-sponsored, large-scale archaeological projects. Further legislation over the next decades required the federal government to take the effect of infrastructure works on archaeology into account and to arrange for mitigation strategies. The National Environmental Protection Act of 1969 placed a concern for archaeological remains at the heart of the planning process, and this was further supported by an Executive Order of 1971 which required federal agencies to co-ordinate their activities in this area and to work effectively towards goals related to trusteeship and stewardship of cultural resources. For Schiffer and Gumerman this represents the end of a frantic period where desperate 'salvage' archaeology would be carried out to extract information from sites before their loss, and the beginning of 'cultural resource management' involving not only investigation but also efforts at mitigating damage, requiring preservation and ultimately 'the least loss of information regarding past lifeways' (Schiffer and Gumerman 1977, 2).

'Salvage' archaeology – or 'rescue', as it is known elsewhere, especially in Europe (Rahtz 1976) – is based on the principles of preservation covered by the discussion in the later sections of Chapter 1. It essentially treats any archaeological site under threat from building work or other activity, whether monumental in the strict sense or not, as if it were nevertheless a kind of monument, a point made expressly for the Netherlands by Willems (1997, 8–9) and for the UK by Carver (1996). The consequence is programmes of investigation – usually by excavation – in order to retrieve as much information about the site as possible before it is destroyed or damaged. The result is a form of 'preservation' as an archive, a collection of reports and publications, also known as 'preservation by record'. As it is classically an archaeological response to the discovery of material without proper prior survey, it is inevitably reactive rather than proactive and is very often carried out with speed and under pressure. It can be criticised for not producing 'good' archaeology and instead producing volumes of 'data' uninformed by a research agenda – hence Schiffer and Gumerman's turn to a 'conservation ethic' (1977) that endeavours to take a longer-term view of the archaeological resource.

Salvage archaeology is typically a response to large-scale development and building work that is perceived as damaging or destroying large amounts of archaeology that would otherwise remain unrecorded. As Lipe (1977, 31) puts it, it should only 'be undertaken as one type of impact mitigation ... after all reasonable alternatives to destroying the site have been explored and when the value to society of the proposed project clearly exceeds the value of keeping the site ... intact'. In the USA, as discussed above, it was born out of large-scale construction and other projects designed to overcome the economic collapse of the post-1929 Depression years. In Europe, and especially in Britain, it was largely a product of the Second World War and immediate post-war activity: military construction during the war years provided scope for prior excavation, and the city-wide clearances attendant on bombing campaigns against civilian targets left areas to be filled with new housing and workplaces. The recognition through the 1950s and into the 1960s that such large-scale remodelling of urban space, together with the rise of highly intensive agricultural practices, the establishment of new woodlands on otherwise open countryside and so on, would have a significant impact on buried archaeology led in the UK to programmes of salvage archaeology in a number of major cities with long pasts – especially London, York and Leicester. Promoted at first by local groups of enthusiasts, this work was seen as distinctive from longer-term 'research' archaeology carried out by university-based academics. The same was true of other territories where the institutional structures involved were different, such as Denmark, where the divide lay between the state service and museums (Kristiansen 1984, 32), and France (Schnapp 1984, 50–51), where it was between national organisation and regional bodies. The increase in rescue work was in many ways the beginning of the perception of a general and permanent divide between 'academic' research archaeology and 'management' archaeology: the one was aimed at sites with a known or assumed capacity to address particular research questions; the other was an effort in crisis management to retrieve 'raw' data from an otherwise unexamined site.

Salvage archaeology was most common as a recourse in territories where large-scale reconstruction was taking place but where the emphasis was more on private enterprise than state control. Where the state was more firmly in the driving seat – although development was as likely to be going ahead – the focus of archaeological authorities was frequently on a more centralised and planned approach. The well-established system of monument protection in India, for instance (as outlined in Chapter 1), tended to focus on exactly that: the concern was for the protection of major monuments from nearby developments and, separately, research and inventory work, rather than salvage excavation (Thapar 1984). In Italy the role of agencies – the Ministerio per i Beni Culturali e Ambientali (MBCA), established in 1975, and the regional *soprintendenze* – has primarily also been that of inventory (see Chapter 4) rather than rescue work (d'Agostino 1984, 78–80). In China (Min 1989; Shen and Chen 2010) the emphasis has been on the protection and preservation of sites discovered during development work rather than on the retrieval of information; during the 1950s, in particular, an attempt at co-ordination of archaeology with development was attempted but clearly impeded development projects. The 1960s saw a shift towards excavation and removal of material before its destruction, and by the 1980s efforts were in place to conduct archaeological investigations prior to destructive activity taking place, something akin to later developments in the UK and the Netherlands (see below). Masson's (1989) review of archaeology in the (then) USSR sings the praises of an 'integrated [development] policy that includes concern for the cultural heritage' and which operates on 'a tripartite progression [of]: conserve – study – use' (Masson 1989, 202). With the fall of the USSR, new laws have placed the emphasis on preservation, with 'rescue' relegated to an extraordinary event (Petrov 2010, 157). Whatever the effectiveness of such systems in practice, the intention in all these territories was to co-ordinate new development with either research into or preservation of the old by ensuring the maximum possible knowledge of the remains of the past. In contrast to salvage work, and whether more successful or not in preserving archaeology either in situ or by record, an attempt was being made at predicting the consequences for remains of other activity.

A key problem that emerged early, and contributed to the search for alternatives to rescue in the anglophone world, was that of the quality of publication resulting from such archaeology. In general, the focus of salvage work would be on the retrieval of information and material from the site as quickly and efficiently as possible, with less focus on its dissemination. The 'marked indifference to standards' in publishing U.S. salvage archaeology commented on by Schiffer and Gumerman (1977, 9) was not restricted to that country. In the UK concerns about the quality of archaeological publication deriving especially from rescue work, and indeed the increasing number of unpublished reports, led to a number of initiatives (Hills and Richards 2006, 311–13). The so-called Frere (DoE 1975) and Cunliffe (1983) reports on archaeological publication sought to specify exactly what material required full academic publication in monograph or journal paper form and what information could be presented in other forms – as microfiche or typescript, for instance. The emergence of the internet has since provided far more opportunities for the dissemination of archaeological material, although most ARM archaeology is still published in paper format, albeit for limited dissemination as 'grey literature' – so called because it is so often contained within grey covers and falls outside the more conventional media for academic publication (and for further discussion of this, see Chapter 4). Such 'grey' material – much maligned in general discourse – provides a valuable basis of research on which to build new syntheses (Bradley 2006).

There is some evidence to suggest that in state-dominated systems of ARM such concerns about publication of rescue work were less common. There is little reference to this topic in the comparative literature of ARM (e.g., Cleere 1984a; 1989; Kobyliński 2001), and national overviews (such as that concerning the Netherlands: Willems et al. 1997) focus primarily on the matters published rather than on what remains unpublished. In part this may reflect an unwillingness on the part of state agencies to confess to failings, however limited and understandable, whereas in a partially privatised system such failings will be clear to observers who are not part of the same organisation. On the other hand, it may also reflect a key difference between state regulation and partial privatisation: in a state-controlled system all aspects of archaeological work will be regulated and – at least officially – provided for, including publication, whereas in the partially privatised systems of the anglophone world those responsible for publication are not those who also rely on them, and emergent weaknesses will be more readily exposed and more widely discussed.

One of the unforeseen strengths of the rise of salvage archaeology across the world was its capacity to create employment. Schiffer and Gumerman refer to the 'depression-stimulated federal archaeology that flourished' under particular legislation and which provided training opportunities for 'many individuals who would later become leaders in the field' (Schiffer and Gumerman 1977, 4; see also Jameson 2004, 28–30). In Australia legislation from the 1960s relating to the preservation of cultural material led to the appointment of government archaeologists across Australia, while other archaeologists established themselves as consultants especially to Indigenous groups in claims over land title. After the recognition of Aboriginal peoples as having prior rights over land, mining companies also employed archaeologists, among other specialists, to co-operate with Indigenous groups over access to resources (Smith and Burke 2007, 9). In the UK in the 1970s and 1980s, the Manpower Services Commission (MSC) – created to provide training and employment opportunities for the long-term unemployed – supplied large numbers of staff for rescue excavations and played a large part in funding such projects by providing the wages for such staff: by the end of its existence the MSC provided almost half of the government funding for archaeology in the UK (Crump 1987). The capacity for rescue work to create employment can be seen too in territories where systems of state-controlled archaeology are in place, as reported on for Denmark (Kristiansen 1984, 32), France (Schnapp 1984, 51), Italy (d'Agostino 1984, 77) and Japan (Tanaka 1984, 83). The economic crisis that has more recently affected the world has, however, seen a marked effect on archaeological employment (Schlanger and Aitchison 2010), and in many countries archaeological work was never very highly paid or respected (see, for the UK, Everill 2007).

In their guide to those seeking archaeological work in Australia, Smith and Burke (2007, xx–xxi) outline the main areas for full-time work as 'universities, museums and government departments' and those for 'casual and temporary work' as consulting. While work in universities will largely comprise teaching with some research, museums will offer a choice between curating particular collections or research, and government departments oversee the work of consultants, who in turn act for developers and others in meeting the requirements of ARM legislation. The same roles are seen in both the UK and USA, although the terminology varies. In the UK the term 'curator' will be applied both to a museum archaeologist responsible for collections and to a local authority or other agency archaeologist responsible for maintaining a register of sites and overseeing the work of contractors. A 'contractor' is an archaeologist (or more usually a commercial firm specialising in archaeological services, referred to as a 'unit') employed by a developer to conduct work in accordance with the requirements of local planning rules. A 'consultant' (*contra* the Australian case) will be an archaeologist who is employed by the developer to advise independently on archaeological matters and frequently to act as intermediary between the curator, contractor and the developer. In the USA agencies such as state authorities, the National Parks Agency and others will employ archaeologists in a role identical to that of the 'curator' in the UK to liaise with, and oversee the work of, contractors working for developers. In state systems the scope for different roles is smaller, although France has also seen the rise of commercial units as well as opportunities in regional and national agencies (Schnapp 1984, 51). The lack of opportunity has been most acute in the countries of the Third World, as documented for Nigeria (Nzewunwa 1984, 106), Togo (Myles 1989, 124–5), Ghana (Myles 1989, 126–7) and the Philippines (Henson 1989, 115), and in countries effectively denied the opportunity to grow by oppressive regimes, such as Bulgaria before 1989 (Gatsov 2001).

The highly reactive nature of traditional salvage archaeology – which typically follows the discovery of archaeological material as a result of construction or other work – is being replaced across the globe by a more 'proactive' approach (see Chapter 6). This seeks to make decisions about the need for archaeological intervention before development work commences, in order to minimise archaeological interference with development projects once they have begun, while still allowing either for necessary investigation to take place or for preservation of the material in situ. The latter option is in theory the one preferred in the UK, where Planning Policy Guideline no. 16 (Department of the Environment 1990, since replaced by several alternatives) came into force more than two decades ago. Its terms specify that significant archaeological material should be left in place and development projects removed elsewhere or redesigned to accommodate it. In practice it has become a device whereby archaeological units may have some time to investigate sites prior to their destruction by construction work, clearly in contrast to Lipe's (1977, 31) strictures quoted earlier (Darvill and Russell 2002). Under such a system of 'preventive archaeology' the likely impact of development projects on archaeological material is required to be taken into account in granting permission for the work to go ahead: this requires that some research – if only into existing archaeological records – be undertaken prior to consent, and may require further work before or during development. Applying the general principle that polluters should pay to redress the harm they cause, the cost of such work is borne by the developer rather than the public purse. Similar principles apply in Japan (Tanaka 1984, 84), the USA and Australia, and are increasingly being introduced into other non-English-speaking territories across the globe (e.g., in France and parts of Africa: Naffé et al. 2008).

An example of a state-controlled service that has moved towards a more managed approach is that of the Netherlands, which saw in 1947 the establishment of a state service for archaeological investigations (Rijkdienst voor det Oudheidkundig Bodemonderzoek, or ROB), whose task was to 'carry out excavations and to document the archaeological heritage' (Willems 1997, 6). Throughout the 1950s and 1960s these largely focused on rescue archaeology related to large-scale reconstruction projects to repair the damage of the Second World War. The work also included larger-scale research projects, and the 1970s saw the first application of systematic archaeological survey (Willems 1997, 9) and an increasing focus on landscapes and settlement patterns at the gross scale, rather than that of the individual site. These, argues Willems (1997, 8), are 'the trademark of ... Dutch archaeology [including] palaeo-ecological investigations and research into the natural landscape and the relations between site and landscape'.

The overall story of archaeological resource management in the years since the Second World War has been of its shift from a focus on monument preservation to short-term 'rescue' excavation of sites on discovery, to longer-term 'management' and 'preventive' approaches comprising the elements to be considered in the next section of this book. Accordingly, ARM is no longer about single, upstanding, spectacular monuments but much more about coping with the threats to more fragile, ephemeral and largely invisible elements that exist within wider landscapes. It takes a longer-term view and seeks to be able to make decisions that can be acted on in advance of actual damage rather than reacting once damage is imminent or has even occurred. This is an ARM that takes further account of the public on whose behalf it works, and the next two sections will consider aspects of this development.

'Public' archaeology as a specialism

Part of the story of the emergence of a recognisable field of ARM has been its gradual separation and distinction from conventional research archaeology. The origins of ARM (as outlined in Chapter 1) made no distinction between the study of the past and efforts at its preservation, or between those involved in either arm of the developing field. This contrasts with the situation today, where the two aspects sit side by side, linked by some common concerns and practices, but for all other purposes (training, career paths, institutional basis and purpose) quite distinct. The previous section has noted the division of constituents of ARM into different roles – curator, contractor and so on. Developing that theme, this section will review the emergence of the division between ARM and other branches of archaeology. It will then go on to consider a further division consequent on this – the separation of a 'public archaeology' proper, concerned with outreach and community engagement, from the wider ARM field.

ARM – otherwise known as 'cultural resource management' in the USA, and more commonly now as 'cultural heritage management' in Australia and elsewhere (Smith and Messenger 2010) – did not emerge from the more general archaeological background until the mid-1970s, as Cleere (1984a, ix) and Renfrew (1983) have indicated. Until then, a concern for the preservation of ancient remains, providing access to them and their interpretation for the wider community and carrying out research into those remains were all seen as part of a (more or less) united but single discipline of archaeology. This was the case in Britain for Lubbock and Pitt Rivers (see Chapter 1); it remained so in 1939 and 1947, when Grahame Clark published the first two editions of his *Archaeology and Society*, which argued the case for active programmes of state-supported archaeological research to build strong nations and educated populations (Clark 1939, 211; 1947, 191; Carman 1993, 44–7; Chapter 8). The change to a separate ARM has been related especially to the emergence of the 'new' or 'processual' school of archaeological theory in the 1960s and 1970s, which has since grown to become the dominant set of approaches in the anglophone world. The proponents of this 'scientific' form of archaeology sought to distance it from any taint of political agendas, including responsibilities to particular communities. As such, ARM archaeology became a matter of applying techniques to retrieve data from material rather than a matter of public engagement at the service of citizenship (Carman 2005b).

The publications that marked the emergence of ARM, although calling it by different names – public archaeology (McGimsey 1972), conservation archaeology (Schiffer and Gumerman 1977), historic preservation (King et al. 1977), CRM (McGimsey and Davis 1977; McKinlay and Jones 1979), rescue archaeology (Rahtz 1976) – all served to emphasise its status as a separate field in its own right. This early literature focused on two areas: justifications for ARM practices and the techniques and methods to be applied. A later explicit concern with ethics (e.g., Green 1984; Vitelli 1996; Scarre and Scarre 2006) represented a shift in emphasis from offering general justifications to the entire archaeological community to offering specific decision-making tools for those working in ARM, one that has since been criticised for its narrowness of approach (Tarlow 2001). As the literature grew, it focused increasingly on narrower concerns: reburial and repatriation issues (Fforde et al. 2002), archaeological tourism (Boniface and Fowler 1993) and contested sites (Chippindale et al. 1990; Carmichael et al. 1994). As Smith (1993, 59) has pointed out, the treatment of certain questions in this way relegates ARM to 'an arena for particular issues' and 'not *necessarily* issues on which the whole of archaeology must engage'. It therefore becomes 'an intellectual "buffer" or barrier between political and cultural issues [on the one hand] and a "pristine" conception of archaeology as an intellectual and "scientific" discipline' on the other. In short, the growth of a separate literature for ARM served 'to create the opinion that [ARM] is separate from archaeology' rather than integral to it (Smith 1993, 59).

The separation of ARM from the rest of the discipline of archaeology has had evident consequences for archaeology, and for ARM in particular. These have not been widely discussed in the literature, since the division is so readily seen as 'normal'. One consequence has been the subdivision of ARM practices into a number of separate roles, as outlined in the previous section: since ARM is itself a separate field of endeavour, it can be conveniently subdivided into constituent parts. This has also allowed a greater subdivision to emerge, as discussed below. A second consequence is that the separation allowed ARM to be dismissed by the academic archaeology community in various ways: as 'applied archaeology' (Embree 1990, 31) that adds nothing to the development of archaeology as a discipline, or as 'a pricing of the past' (Shanks and Tilley 1987, 24) consequent on the adoption of a management role, or as the chosen career of those who prefer unintelligible acronyms for complex technology to doing 'real' archaeology (Binford 1989). Accordingly, in the textbooks of the discipline it has been either not addressed at all or is relegated to separate chapters, unrelated to the remainder of the discussion. At the level of the education and training of archaeologists it is rarely integrated into the curriculum: at some institutions this branch of archaeology will be ignored; at others it is treated separately. A third consequence – partly deriving from the second – was the emergence of quite separate discourses between research archaeology and ARM, together with separate loci for those discourses to take place. Each area would usually have its own range of conferences and colloquia; where they share the same venue – as at meetings of the World Archaeological Congress, the European Association of Archaeologists, the Society for American Archaeology and others – they would nevertheless comprise separate sessions, frequently within entirely separate sub-themes. Opportunities for integration – and the willingness to take them – although growing (see Chapter 8), are rare, and when taken, less likely to attract participation than to limit it. It is still quite possible for an archaeologist to attend many conferences over a career and, as an ARM specialist, never encounter an academic researcher, and vice versa.

Despite the title of McGimsey's (1972) key publication on *Public Archaeology*, his book was less about the interpretation of sites, as might have been expected, than about the standard components of ARM practice: laws, organisation and preservation practices. However, over past decades, and despite the use of the term 'public archaeology' to mean different things to different people, the preservation and management of archaeological resources have separated from their sister-service of engagement with the public that archaeologists serve, to allow the emergence of a public archaeology 'proper' – one specifically concerned with issues of public interpretation, outreach and education. What follows will outline this shift in emphasis and some of its implications, while Chapter 7 will examine the current practices of public engagement in more detail.

The history of archaeology's engagement with a wider public goes back to the origins of the field. In late nineteenth-century Britain, Pitt Rivers established his museum at Farnham to educate the workers on his estate into the inevitability of change through evolution rather than by revolutionary means, an aim (or at least an approach) that persists in the Pitt Rivers Museum in Oxford (Hudson 1987). At this period – and indeed earlier – the distinction between a concern for the protection of ancient remains and providing public access to them did not yet exist: preservation inevitably allowed access, while the provision of public access justified efforts at preservation. Jameson (2004) charts the rise of two distinct public archaeologies in the USA: from the pioneering work of Jefferson in promoting the heritage of Virginia, through the involvement of state and federal institutions in studying America's past, to an increasing focus on preservation and the ultimate dominance of the latter in federal programmes. He argues that it was theoretical debates about interpretation among

archaeologists themselves – academic and professional – that led to a
revived interest in public engagement in the 1980s. In the same volume
Frost (2004) outlines the range of public education programmes in archaeology that have developed in the USA over the past two decades, and
Copeland (2004, 132–3) does the same for Britain.

Merriman (2004a, 3) also outlines the distinction that emerged between
public archaeology as archaeology on behalf of the wider community and as
engagement with the members of that community: 'public archaeology ...
relied upon public support in order to convince [decision-makers] that
archaeological sites needed protection or mitigation'. On this basis the
case has been made by Cleere (1984b, 61–2; 1984c, 128) and McGimsey
(1984), among others, for programmes of public education, and it is as public
education that so much public archaeology 'proper' is seen in the anglophone world. Both Jameson (2004) and Frost (2004) discuss it in these terms
in Merriman's (2004b) edited volume on the subject, and the US-based
Society for Historical Archaeology (SHA) and Society for American
Archaeology (SAA) each delegate consideration of such issues to a Public
Education and Interpretation Committee and a Public Education
Committee, respectively. Such an approach, drawing on wider debates on
the public appreciation of science, has been called by Merriman (2004a,
5–6) the 'deficit' model of engagement with the public, in which non-
archaeologists are assumed to be deficient in their understanding and
appreciation of the field, and accordingly in need of education and thereby
improvement. The alternative model (Merriman 2004a, 6–8) is the 'multiple
perspective' model, in which recognition is given to the competing needs of
different communities of relating to their pasts and to the different interpretations and uses to which such pasts can be put: rather than offering a
single (and 'true') archaeological past to our constituency, the aim is to offer
the essential tools to evaluate the range of different interpretations on offer.

A discussion which, although not specifically concerning public archaeology in the sense used in this section, nevertheless supports this shift from
ARM as a purely professional concern to a broader public interest is that
offered in Briuer and Mathers's (1996) review of U.S. 'significance' literature from 1972 to 1994. They point out that there is a clear sequence of
changes in emphasis in the literature under study, 'from

(a) an early and heavy concentration on contemporary archaeological
    research to,
(b) future archaeological values to,
(c) the importance of cultural resource to other (allied) disciplines to,

(d) the value of cultural resources to all disciplines *to*,
(e) consideration of broader public and social values (Briuer and Mathers 1996, 27).

They attribute this shift in valuation strategies to a rise in concern for the 'stewardship' of archaeological resources, whereby archaeologists are seen less as the primary stakeholder in relation to the management of archaeological remains – that is, as the main beneficiaries of ARM practice – and more as custodians of such material on behalf of a wider community. This is in one sense a return to the original conception of 'public archaeology', which combined ARM practice to preserve sites with their public availability, but also marks another: the incorporation of 'public' or 'community' concerns into ARM practice, thus allowing ARM to develop as a particular arm of archaeology rather than accepting that public interest should be allowed to dominate archaeological endeavour as its raison d'être. As will be seen in the central (main) part of this book, it also becomes quite possible to separate out public outreach and stewardship from mainstream ARM activity: this is not to suggest that we should do so, but it is important to be alert to the realities of ARM practice.

Third World archaeologies offer two competing models that reflect, but do not entirely replicate, the anglophone experience outlined above. Mapunda and Lane (2004) argue that, despite long-standing research into East African archaeology and the establishment of agencies responsible for preservation and for outreach, some of which operate with high effectiveness, general public interest in local archaeology remains low. They blame a number of factors: the distance of responsible agencies from local concerns, the poor quality of interpretive material and the failure to involve locals in ongoing research programmes. The result is that archaeology is seen as something alien and as the concern of others than of the local population, and ultimately as an inconvenience that interferes with local life. Similar concerns are reported for southern Africa by Segobye (2008). Funari (2004) outlines the separation of the majority populations of Brazil from the country's archaeology, which has been largely conducted by, among and mostly for other archaeologists. Nevertheless, he also is able to chart the acts of archaeologists against oppressive regimes and genocidal practices against the Indigenous population. As for other South American countries (Politis 1995), the firm establishment of democratic civilian rule allowed the emergence of archaeologies that considered subordinate and excluded peoples, that addressed contemporary issues and that introduced schoolchildren to Indigenous archaeology as part of the curriculum.

The separation of direct public engagement in archaeology from preservation and management of the resource is at once testimony to and a product of the professionalisation of the field in the closing decades of the twentieth century. As archaeology increasingly becomes a specialist activity of those specifically trained and educated to undertake it, the discipline simultaneously subdivides into further specialisms. As well as the various branches of academic archaeology, and the division of those involved in the management of archaeological resources into curatorial, investigative and consultancy roles, engagement with the public also becomes a specialism in its own right. Many institutions responsible for public engagement – national agencies, museums, etc. – employ specialist staff, very often trained as educators, to undertake the role (Cracknell and Corbishley 1986). Where more generalist archaeologists become involved, they find themselves increasingly involved in this aspect and more distanced from archaeological investigation itself (e.g., McDavid 2000; Pryor 1989). The consequence is that – despite the best intentions of archaeologists themselves and in defiance of much disciplinary rhetoric – public outreach becomes something apart from the mainstream of archaeological activity. As Hills and Richards (2006) and Parker Pearson and Pryor (2006) demonstrate for British archaeology, the means of disseminating ideas and understanding of the subject are increasingly removed from the hands of archaeologists. Chapter 7 will review nonetheless the means archaeologists apply in this area and their benefits and consequences for the field.

Systems of selection and valuation

Chapter 5 will review the ways in which the archaeological resource may be evaluated. As Briuer and Mathers (1996, 6–9) indicate, ARM literature on the topic of such valuation in the USA was significant during the period from 1972 to 1996, reaching peaks in the late 1970s and in 1990. Similar discussion was also taking place in other territories (e.g., the UK and Australia) in the 1980s and into the 1990s (see, e.g., Carman 2002, 155–78; Smith 1996). Virtually all formal academic debate of the issues involved ceased after 1996, the reasons for which are not entirely clear, only to revive within the last few years. Nevertheless, the valuation of archaeological resources (however called) has been a central practice of modern ARM since its invention, although the methods applied and the principles behind it have varied considerably over time. In this respect there has been consideration of the changing approaches to the value of archaeological remains in the UK (Darvill 1993; 1995; 2005; Carman 2005b). Darvill

(1993) has chosen to take a long-term approach, identifying differing value schemes in operation from medieval to modern times. While the medieval period was characterised by a concern for the monetary and curiosity values only of field monuments, the Renaissance focus was on values associated with the aesthetic and historic attributes of monuments and objects; the twentieth century by contrast sees the rise of values defined in terms derived from economic theory – as 'use' values, 'option' values and 'existence' values. My own scope was narrower, focusing on the period from the late nineteenth century (Carman 2005b). For me the crucial shift was from values associated with social reform and the making of 'good citizens' to a concern for tangible and measurable outcomes. Accordingly, both approaches see a shift in valuation schemes from one ideological scheme to another, despite some disagreement about the probity or consequences of the changes identified.

Contrasting approaches to changes in archaeological value have been taken by others. Deriving from the experience of endeavouring to make judgements about particular sites in real-life situations, practitioners have been keen to develop evaluation schemes that are at once meaningful in archaeological terms and can ensure parity between different contexts and the treatment of different objects. In the UK this led to the development of a specific set of criteria for application by responsible agents in making decisions about the legal preservation of sites (first promulgated in 1983: DoE 1983; see also DoE 1990). In practice the eight criteria listed in official documents are supplemented and supported by a more developed, more complex and more sophisticated set of factors to be applied by their profes-sional advisers (Darvill et al. 1987). In the Netherlands a similar approach to site evaluation has been taken, with the development of criteria not unlike those used in the UK (Groenewoudt and Bloemers 1997), a developed version of which has since been offered as a general solution for application throughout Europe (Deeben et al. 1999). By contrast, no such systematisa-tion has been at work in North America, despite the influence of the region on other parts of the globe, and despite the legal imperative to protect sites of 'scientific significance'. Instead, the literature of American ARM is replete with individual attempts to define the characteristics that mark a site as 'significant' for legal purposes (e.g., contributions to Schiffer and Gumerman 1977, 241–92; Hardesty and Little 2009). A review of the literature (Briuer and Mathers 1996, 14) produced a list of criteria similar but not identical to those used elsewhere in the anglophone world, but this is not offered as an approach to assessment to be taken up by all, merely as an indication of the kinds of criteria applied in practice.

Criticisms of efforts at the professional evaluation of sites by the application of specific criteria have focused on a number of issues. The first – to
receive most attention in the literature – has been a general agreement that
the measurement of the archaeological value of a site is dynamic and
relative; that is to say, it depends on context and will vary over time
(Briuer and Mathers 1996, 11). One of the problems with the application
of criteria for measuring the significance of sites identified from early on was
that they can only reflect current concerns and cannot foresee any that may
emerge in the future. Such an idea is contained at the heart of one of the
seminal papers concerning archaeological value, in which Lipe (1984, 3)
outlines how different values derive from particular contexts of use, and how
these in turn feed particular institutional structures and result in the preservation of particular kinds of remains. These preserved remains then form
the 'cultural resource base' from which items will be selected in the next
'round'. In part this consensus as to the dynamic and relative nature of the
evaluation process derives from a general feeling that 'significance' is the
servant of archaeology rather than its determining master and should reflect
specifically archaeological concerns. Accordingly, the second most discussed aspect of American ARM practice is the need for regional research
designs, representing

> a continuing consensus ... for developing well-defined and intellectually
> rigorous regional frameworks for evaluating cultural resources, rather than
> restricting ... units of analysis to ... site-by-site phenomena or narrow and
> highly idiosyncratic criteria. The continued and widespread popularity of
> this concept is probably a function of its relationship and overlap with
> other frequently cited concepts ... that have become central to discus-
> sions of cultural significance (Briuer and Mathers 1996, 15).

The similarity in measures of significance and representativity across the
world leads to another of the charges levelled at significance evaluation:
that it has nothing to do with archaeological research as such but is instead a
bureaucratic practice (Carman 2000, 10–18; Faulkner 2000). There are two
counter-arguments to this. One is that the purpose of establishing protected
sites, or archaeological preserves (Lipe 1974), is to maintain a stock of
undamaged sites for future investigations which will apply new techniques
and different research agendas. The other is that 'with one notable
exception ... none of the publications [reviewed in the USA] take the
position that [ARM] is not research' (Briuer and Mathers 1996, 17). That
exception (Dunnell 1984) equates research with inevitable destruction
and ARM with a stark choice between preservation and destruction

without recording, since the sites themselves are not sought on the basis of relevance to research but only because they face destruction.

In seeing the world in such a way, archaeological value is no longer an absolute, nor is it primary; it sits alongside other values which are hostile to, and some of them more powerful than, archaeology. Accordingly, it becomes necessary to define archaeological value in meaningful terms: for Carver this means it must be anticipatory, in the sense of being ready at the point of decision as to the future of a particular place; it must be professionally made and presented, both to document fully its content and to carry authority; and it must be able to claim the '"global" . . . character of its definition and the universal nature of its clientele and thus . . . claim that it represents the interests of the largest but least influential constituency of all, that of the unborn' (Carver 1996, 48). The objection to professional systems of archaeological valuation is that 'behind the concerns and definitions, laws and regulations adopted by virtually all countries for the care of their "archaeological heritage" is a belief that the past is composed of "monuments"' (Carver 1996, 50), and it is these that are assessed under systems of archaeological resource management. Assessment and evaluation criteria 'are designed to apply to identified sites, for which . . . attributes . . . can be assigned, rather than deposits which are still unseen' (Carver 1996, 51). Accordingly, 'the concept of the monument and the ways used to define monuments contain a built-in obsolescence, because both tend to endow the future more liberally with examples of the identified, rather than the unidentified archaeological resource' (Carver 1996, 51). Carver's answer is to promote the research value of unknown and unassessed remains over that of value as measured in terms of 'importance', which is grounded in the already known and established.

Carver's argument is not unlike that of Schaafsma (1989) and others (e.g., Lynott 1980; Tainter and Lucas 1983) in certain respects, in particular in their focus on 'insignificance' as the only alternative to marking a site as significant. Tainter and Lucas (1983) point out that significance is not an inherent attribute of material but depends on the context within which the judgement is being made. Accordingly – and as mentioned earlier, as a factor on which many seem to agree – site significance is a dynamic and relative concept. The issue, however, is that while a designation as significant will result in preservation or investigation of the site, a failure to achieve significance may result in its loss. At the same time, and drawing on Carver's (1996) argument, significance is measured in terms of the already known rather than the yet to be known. Schaafsma's (1989) answer to this is to abandon the search for 'significant' sites and instead to treat all sites as 'significant until proven otherwise'.

Throughout their arguments Carver (1996), Schaafsma (1989) and Tainter and Lucas (1983) all emphasise that the evaluation of remains is a procedure whereby value is given by the process of evaluation rather than inherent in the material. In taking the same line, Leone and Potter (1992) accuse ARM of essentialism, by which the values placed on archaeological material are those that relate to archaeology alone – ignoring the ways of valuing objects that other people may adopt – and are accordingly fixed and static rather than contingent and relative. By adopting 'not only the "scientific rigour" and methodology of [processual archaeology] but also the authority given to archaeology by its new identity as a Science' (Smith 1993, 58), ARM archaeology became institutionalised as a powerful discourse able to dominate the voices of others. Accordingly, to make archaeology at once more democratic and more representative of those it serves, Leone and Potter (1992) argued for the creation of a dialogue 'of equals' between archaeologists and others interested in a site, and taking their ideas of its value into the significance evaluation process.

Some more recent developments in issues of value have gone directly down this route. The 1999 version of the Australian ICOMOS Charter for the Conservation of Places of Cultural Significance (otherwise known as the 'Burra Charter') places a specific responsibility to include non-archaeological values – especially those relevant to Indigenous and local populations – when assessing sites for preservation. It is in effect a recognition of what has been termed 'cognitive ownership', defined as 'the interest in or association with a cultural site claimed, even implicitly, by any person or group who attaches some value to that place' (Boyd et al. 2005, 93). Such interests and associations are variable, and may be economic, intellectual, spiritual or conceptual, among others. As Boyd and his colleagues put it, 'for every place a wide range of "owners" and meanings can be identified, each with particular relationships with the place [or object] and, importantly, with every other owner' (Boyd et al. 2005, 93). To some extent this recognition is a return to the kinds of values identified in the past by Darvill (1995) and Carman (2005b) – values ascribed not by a particular category of person (the archaeologist), but by society at large – but it also marks a shift away from the professional evaluation of resources towards more general concerns. Clark's (2001) *Informed Conservation* of historic buildings and landscapes specifically incorporates issues of local interest, amenity values and stakeholder concerns in constructing arguments for the significance of sites. A still broader approach is taken in the idea of assessing the total *Public*

Value of resources (Clark 2006), which incorporates a mix of professional, social and economic measures of value in a single scheme. In all these cases the purely archaeological evaluation of sites is considered as part only of a broader social process, returning archaeology to its wider social context and inevitably placing additional responsibilities on practitioners. ·

Archaeological resource management as politics

Laurajane Smith's (2004) discussion of archaeology as a tool of contemporary governance identifies three process during the 1960s and 1970s that facilitated the rise to prominence of archaeology as a tool of governance, especially (but not exclusively) in North America and Australia (Smith 2004, 4–6). First, she points up the increase in demands by Indigenous populations for recognition and for control over land and other resources, putting such questions directly on the political agenda. The challenges these posed for 'traditional' archaeology have been seen by a number of commentators as reflecting the development of post-processual archaeology, which emphasises the political role of archaeology in the present, although for Smith (2004) it has more to do with the rise of processualism as reflected in the professionalisation of the discipline. Second, she points to an increasing concern with 'heritage' in Western countries, whether as part of a wider concern for the environment, a response to increasing opportunities for cultural tourism, a nostalgic attempt to reclaim a lost past, as part of conservative political agendas, or as a challenge to established forms of identity politics and nationalism: all this served to put the past on national political agendas across the globe. Third, and finally, she points to the way in which archaeologists became active in these debates, lobbying for preservationist legislation, with some acting as consultants and advisers to those on either side, while at the same time developing formal professional bodies to represent the interests of practitioners and establish codes of ethical conduct to regulate archaeological activity. She sums up these developments in Australia and North America as 'the uptake of archaeological knowledge [as a discourse of rationality and objectivity that was easily understood by the modern liberalism of Western governments, and thereby] as a technology of government by providing . . . a social problem complete with a truculent population that needed identifying and defining' (Smith 2004, 6). In short, by managing claims to heritage one could also manage the populations making claims on that heritage.

The last British Labour government also subscribed to the same idea, although for them it was a means to establish a more communitarian spirit in a nation they saw as having been divided by neoliberal economic policies and class politics. So-called 'essays' by the UK minister responsible for cultural matters in 2004 and 2005 (Jowell 2004; 2005) sought to outline an approach to valuing cultural resources in terms of their usefulness to creating viable communities and promoting good citizenship. Speeches by both the senior and junior ministers for culture at the Capturing the Public Value of Heritage conference in January 2006 developed the theme. The way they talked about these issues was at once instructive and redolent of their nineteenth-century forebears (see Chapter 1). Within the context of developing an idea of a national identity for all of Britain (rather than its constituent countries: see Schofield et al. 2011, 6–7), Jowell wished to 'explore the links between public value and heritage and the public benefit that comes from developing a sense of shared identity'; and she declared that she had 'always regarded our historic environment as being a vital part of the public realm – part of what [she] would define as those shared spaces and places that we hold in common and where we meet as equal citizens' (Jowell 2006, 7–8). Her colleague explicitly referred to the work of William Morris, John Ruskin and Octavia Hill in promoting 'a radical desire for the British people to enjoy their national heritage [quoting Octavia Hill] to "make lives noble, homes happy and family life good"' (Lammy 2006, 65) and described his own task as 'to revive that radical, empowering conception of heritage ... and to help build a Britain at ease with its present because it understands, values and is able to access its past' (Lammy 2006, 69).

The Tony Blair government's vision of 'heritage' as a way to build a good society was not new for post-Victorian Britain. Grahame Clark's *Archaeology and Society* – first published in 1939, reissued with a slightly different focus in 1947 and then in new editions up to the 1960s – was explicit about 'the social value of archaeology' (Clark 1939, viii) as a means of building strong nations, and from 1947 as a means to build a new international order that would obviate war. Recent commentators in Britain have written to support such developments, arguing that thereby 'archaeologists can create new alliances, enhance trust in their work and participate in novel kinds of active engagement with the wider world' (e.g., Darvill 2010, 402). On the basis of these developments it can be argued that archaeology – at least in the English-speaking world – has ceased to be an elite or specialised subject and has become one that belongs to all. Accordingly, the rise of 'community', 'collaborative' and 'democratic' archaeologies is now well documented (*World Archaeology* 2002; Field et al. 2000; Moser et al. 2002; McDavid 2002; Faulkner 2000; McDavid

2004) and recent discussions in the UK (e.g., Clark 2006) have focused on the 'public value' of archaeology as part of 'social inclusion' policies and the creation of a sense of national identity based on shared values rather than ethnicity. Whether it is called 'emancipatory' archaeology, 'engaged archaeology' or 'critical archaeology', what is promoted is an archaeological practice representing a politics that 'argues through the medium of [archaeology] to detach the power of truth from the present social order' (McDavid and Jeppson 2007), using archaeological interpretation to challenge conventional and expected understandings of current norms.

Such is the approach proposed by Bernbeck and Pollock (2007, 227) in their 'archaeology of perpetrators' of crimes against humanity – an explicit attempt to provoke 'controversial public discourse' by avoiding the creation of a 'closed' 'coherent narrative of the past' based around identification with victims and to put in its place 'a critical distance . . . that seeks to preclude a desire to identify' and, at the same time, 'an uncanny awareness that this distance is unjustified because one's own forebears were' not neutral in the oppression or abuse of others. An 'archaeology of perpetrators' puts complicity and unwillingness to recognise the dark side of human nature centre-stage. Similarly, Dean Saitta's work at the Ludlow coalfield in the USA challenges accepted interpretations of the past to make connections with the present: in working on an example of the use of force to support capitalist exploitation, Saitta distinguishes between the 'descendants' of those involved – who are the current white middle class of middle America – and the 'descendant community' who are the 'unionized working class of southern Colorado', some of whom are white but the majority of whom are Chicanos (Saitta 2007, 275). This project forces recognition of the processes of inequality and exploitation that created (and arguably continues to create) modern America, and creates the space to rethink the outcomes of capitalism. A similar approach is taken by some who use archaeology to study the contemporary world. As Harrison and Schofield (2010, 146) have recently put it, 'An archaeology of the contemporary past must always be a critical intervention in the present[, turning] the lens of archaeology on our own society', especially the 'hidden, abject, obscured, clandestine, or forgotten' – whether it be the impact of militarisation on landscape and people, studies of the homeless, the application of forensic studies or merely to look with a new set of eyes at the familiar and ubiquitous.

Others have involved non-archaeologists directly in the processes of archaeological work. They work to challenge the idea that professionally trained archaeologists are the sole providers of archaeological interpretations and the only people qualified to undertake archaeological investigation.

Such a process involves abrogating some or all professional authority and putting our skills and knowledge at the service of others who direct what we do. Not only does this provide them with access to what they may consider their past (and not that of the archaeologists), but it also serves to undermine in a very direct and manifest way the structures of authority and power that are part of the modern order and in part invested in academic disciplines and agencies (such as those employing archaeologists) operating under the authority of law and government. An example is the work of Maggie Ronayne (2007) on the Ilusu Dam Project, where the connection was made between archaeological sites under threat, continuing traditions and current ways of life, extending the definition of archaeology into the present. Elsewhere community archaeology has been used to open up discussion of issues otherwise silent, such as issues of 'race' in the southern U.S. states raised by the investigation, preservation and presentation of former slave plantations in Texas (McDavid 2002).

From these perspectives the purpose of archaeology was never intended to be an 'objective' engagement with a past that was gone, but was rather meant to take advantage of the past for present purposes. In engaging in 'community' archaeologies that challenge the present its practitioners claim to be following the true purpose of their calling. In this, the professional interpretation of material culture is only the beginning: the true work is perceived as engagement with others in the present.

Conclusion

This chapter completes the work begun in Chapter 1 by taking ARM practices over the course of the last fifty years and bringing them to their current position. The overall story is one of the separation of what we call ARM from the mainstream of archaeology in which it was embedded up to the twentieth century, of the increasing professionalisation of the field and the further subdivision of ARM into specialisms of its own. What has ultimately emerged is an international consensus on what ARM should be, how it should operate and what it is for. This is reflected especially in the international conventions and charters relating to archaeology adopted and promulgated by global agencies such as UNESCO and its daughter organisations the International Committee on Monuments and Sites (ICOMOS) and the International Committee on Archaeological Heritage Management (ICAHM), and regional organisations such as the Council of Europe and the Organisation of American States (Carman 2002, 68–71). As has been outlined in this chapter, these represent the agreed basis of procedures to be adopted towards archaeological remains and their collection, retention and preservation. The precise means may vary from context to context, but the essential core is shared across the world. The final section outlined more recent developments in the field that relate to a particular understanding of the role of archaeology in the present that goes beyond the mere practice of ARM. The chapters in the next part of the book will look in detail at the core practices of ARM, with an aim of understanding what they achieve not only for the material remains of the past but also for the wider society on whose behalf they are carried out. First, however, we turn to a review of one of the underlying mechanisms for the management of archaeology: law.

CHAPTER 3

Systems of regulation

Every country in the world has some form of law relating to its cultural heritage. These range from the draconian (and sometimes relatively ineffective: Cleere 1984c, 130) to the more loosely formulated and generally respected. In between lie the majority, more or less complex and more or less complied with. Some are 'home-grown' and reflect particular local circumstances; others elsewhere are copied from neighbouring or more distant places; others again have been adopted from past rulers but remain in place nonetheless. We saw in Chapter 1 how important the passage of law has been to the development of the idea of preserving material from the past: in every case, laws proved a key means by which that preservation was effected. Laws, as the next section will discuss more fully, also serve to legitimise the idea of that preservation.

This chapter will conclude the thrust of this part of the book by looking at the different kinds of law that apply to the material heritage in different parts of the world and how they operate. As before, it is an exploration and celebration of difference rather than similarity. The common thread, however, lies in the adoption of law – of whatever kind and however written – as the key method of dealing with the cultural heritage. As has been seen in Chapter 1, it is the promulgation of laws to preserve old things – whatever the motivation driving it – that turns a mere private or sectional interest into something like ARM as we know it. In the current state of ARM, laws are even more crucial to the preservation of our heritage: without them, it can be cogently argued, there is no ARM. At the same time these laws need to be overseen and put into effect by appropriately empowered agents, whether of the state or independent. These agents too have their powers and duties defined by the laws that govern them and the material on which they act. Accordingly, even in so-called 'non-statutory' systems of ARM, law is the underlying mechanism and the ultimate repository of authority.

The sections of this chapter will offer introductory outlines to some of the forms which laws in this area can take, how they are organised and to be interpreted, and the relations between laws at the national and international level. The opening section will examine some of the justifications for laws in this area, a truly global discourse. A section on interpretation of laws will expose the clear differences that exist between legal systems, and which necessarily affect our understanding of them and any attempt at international comparison: these include the legal structures of federal versus unitary states, laws derived from traditions of Roman (and other) law and those grounded in English 'common law'. An overview of international regulation – global in nature but subject to interpretation at the national level – follows. The laws of national territories will then come under scrutiny, representing different systems of laws: those assuming the state to be the proper owner of material versus those where private ownership is held to be the ideal, those favouring direct intervention and control versus more indirect and administrative mechanisms and so on. Overall, the paradox of the ubiquity of laws to achieve the same ends that take a remarkably diverse set of forms will become clear. A final section will review the effect the promulgation of legislative control has had on the field in terms of the development of professional agendas and associations, both national and international, and the ways these too regulate the practice of ARM.

Unlike the content of the previous chapter, this aspect of ARM is very well documented. This is partly inevitable: laws are usually written documents and to ensure compliance must be made widely available to their intended audience. The literature of ARM, therefore, abounds with summaries and commentaries at the national level (for the UK, see Carman 1996; Pugh-Smith and Samuels 1996; Hunter and Ralston 1993; 2006; for the USA, U.S. Department of the Interior 1989–90; for France, Rigambert 1996; for Austria, Hocke 1975; for German states, Dörge 1971; Eberl et al. 1975; for Switzerland, Hangartner 1981; for Mexico, King et al. 1980; etc.) and at the international and comparative level (Burnham 1974; O'Keefe and Prott 1984; Cleere 1984a; Carman 2002, 68–76; and on underwater archaeology, Dromgoole 1999).

The role of law

Despite the ubiquity of legislation as a foundational tool of ARM practice, very little of the literature of the field concerns the purpose of such laws or, to put it another way, explains why we pass laws on this matter rather than tackling it in another way. McGimsey (1972), for instance, argues power-fully for legislation as a key component of a state preservation programme, but also argues against legislation alone since it would be an entirely 'negative approach' (McGimsey 1972, 33 and 46), lacking the necessary support from the wider public. O'Keefe and Prott (1984) go further: they argue that the dangers facing the archaeological resource are ever greater and that accordingly 'some of them can only be controlled by governments' and therefore require legislation (O'Keefe and Prott 1984, 13). At the same time they recognise the valuable role that laws play in resolving key con-flicts over material – especially issues of ownership and control – and the setting of policy aims, as well as the increasing requirements of national governments to comply with international treaties concerning the heritage (O'Keefe and Prott 1984, 14). None of these is, however, a reason for law *as such*: both McGimsey and O'Keefe and Prott offer programmes of public education and the mustering of political support as alternatives (McGimsey 1972, 29–31; O'Keefe and Prott 1984, 145–50).

In so far as McGimsey does provide a reason for legislation, it must be as part of the requisite 'administrative structure' (McGimsey 1972, 27) for such a programme, which includes its establishment as a legally recognised authority with its own budget. Pickard (2001a, 4–10), reviewing a sample of European states with a view to their response to new international agreements on cultural heritage, expands on this theme by presenting a number of areas where legislation has a valuable defining role:

- definition of the heritage, concerning the attributes and characteristics a heritage object should have or be deemed to possess;
- identification of the heritage, especially the means available of inven-tory and recording, and the making of lists and schedules;
- preservation and protection of the heritage, whether through systems of designation or by regulating development;
- the philosophy of conservation in place, including attitudes to restora-tion and reconstruction;
- appropriate sanctions against breaches of the law and the means – coercive or otherwise – to encourage compliance;
- the integration of cultural preservation with other government policies and imperatives;
- financial aspects;
- the specific powers and duties of government and non-governmental agencies in respect of the heritage; and
- educational and other aspects.

From this functionalist perspective the law in this area can be seen not as a mechanism of ARM but as a facilitator for systems of ARM to come into being: on its own, it seems, law does nothing, but requires other agencies in order to put ARM into effect. This is perhaps one reason why law should so often emerge first in systems of ARM as described in Chapter 1: it provides the framework on which the other aspects of ARM can hang. On the other hand, it would seem that other components of an ARM system could exist independently of legislation to put them into place. The question 'Why law?' remains.

Although in general sympathetic to ARM as a practice (and whatever they may choose to call it), others have taken a more critical view of the role of law in this field. A study of English law in this area (Carman 1996) concluded that its main purpose was to give value to archaeological remains. Though a continually reductive process of selection of certain kinds of object from all the things in the world, subsequent categorisation of those things into legal terms and allocation to particular agencies for a limited range of treatments, archaeological sites and monuments would emerge with a new meaning and a new set of values placed on them. In the process they became officially recognised as important and worthy of protection and preservation. This is a reversal of the usual understanding of the sequence, whereby things that are important are chosen to be preserved by law: here it is the law that makes certain things important. A similar view was reached in respect of legislation to govern the heritage of Indigenous populations in Australia and the USA (Smith 2004, 125–55). As Smith puts it, legislation 'plays a key role in the management of Indigenous material culture, as . . . it establishes the need for management procedures and processes' (Smith 2004, 125). Such law therefore goes on to define who will manage Indigenous culture and how those involved – archaeologists, Indigenous people and government agencies – will interact. This means law sets 'the parameters of acceptable management practice . . . [and] the scope of policy debate, and influences the way in which debate is con-ducted between the three actors' (Smith 2004, 125). Overall, 'legislation provides governments and bureaucracies with terms, concepts and guide-lines against which competing claims to material culture may be assessed' (Smith 2004, 126) and ultimately 'provides the conceptual frameworks that must govern debates within' ARM which 'institutionalize and regulate the discipline [of archaeology] as a technology of government' (Smith 2004, 154). Similarly, Fourmile (1996) has reviewed the role of Australian legislation in denying the Indigenous population any access to or control over their cultural heritage. These readings of the place of legislation in

ARM locate it at the service of requirements external to the discipline itself and closer to those of government. In other words, rather than law serving the needs of archaeology, archaeology is made to serve the needs of government.

Interestingly, however, it not just those who are critical (or indeed suspicious) of law who see it in this light. Breeze (1996) – writing on the definition given in Scotland to the British legislative category of 'national monument' – is clear that the purpose is 'to ensure that all people have access to [Scotland's built] heritage [of all periods] and are able to enjoy it, regardless of their own origins and background' (Breeze 1996, 102). He also acknowledges that 'preserving monuments . . . is not entirely an end in itself' and cites government reasoning behind it (Breeze 1996, 102). Accordingly, the idea of a 'national' archaeological resource based in law is seen here not as a limiting and exclusive concept but nevertheless as one that remains at the service of government agendas. This same idea is reflected in Knudson's (1986) review of cultural resource management practice in the USA. As a result of success in 'persuading the major policymakers . . . of the public significance of archaeological resources . . . the implementation of such policies will not leave anyone . . . out of the process of public accountability for the treatment of those resources', and 'this will be conducted within the context of multiple public objectives' (Knudson 1986, 399). The public referred to here is taken to be the Euro-American population of the USA, excluding its Indigenous population whose cultural works are under discussion. Accordingly, even though it is acknowledged that conservation of cultural remains is a globally endorsed project, the target of conservation practice in the USA and what flows from it is directed at a particular audience, at least partly the result of 'a lack of genetic continuity between the dominant political community in the United States and prehistoric Americans' (Knudson 1986, 396). Here, as in the UK, law drives the ARM process rather than providing support for it.

In most writing on ARM a legislative basis for preservation practice is taken for granted. The literature is therefore for the most part descriptive rather than critically discursive and does not ask why laws are in place in such profusion. One reason is simply historical, as is evident from the previous chapters: it is 'the way it is done'. Other reasons emerge from a closer reading, however, whether from an overtly critical or a more sympathetic perspective: laws serve, as it turns out, not the needs of ARM but rather the agencies – and, in particular, national governments – who promote them. This is not an issue of effectiveness but may have an impact on the way ARM is done in different contexts.

Reading and interpreting laws

Laws are technical documents rather than discursive texts, which means they are not only written in a particular way but also designed to be read in a certain way (see, e.g., for the USA, Dickerson 1975; for the UK, Cross 1995; for Italy, Tarello 1980; for international comparisons, MacCormick and Summers 1991). Indeed, 'reading' in its conventional everyday sense may not be quite the right word: laws are usually designed to be used more like a technical manual than read as a linear narrative. Moreover, the particular manner in which such texts should be read varies from jurisdiction to jurisdiction, so that an ability to operate in one legal system does not automatically imply an ability to so operate in a different one. The aim of this section is to outline some of the ways in which laws relevant to archaeology can vary from country to country across the globe.

As I have argued elsewhere (Carman 1996, 17; 2002, 102–3), to have a truly meaningful comparison between the practices of archaeological heritage management it is necessary to take three factors into account:

- differences between legal and regulatory systems;
- differences in the nature of the material record of the past between one territory and another; and
- differences in the traditions and historical development of archaeology between one territory and the other.

The first of these covers such things as the basic assumptions relating to the interests to be served by law, the degree of appropriate state control held to be applicable in an area, the weight to be given to private property laws or the expected powers and duties of state and other agencies. All of these will differ between one territory and another, or one legal system (e.g., common or Roman) and another. In the UK or USA, for instance, the usual style is to provide for legal protection without taking material directly into state ownership, but in other territories all archaeological remains and other heritage objects are held to be the property of the state. In the UK, the USA and Australia this reflects the ideological authority of private property upheld by a system of common law, as against the authority of the state more typical of systems deriving from the European continent. Here the difference lies in expectations of what is right and proper and more fundamental social values. Where it is expected that heritage objects should belong to the state, the kind of ARM system operated in the UK or the USA – where archaeology can be carried out by private contractors or amateurs – makes no sense; in the UK or USA the adoption of a system of generalised state ownership would be seen as an attack on private property. An attempt to assess the merits of one system against another therefore runs up against these fundamental differences in understanding what laws can and should do, and to whom legal authority should be given.

The second and third factors are linked. They concern the nature of the archaeological record and how it inevitably differs in different territories, and the understanding given to the purpose and focus of archaeological research, which will differ in one country from another, so that very different research traditions may exist, leading to a differential emphasis on types of material. In the UK, for instance, the treatment of different types of material is very often the same, regardless of physical form or age. Prehistoric structures in the countryside can be treated in exactly the same way as medieval ruins in a city; and ancient monuments (a legal category that in England now includes some material from the twentieth century) can be placed on a schedule while standing buildings can be placed on a list, both of which offer some form of legal protection. There are other territories, however, where differences in age make a substantial difference. Material from a preliterate past may be treated very differently from material emanating from historical times, or one period of history – or material representing one particular way of life – may be more highly valued than another, making one subject to legal control and protection while the other is abandoned to its fate. In the USA, for instance, buried remains of the Indigenous population are subject to forms of federal legal control while the remains of (sometimes contemporary) colonising Europeans are excluded from this coverage. Such differences will make any direct comparison of UK and U.S. laws rather meaningless, since they are grounded in very different historical circumstances, are driven by very different political and cultural imperatives, and concern significantly different categories of person. At root, therefore, UK and U.S. systems of legislation in this area do not concern the same types of material.

Any set of national laws will also need to be read in accordance with specific standards. These 'rules of construction' are quite precise and are often themselves enshrined in law, ensuring that any law of the particular state will be interpreted in the same way as any other and thus guarantee consistency in application. These rules do not, however, cross territorial and jurisdictional boundaries. A brief introduction to some of the key differences that can exist is set out by O'Keefe and Prott (1984, 150–51) and another by Summers and Taruffo (1991, 501), but for specific advice on how to read laws in particular jurisdictions more precise legal guidance needs to be sought. In particular, there are gross differences between the manner of interpreting laws between systems of legal codes and the principles of common law. All start from the premise that laws are written and composed of words: the question arises as to how to understand the meaning and intention behind certain words and phrases.

Codification of law: France

As conveniently summarised by Troper, Grzegoczyk and Gardies (1991, 171), a distinguishing feature of French legal culture is that it is 'one of written law ... to a large extent codified'. The effect of codification is to offer a body of law that is complete and contains no contradictions or elisions; it therefore does not allow opportunities for avoidance or evasion, or for circumstances that are not covered by it. Accordingly, where the law is silent on an issue, it becomes the task of interpreters to fill that silence, either by simply not recognising the omission or – more probably – by recognising that the 'gap' in legal coverage is a result of the legislator's inability to think of everything in advance and thus prevailing on the interpreter to do so (Troper et al. 175–6). It is generally assumed that the legislators intend all laws to comply with the constitution, and so laws will be interpreted to ensure this (Troper et al. 1991, 195), and that the administration works for the good of the common interest (Troper et al. 1991, 196), although laws restricting liberties are interpreted more strictly (Troper et al. 1991, 202).

Although, as elsewhere in the world (see below), interpreters seek the 'true' meaning of a law and the intention of the law-maker, the materials they are allowed to draw on is very wide rather than being constrained (as elsewhere) by tight legal rules (Troper et al. 1991, 184–9). These may include:

- the historical background to the law
- documents used in drafting the law, including drafts and consultations
- interpretations by users of the law, especially public officials
- the language of other, related, laws
- the language of laws amended by the one in question
- the history of legal terminology
- the effect particular interpretations would have in terms of the national constitution or international treaty obligations
- customary procedures and practices that would otherwise be affected.

Interestingly, especially for comparison with the USA and UK (see below), interpretations by other courts are rarely drawn on, although those of superior courts within the same hierarchy may be.

Overall, French law is seen as a unity that governs all those it rules. Interpreters of law – that is, the courts – are seen not at all to make law but simply to seek the law-maker's intention. Accordingly, in filling 'gaps' not covered by a specific legal phraseology, they are seen only to be expressing the will and intention of the legislator rather than as making new law or extending its coverage. All laws are interpreted in the light of the over-arching code of which they are a part: it follows that no French law 'stands alone' but must be read as part of a coherent and cohesive system that effectively recognises no differences of status or standing or of exception. As Summers and Taruffo (1991, 501) see it, in French law there are no genuine issues of interpretation, and only one meaning is ever possible, and it is this that interpreters must seek.

A federal common-law state: the USA

The American case is very different from that of France. While France is a single state, the USA is a federal one, divided into fifty jurisdictions governed by a federal constitution. All laws of every state and federal law (a jurisdiction in itself) must ultimately comply with the constitution: as in France, compliance will generally be assumed unless demonstrated otherwise (Summers 1991, 443–4). In the case where a state law is in conflict with a federal law, the federal law prevails, but a statute will prevail over administrative regulation and usually the common law, which underpins all law (Summers 1991, 444–5). Whereas in French law gaps in legal coverage are acknowledged and addressed in interpretation, in the USA such gaps are generally treated as if they are simple matters of textual interpretation (Summers 1991, 411–12): the issue is one of particular words and their meanings rather than attempts to meet the standards of an overarching code.

The materials that a U.S. court may draw on in making interpretations is at once wider than that in other territories and more tightly regulated. Materials that must be taken into account include:

- the language of the text and any titles, sub-headings and other terms relating directly to it (compare with the UK, below)
- dictionaries and grammars which set out the 'ordinary' meanings of words under examination
- any legal definitions of terms
- the text of other related statutes
- any prior, repealed or modified laws
- any official history of the passage of the law

- particular historical circumstances the law was intended to address, which may now have altered
- general legal principles
- interpretations by similar or higher courts
- interpretations by officials charged with administering the law (Summers 1991, 422–7).

In addition, interpreters are expected (but not required) to take into account interpretations by other (non-official) users of the law, by courts in other jurisdictions and those of senior legal academics. There are also materials expressly forbidden from consideration, such as the testimony of legislators as to what they believed the law to be and non-official documentation relating to the history of the legislation; by implication the latter excludes the historical background to the law's passage (a direct contrast with the French case).

By contrast especially with France, the U.S. system is one that openly acknowledges the possibility of alternative readings of legal texts (Summers and Taruffo 1991, 501). It follows that U.S. courts have more of a law-making role than their French counterparts. The prior interpretation by other courts also has a much more important role here than is evident in the French system, and the authority of officials over legal interpretation is much less evident. Similarly, no requirement exists to make the law fit part of a broader code, despite the overarching commitment to constitutionality.

A unitary common-law state: the UK

The role of the courts in the UK is not to make law but, similar to their role in France, only to interpret it. Accordingly, it is not the place of the courts to fill gaps in coverage, which are left to legislators (Bankowski and MacCormick 1991, 362). The law is not codified, and therefore, in large measure, each piece of legislation stands alone and separate from others, except where connections are expressly drawn (Bankowski and MacCormick 1991, 363): the focus of interpretation is therefore very much on the strict interpretation of particular words and phrases rather than on seeking to contextualise the whole (Bankowski and MacCormick 1991, 382). Interpretation is therefore an essentially pragmatic process of seeking the 'ordinary signification' of words (Bankowski and MacCormick 1991, 382–6) rather than being driven by broader principle, as in France, or by constitutionality, as in the USA. Nevertheless, there are certain underlying presumptions that guide the interpretive process: that absurdity is not an intention of legislators; that laws are designed to operate fairly; that laws do not (unless specifically indicating otherwise) operate retrospectively; and that existing laws remain unaffected unless the law specifically indicates otherwise (Bankowski and MacCormick 1991, 391–2). In the UK system statutes will prevail over all other kinds of law but increasingly need to comply with laws made elsewhere: in particular, EU legislation and certain international treaties (Bankowski and MacCormick 1991, 375).

As in the USA, interpreters may draw on certain materials, must use others and are barred from using others; however, the range of materials differs from that elsewhere. The primary source is the specific substantive language of the law itself, excluding any sub-headings, titles or marginal commentary that is only present to guide users to relevant texts and not to determine its meaning (Cross 1995) but including any 'Interpretation' section which sets out the precise meanings certain words and phrases may carry. Any previous interpretation by a similar or higher court must also be drawn on, together with any relevant subsidiary legislation which may bring the law into force (Bankowski and MacCormick 1991, 375). They may (but are not required to) refer to other laws on the same topic, government guides on good practice, any previous legal history of the terms, current usages of officials and scholarly writings (Bankowski and MacCormick 1991, 376–80). Material expressly barred from consideration includes any information on the history of the law, and economic or sociological data on the effects of particular readings (Bankowski and MacCormick 1991, 380–82).

In general, UK law is seen as a body of separate regulations, some of which stand entirely alone and others which are grouped together, and are interpreted accordingly. Although general principles and assumptions guide the process, the focus is very much on the specifics of individual provisions rather than the creation of a unified whole. Only those materials directly relevant to the point at issue are taken into account: extrinsic factors are barred because the courts would then be involved in making policy, which is not their role. The assumption – as in France – is that there is a single meaning lying behind a particular provision, and the function of interpretation is to find it.

Differences in reading laws

These three examples offer a taste – albeit a small one – of how different sets of laws represent different legal ideologies and are therefore to be read differently from one another. In particular, the clear differences between laws that operate as part of a codified system and those that stand alone need to be taken into account, as do the specific materials that can be drawn on for interpretation and those that cannot, and the extent to which underlying principles regarding the presence of 'gaps', absurdity and contradiction may be applied. Although Summers and Taruffo (1991) take France and the USA as exemplary of opposed legal systems, here I have used them merely as examples, placed alongside a third, to illustrate diversity. It is worth noting, however, that this has been written neither by a lawyer nor a legal philosopher: any advice on how to read UK, U.S. or French law that can be extracted from this should be treated with caution, and an appropriate legal text or guide should always be consulted for firm advice. An area not mentioned here has been international law, which is the topic of the next section. There are specific rules of construction for these too, which will be covered there.

International laws and their coverage

Technically those materials referred to by (especially but not exclusively) heritage practitioners as 'international law' in the field of heritage are not in fact law: rather, for the most part, they are sets of agreements between nation-states whereby those states agree to a common standard of treatment for certain classes of object, either generally or in defined sets of circumstances. They may be agreements that are designed to operate globally – such as those promulgated by the United Nations or UNESCO – or regionally, such as those relating to Europe or the Americas. These laws are important in the field because they are taken to represent the global principles to which all those concerned with the heritage subscribe. Increasingly they are also taken as the basis for the passage of law at the national level. The main international laws in force at present are set out in Table 3.1.

Since they are promulgated by organisations composed of individual nation-states, these international agreements are binding only on the states acceding to them: they cannot be enforced against individuals or agencies unless they have also been incorporated into national laws, although this does not lift the responsibility from national governments to put in place appropriate arrangements to ensure compliance below the level of government. They are to be read and interpreted in a distinctive manner which reflects in many ways their purpose as setters of norms and guidance. Each such document begins with a preamble which sets out the conditions under which it was brought into existence and the purpose it serves: its specific

TABLE 3.1 *Main international instruments relating to the cultural heritage*

Date	Promoted by (international organisation)	Title
1954	UNESCO (portal.unesco.org)	Convention for the Protection of Cultural Property in the Event of Armed Conflict (Hague Convention)
1970		Convention on the Means of Prohibiting and Preventing the Illicit Import, Export and Transfer of Cultural Property (Paris Convention)
1972		Convention concerning the Protection of the World Cultural and Natural Heritage
2001		Convention on the Protection of the Underwater Cultural Heritage
2003		Convention for the Safeguarding of the Intangible Cultural Heritage
2005		Convention on the Protection and Promotion of the Diversity of Cultural Expressions
1971	RAMSAR (www.ramsar.org)	Ramsar Convention on Wetlands
1995	UNIDROIT (www.unidroit.org)	Convention on Stolen or Illegally Exported Cultural Objects
1954	Council of Europe (www.coe.int)	European Cultural Convention
1969 (revised 1992)		European Convention on the Protection of the Archaeological Heritage
1985		European Convention on Offences Relating to Cultural Property Convention for the Protection of the Architectural Heritage of Europe
1976	Organisation of American States (www.oas.org)	Convention on Protection of the Architectural, Historical and Artistic Heritage of the American Nations

provisions must be read in the light of these opening statements as to function rather than as stand-alone imperatives. This contrasts with the way in which laws are read at the level of some nation-states which are binding on individual citizens and state and non-state agencies.

In addition to conventions, the membership of international bodies such as UNESCO and the Council of Europe may also adopt resolutions, which have much less legal force than a convention but which nevertheless provide guidance as to norms and expectations. These too are not binding on individual citizens, etc. unless their provisions are adopted into national law, but they may also provide the basis on which future conventions are constructed. Other international organisations also contribute to international law in this area, in a more substantive manner. The European Union is concerned primarily with economic and political issues, leaving matters of culture to the broader membership of the Council of Europe, but recent changes in the EU have allowed it to consider cultural matters, and these may become more significant as time moves on. However, as part of its economic remit, it brought forward in 1992 two legal instruments relating to the movement of cultural items into and out of the EU and between member states. The terms of the Directive on the Return of Cultural Objects Unlawfully Removed from the Territory of a Member State will need to be incorporated into national laws before it takes full effect, but this must be done to a set timetable; the regulation on the export of cultural goods – which places limitations on the export of such items outside the EU – had immediate and direct effect on member states and their citizens.

Like all legislative arrangements, some international instruments purport to relate to all aspects of heritage, such as the UNESCO World Heritage Convention, the European Cultural Convention and the Organisation of American States Convention. Others concern all matters relating to particular types of heritage object, such as the Ramsar Convention on Wetlands, the European conventions that separately treat the archaeological and architectural heritage, and the UNESCO conventions on underwater and intangible heritages. Others attempt to address particular issues that affect cultural objects, such as the UNESCO Hague and Paris conventions, the UNIDROIT Convention and the European Union measures in relation to the movement of cultural objects. The Paris and UNIDROIT conventions and the EU measures all relate in particular to the issue of the illicit acquisition, movement and transfer of cultural objects from one state to another: whereas most international law seeks to provide guidance and to set standards, these measures endeavour to go further, by regulating behaviour. In this way they are acting much more like national laws.

Not all states choose to accede to all international laws in this field. In some cases it will be because they consider they lack the resources to meet the standards required by that law; in others – particularly developed states in the West – it will be that they already have laws and mechanisms in place that meet or surpass those of the particular instrument. In some cases it may be felt that the particular instrument – although perhaps introduced by the state in question – is aimed at the practices of other states that do not meet the standard set. In others it will be because it challenges or threatens a particular national interest, such as an economic interest. Failures to accede inevitably weaken the effect of such laws, since they cannot be enforced against states that have not done so. In turn this may affect the capacity of the instrument to act as a measure of minimum performance and an international standard. At the same time such laws have been criticised for adopting a specifically Western approach to ideas of cultural heritage, constructed around notions of the built and monumental heritage, rather than heritages of practice and belief. Such criticisms have led to a refocusing, especially by UNESCO, on such ideas as the 'intangible heritage' and 'cultural diversity', reflected in instruments promulgated in the early part of this century (see, e.g., Smith and Akagawa 2009; Taylor and Lennon 2012). These represent new approaches to the cultural heritage which can be expected to have influence at the level of the nation-state, although not all Western states have yet acceded to these new principles.

National laws and their differences

Although references in the literature of the field to international measures are extensive and such laws are invariably treated in the literature of the field as significantly influential (e.g., Cleere 1989; Skeates 2000a; Carman 2002; Smith 2004, 106), attempts to assess their effect on law and practice at the key level of the nation-state are nevertheless limited. A project by the Council of Europe, however, attempted to do this for the European conventions relating to the archaeological and architectural heritage, by a process of comparison of how different states put the requirements of the conventions into effect (Pickard 2001b). As would possibly be expected, the range of thirteen countries from all parts of Europe – some well established, others newly emergent – provided evidence of a wide diversity of treatment, organisation and focus, together with different levels of compliance with the conventions. The project focused, in particular, on the following aspects of heritage management in each territory:

- definition of the heritage, including systems of categorisation and selection criteria
- processes of identification, and styles of inventories and recording

- measures to protect, preserve and prevent damage
- conservation philosophy, including attitudes to reconstruction and refurbishment
- sanctions for breach of regulations, and coercive measures in place
- integration of conservation with other planning and land-use regulation
- financial provisions, including sources of funding, tax regimes and economic development programmes
- the role and structure of relevant agencies and organisations
- provision for the education and training of staff.

The discussion usefully highlights differences between individual countries but also indicates areas few or none have yet addressed, pointing to the future influence likely to be wielded by regional rather than purely national approaches (Pickard 2001a, 4–10). Several of these areas – especially those of inventory, preservation measures, finance, organisational matters and education – will be further addressed in the remainder of this book. Here I wish to outline the areas where legislative provisions can take a different approach in different parts of the world. These areas are, in particular:

- ways of defining and specifying the object of such laws
- how different bodies of material are addressed in laws
- issues of rights of ownership and control
- the kinds of sanctions which may be applied.

Depending on the system of law in place, the approach taken in these areas will correlate quite closely.

Defining and specifying material

There are several ways in which the material covered by a law or a body of law may be described, set out by O'Keefe and Prott (1984, 184–7) as enumeration, categorisation and classification. *Enumeration* is a system of lists of the kinds of material to be covered: this is typical of U.S. federal laws in this area (US Department of the Interior 1989–90) and has been to some extent adopted in the UK for the purpose of describing the kinds of objects that can be considered for the purposes of legal protection (Carman 1996, 120–24 and 187–92). The problem with this approach is that it leaves open the question of whether items not on the list but of a similar kind can be included: for example, if the list specifies 'graves and burial sites', does this also cover above-ground disposal of the dead? *Categorisation* is a looser approach whereby a broad description of types of material is provided, into which a range of particular objects may fall. The problem of this approach is that too narrow a definition may exclude objects of concern, while too broad a definition may include too much material. Unlike enumeration and categorisation, *classification* is concerned not with the form of the object but with actions taken towards it: in such a system, only those objects officially recognised and designated as such by a responsible authority can be granted protection. While convenient and transparent, the system has the flaw of only recognising those objects that have been specifically designated, leaving others of similar nature to their fate. At the same time, it is worth noting that these different systems are by no means exclusive. It is possible to use them in combination, so that the list under an enumerative scheme may include categories, while a scheme of categorisation may also enumerate particular types of object, and a classificatory scheme may operate in respect of items enumerated or categorised.

These differences represent contrasting approaches to the cultural heritage as a phenomenon as well as the structure of law. Where only designated material is covered by law, the emphasis is placed on the relevant authority and its decisions; where material is enumerated, anything included is automatically covered, removing authority from agencies and placing it more generally; under schemes of categorisation a measure of interpretation is required, placing some but not all of the focus on agencies. An enumerative scheme assumes a solid understanding of the kinds of materials and places constituting the heritage: by its nature, anything not listed is excluded. A scheme of categorisation has a greater capacity for the inclusion of new types of material, especially if the categories are drawn not on the basis of physical form or attributes (e.g., state of ruination or age) but on value ascriptions (e.g., 'of architectural, archaeological etc. interest or importance'). Paradoxically, the greatest flexibility may exist under a scheme of designation, so long as the capacity to designate is drawn widely: if it is limited by enumeration or categorisation, then it is significantly less able to include new types of material.

Addressing different bodies of material

The range of objects that can be classed as cultural resources is wide, ranging from individual movable objects singly or in groups, to upstanding buildings in use, ruined buildings and structures, earthwork sites, buried features, scatters of material and natural features used by humans to entire landscapes, built and natural (Carman 2002, 30–57). Under systems of law the ways of treating them may be as varied as the material itself. In some regimes all cultural material of whatever kind is treated under the same body of law: while different objects may be treated in particular ways, the overall scheme is common to all classes of material. By contrast, others make a clear distinction between particular kinds of object, so they are not only treated differently but are also subject to different bodies of law. In those cases where a single, overarching national antiquities law covers all cultural objects, no distinction is drawn between individual bodies of material. Regardless of whether the object is a movable object, a scatter of material, a ruin or a buried feature, an upstanding building or a landscape, it will be subject to the same regime, effectively rendering them all a single class of object for legal purposes.

By contrast, other regimes make a clear distinction between particular kinds of object, so they are not only treated differently but are also subject to different bodies of law. Distinctions may be drawn on the basis of the physical properties or attributes of the material, so that movable objects are differentiated from fixed monuments and sites, and the latter perhaps from upstanding buildings in use. While movable objects are subject to laws concerning ownership and their placement in museums or other archives, fixed sites and monuments may be subject to official protection in the care of the state, while buildings in use are subject to controls on use and alteration. Alternatively, distinctions may be drawn on the basis of whose heritage the object represents: in states where an Indigenous population may claim rights over its cultural material, such as the Americas or Australia, such material will be treated differently from the historic heritage of the incoming European population. Here a distinction between prehistoric (i.e., pre-European contact) material and historic (colonial-period) material is effectively drawn, but it is in fact a distinction based not on age but on putative cultural origin. European states – except those where an Indigenous population dwells, such as in northern Scandinavia and Russia – and numbers of states in Africa and Asia (although not all), generally have no need of such a distinction, and material of all periods is capable of treatment under the same regime, although distinctions between different types of object may also be maintained.

Ownership versus control

As O'Keefe and Prott (1984, 189) point out, 'it is not usually necessary to have ownership of [material] in order to regulate what may be done in relation to it'. Nevertheless, as they go on to add (O'Keefe and Prott

1984, 191), a number of states across the globe do claim a right of ownership of certain classes of cultural material from the moment of discovery. While in most cases this right of ownership applies only to removable material – which will probably find its way into a museum or archive – in some cases it applies also to the land on which they were found (O'Keefe and Prott 1984, 195). Alternatively, material and land may become subject to compulsory acquisition by the state unless certain conditions (such as the deposition of material in a suitable archive) are met. This 'nationalisation' of the cultural heritage has a number of advantages:

- it is a coherent and transparent process applied equally to all
- it ensures full control by appropriate agencies over the fate of material
- it associates such material with the entire community as represented by the nation state (see also Chapter 1)
- it is simple.

However, it rides roughshod over private rights and may encourage finders to fail to report or record finds.

An alternative to state ownership is to provide for the regulation of the treatment of cultural material while allowing private ownership of that material. This may involve drawing distinctions between material on the basis of its type or circumstances of discovery, so that some material is the property of the state while other material of a similar kind is not: this is the case, for instance, with the laws of Treasure Trove and Treasure in England (Palmer 1993; Carman 1996, 55–61; Bland 2004). Alternatively, the 'cultural' component of the material may become controlled by state agencies while the object itself remains the property of another: this is sometimes the case with upstanding monuments, where the land on which a monument stands and in which it is rooted remains the property of the landowner but the monument itself passes into state control; in such cases the landowner continues to have use of the land but is subject to limitations on treatment of the monument. A third way is to place controls on the use of land either to prevent damage to existing archaeology or such that the presence of archaeology is taken into account as far as possible before the discovery of cultural material; decisions regarding the fate of any such material will therefore have been taken before any work commences, and where significant material is to be encountered work likely to damage it may be completely prevented. In cases such as these, laws and administrative arrangements to put them into force will be more complex and potentially more costly; but, if effective, they can develop a measure of public support for the project of cultural heritage protection, limiting the problems of avoidance.

Public and private agencies

The role of state agencies will differ according to whether the laws provide for state ownership or for state controls on private ownership of cultural material. In the first case, all authority over cultural remains will lie with the state. In the second, state agencies will need to interact and compromise with others who retain an interest in the material.

By far the most common approach is that of central regulation by state control, in which heritage objects are deemed to be the property and thus the responsibility of the nation-state and its agencies. Under such a system only those accredited by the state – frequently its employees, but also those granted specific licences – are entitled to conduct archaeological or conservation work. Accordingly, excavation by anyone else is commonly a criminal activity. In theory, at least, all building and other work will cease when archaeological remains are encountered, and state-employed archaeologists will move onto the site. In practice, however, limitations apply on this potentially draconian system. Small developments will be allowed to proceed unhindered, government-sponsored projects may also proceed without the interference of an archaeologist, and in many countries where such systems apply lack of resources will result in incomplete coverage. Nevertheless, the ideal behind such a system is a very powerful idea and dominates much thinking in the heritage field. It is the ideal assumed to exist by most international agencies, such as UNESCO, and very often those territories or areas not applying this approach can be thought to be deficient. Here archaeology is a cost carried out of taxation levied on the entire community in whose service it is deemed to exist.

The alternative system, which applies mostly in anglophone countries such as the UK, USA and Australia, is that of a partially privatised archaeology. This is essentially a private enterprise system under a measure of regulation by state and state-empowered authorities. In general there will be no limitation on who may carry out archaeological work, although professional bodies (see below) will seek to encourage the employment of those accredited by them. Excavation itself will most often be carried out as a result of the need to mitigate the damage of archaeological remains by development projects. In the USA material of 'scientific significance' may need to be retrieved or preserved; in the UK the emphasis is theoretically upon preservation in situ but frequently results in rescue excavation and

so-called 'preservation by record'. Where development work reveals archaeological remains, the developer will be responsible for employing archaeologists to carry out appropriate work, monitored by the local authority to
ensure proper standards of recording. Here archaeology is a cost levied on
the developer, treating damage to the heritage as a form of pollution and
applying the principle of 'the polluter pays' for restitution. This is archaeology as private enterprise, although never completely unregulated, and
much of the discussion of such systems turns upon issues of regulation
and control rather than freedom of action (see, e.g., Jansen 2010; Trow and
Grenville 2012).

Sanctions and penalties

There are two aspects to the issue of sanctions and penalties applied for
breach of laws relating to the archaeological resource: the kinds of offences
to which they relate; and the types of sanction applied. Depending on the
kind of regime in place – a state-ownership regime or a 'privatised' regime –
particular attitudes as to the severity of breach and what types of breach are
more serious will prevail, reflected in the sanctions applied both theoretically and in practice. The range of available sanctions runs the full scale of
penalties for breach of any kind of law: from prison terms through fines
where breach is considered a criminal matter to civil remedies such as
damages and carrying the cost of restoration and repair and the confiscation
of material. Such penalties may be combined, so that a person in breach
may have to carry out reparation and pay a fine or serve a prison term. As
Pickard (2001c, 329) points out, however, such powerful sanctions tend
not to be applied: prosecutions may be rare, and the penalties imposed
relatively light.

Where archaeological material is held to be the property of the state,
criminal sanctions are more likely to apply to those who claim it for
themselves. It is frequently a breach of criminal law to export such material
without the proper authority, and sometimes any private appropriation of
such material will be considered a form of theft. In some territories,
although private ownership is allowed, penalties apply for the non-
reporting of finds (O'Keefe and Prott 1984, 209–10, 215–16). An alternative
is to reward finders for reporting: they may be allowed to retain the find
without penalty, or may receive payment for its delivery to a suitable
repository. Where private ownership of material is the accepted norm,
specific provisions may apply to particular classes of material – either on
the basis of its attributes, such as its form or material, or on the basis of its

context of discovery, such as its location when found, or the process by which it came to light. Accordingly, for the bulk of archaeological material, normal rules for the allocation of ownership will apply, but certain material may become the property of the state. In such cases a need to report may apply to all material or only that owned by the state: in the latter case, provision may nevertheless be made for the voluntary reporting of finds.

Penalties also apply to those who may damage or destroy archaeological sites and monuments and historic buildings. In some cases, where these are owned by or in the care of the state, the penalties will be criminal, involving fine or prison. In other cases they will be civil, such as reparation or damages. Where arrangements are in place for the control of construction and development work, archaeological remains may be included among those factors to be considered. In such a case, where the likelihood of damage to archaeological remains is envisaged, the proposed work may be prevented altogether, but is more likely to have controls placed on it: for redesign to avoid affecting significant archaeological material, or for advance investigation of such material at the cost of the developer. Failure to comply may result in a fine or the imposition of further controls on development work. In similar vein, some Latin American states may apply sanctions to unsatisfactory excavators for poor-quality archaeological work (O'Keefe and Prott 1984, 305): such penalties will involve the cancellation of licences to conduct work in the territory concerned.

Summary

It is likely that the kinds of differences between national laws outlined briefly here in some way correlate. Accordingly, where a single body of law applies to all cultural objects, they may also be subject to direct state ownership and control, allow for no non-state agency involvement and apply at least theoretically strict criminal sanctions. Where distinctions are made between types of object, different ownership regimes may exist side by side, there may be a measure of non-state involvement in archaeology, and sanctions may be relatively light and civil rather than criminal. To date, however, and despite the work of O'Keefe and Prott (1984) and others (e.g., heritagelaw.org), no substantial work of this nature has yet been completed so these suggested likely correlations remain only as plausible assertions. Nevertheless, whether or not these types of correlations exist in reality, the crucial point is that differences between legal regimes are not mere matters of administrative convenience: in the same way as the differences of legal interpretation covered above, they represent fundamental differences of ideology in terms of what law is for, where authority resides and the nature of the cultural heritage. In thus approaching national laws, it is necessary to be sensitive to the kinds of ideology represented and the attitudes towards and expectations of both law and heritage that they carry.

The professionalisation of archaeology

The application of legislation in the field of archaeology and its regulation under law is one of the factors that has encouraged the increasing professionalisation of the field. The regulatory influence of official organisations allows them to produce standard-setting documentation which influence practice and require to be met if work is to be granted to those at whom they are aimed: a number of state agencies accordingly have adopted such a non-legislative approach to controls on archaeological work. Parks Canada, for instance, publish as part of their website (http://parkscanada.pch.gc.ca/library/PC_Guiding_Principles/) their Cultural Resource Management Policy, setting out the principles guiding their treatment of the historic places in their care. In the UK, English Heritage seeks to guide the conduct of publicly funded archaeological work by encouraging a particular managerial approach (English Heritage 1991). English Heritage was also responsible for producing the nationally applicable guidelines for local authorities on the treatment of archaeological sites under threat from development projects (DoE 1990), and monitors their application and effectiveness. The message of such products – whether international or national – is that of the particular expertise of the people responsible for them, which in turn further encourages the professionalisation of the discipline as a whole.

As seen in Chapter 2, the increasing professionalisation of archaeology over the past decades has had an impact in terms of self-regulation. As bodies come together to represent archaeologists as professional specialists working in a broader environment than pure academic research, they also promote their own standards among their membership. In particular, they will require of their members adherence to basic minimum standards of ethics and performance. These usually lack any legal power but nevertheless derive authority from the overall professionalisation of the field encouraged by the emphasis placed on expertise and specialist knowledge by national and international heritage agencies. These professional associations are established to serve the interests of archaeologists themselves and often do more than merely offer standards of performance, by providing opportunities for archaeologists to meet and discuss matters of common

TABLE 3.2 *Professional responsibilities of archaeologists*

Professional responsibility owed to:	Associations/professional bodies in				
	USA			Europe	UK
	SAA	AAA	RPA	EAA	IfA
The public	•	•	•	•	•
Colleagues		•	•	•	•
Archaeological record	•	•	•	•	•
The past					•
Students		•			
Clients		•	•	•	•
Laws		•	•	•	•

interest at conferences and congresses. Membership of some such bodies may also indicate that a particular individual has achieved a certain level of expertise as an archaeologist and is therefore a suitable individual to undertake particular kinds of professional task. In contrast, some are primarily academic institutions, membership of which says little or nothing about the capacity of the individual. By offering codes of ethics or standards of performance, however, they seek to confirm the expertise and professionalism of archaeologists as a whole. An overview of the statements of good practice produced by the bodies listed in Table 3.2 reveals a close similarity of idea as to those to whom (or to which) archaeologists should consider themselves responsible. This reflects the global nature of archaeology as a discipline, but also the ease with which aspects of archaeology related to heritage issues become accepted throughout the globe. Here the Society for American Archaeology (SAA), the American Anthropological Association (AAA) and the European Association of Archaeologists (EAA) are primarily academic institutions, the main activity of which is to organise annual meetings for academic and professional discussion; the U.S. Register of Professional Archaeologists (RPA) and the UK Chartered Institute for Archaeology (IfA) work to represent the commercial archaeologist working in a partially privatised system of development control, their main task being to provide assurance to clients that the archaeologists undertaking work are qualified to do so.

In combination with laws and regulatory procedures, these systems of self-supervision and oversight create a climate where archaeology operates inevitably as part of systems of governance. Although not widely discussed in these terms (but see Smith and Campbell 1998; Smith 2004, 58–80), the point is recognised by others with an interest in the material remains of the past. Especially in those jurisdictions governed by a tradition of common law and private property rather than state control and ownership, those who object to giving control over the past to a 'closed' profession, and despite their own inclination towards individualism, organise themselves into groups who may then propagate their own codes of practice and standards of behaviour, effectively 'professionalising' an anti-archaeologist stance. This is to some extent the situation in the UK in respect of amateur metal-detectorists and treasure-hunters, many of whom work in association with archaeologists and others (Thomas 2012). The voluntary Portable Antiquities Scheme – whereby finds are reported and the information made publicly available (www.finds.org.uk; Bland 2004) – is given support by the code of practice of the National Council for Metal Detecting (www.ncmd.co.uk), among others.

Conclusion

This brief outline of how laws and regulations impact on archaeology will be developed further in the book as particular aspects are addressed. The key points to note, as in Chapters 1 and 2, are the variations in approaches to law in the field: these in turn represent not mere habit and local practice but real differences in ideology and approach. Where a system is based on close control by central government, it represents a very different understanding of the purpose and role of archaeology in society from one where private ownership is upheld and regulations are looser and more flexible. These are differences that matter, especially in relation to study or work in an area new to one: ideas that are the norm in one territory do not transfer simply to another. Such differences are reflected in how archaeologists are trained and qualified, the relations between archaeologists and the state, relations between archaeologists, between archaeologists and others interested in the past, and between archaeologists and the wider public. They are also reflected in the literature, by the provision of national and regional guides to archaeological practice (see, e.g., Smith and Burke 2007; Schofield et al. 2011).

PART II

PRACTICES

CHAPTER 4

Inventory

Inventory and recording are rarely mentioned in the international comparative literature of ARM (see, e.g., chapters in McManamon and Hatton 2000; Layton et al. 2004; Messenger and Smith 2010), and, where mentioned, they are glossed over or combined with other activities such as survey (e.g., chapters in Cleere 1984a). They are also rarely given their proper status in reviews or discussions of national systems of ARM (see, e.g., Sebastian and Lipe 2009; Smith and Burke 2007; although for an exception see Fraser and Newman 2006), and there are occasional explicit international approaches to the topic (e.g., National Museum of Denmark 1992). However, even where inventory and recording are mentioned among other aspects of ARM, they are frequently given rather short shrift (see, e.g., Schofield et al. 2011, 83–4) and are therefore assumed to be unproblematic in nature. The most common location for an explicit discussion of inventory and recording is in the field of applying computer systems to archaeology (e.g., Lagerqvist and Rosvall 1991; Kerrel et al. 1991; Fitz 1991; Corazzol 1991; Stancic and Veljanovski 2001; and other proceedings of the Computer Applications in Archaeology conferences), which separates them from the field of ARM and locates them in other sub-fields of archaeology.

The process of recording the heritage is nevertheless a key function of archaeological agencies at every level of organisation. The justification behind inventory is that no decision about the future of the archaeological resource can be taken unless there is clear knowledge of what it comprises (Thornes and Bold 1998, 1). As emphasised in Chapter 3, it is one of the roles of laws in the field to determine what particular characteristics heritage objects and places must have. Accordingly, the task of inventory is to match objects and places with that list of usually legally approved characteristics. Table 4.1 sets out the difference between the archaeological record and resource in this respect: whereas the archaeological record (the

TABLE 4.1 *The archaeological record and the archaeological resource*

Characteristic	The Archaeological ...	
	Record	Resource
Serves the purposes of	researchers	the public
Key attribute	variability	finite/non-renewable
Used for	research	public purposes
Creation of	archaeological theory/ method	regulation
Considered as	evidence	resource
Identified by	survey	categorisation
Selected for	relevance	significance

object of research activity) is identified by survey, the resource (the object of management) is identified by a process of categorisation. This involves, in particular, the matching of objects and places with the particular and predetermined attributes they need to have in order for them to be classed as archaeological objects. Such inventories of 'approved' ARM objects exist at every level of organisation. The UNESCO World Heritage List promoted and managed by ICOMOS is an inventory of those sites and places considered by individual nation-states to be of particular importance (Askew 2010). Similarly, at the national level in every state of the world certain sites are marked as being of particular importance or significance (an issue to be addressed in Chapter 5). However, in order that sites and places can be separated out as special, there also needs to be a general background inventory of all those things and places which fall into the remit of ARM.

In most countries of the world there is a single national database of sites (National Museum of Denmark 1992; chapters in Messenger and Smith 2010). In federal states, such as Australia and the USA, responsibility for recording archaeology falls on federal and state agencies together, and often in addition with others, such as organisations representing Indigenous peoples. Here, co-ordination will be carried out by one particular federal body – in the USA it is the National Park Service (Canouts 1992), and in Australia the Australian Heritage Council acts as an advisory body to the federal Department of Environment and Heritage (Smith and Burke 2007, 12). In the UK this general inventory is referred to as the Historic Environment Record (HER), kept by the archaeologist employed by each county local authority. Ideally – although it is likely that none is entirely complete or up to date – these records comprise the details of all monuments, find-spots for antiquities, archaeological sites and sites where archaeological work has been conducted throughout the county. In addition to the HERs, the national heritage agency of England, English Heritage, has responsibility for the National Monuments Record, which acts as an index to the more detailed local HERs. Taken together, they are considered an almost complete record of the nation's archaeology (Aberg and Leech 1992; Fraser and Newman 2006).

In all cases of inventory, the emphasis is strongly placed on the completeness and accuracy of the records held, and the methods of recording applied. Further emphasis is also placed on methods of retrieval of the information held and the uses to which it is put. To some extent these interrelate, especially with the increasing use – and planned use – of information technology, (see, e.g., Lagerqvist and Rosvall 1991; Kerrel et al. 1991; Fitz 1991; Corazzol 1991), and all are subject to the promotion of common standards (e.g., Thornes and Bold 1998). These issues become of even greater importance where separately compiled sets of records are intended to be united to form a single overarching record. Here the problems of co-ordinating record types and translation from one system to another become very evident and very important (National Museum of Denmark 1992). Accordingly, this chapter will offer an overview of processes and systems of inventory, the kinds of material covered and the maintenance of records. Some of the specific content will be evident to those reading it, and even obvious: nevertheless, standard principles will be emphasised.

Defining the archaeological resource

While the material with which archaeologists are concerned varies only in terms of its particular period and regional interest, the material classed as 'the archaeological record' and that classed as 'the archaeological resource' are always identical. The differences between them relate to the uses to which they are put and the purposes they serve. Anything that can be classed as 'archaeological' will fall into both categories at once: the difference will emerge in terms of the attitudes taken towards it and the treatment it receives. Chapter 2 reviewed the separation of ARM from the host discipline of archaeology: the distinction between the 'record' and 'resource' is at once symptomatic of that division and a consequence of it.

The two phenomena can be distinguished on the basis of a number of characteristics in which they differ, as summarised in Table 4.1. They are of concern to two different groups of people. As 'record', archaeological material is primarily of concern to field archaeologists researching into the past. As a 'resource', however, it is primarily considered to be of concern to the public (McGimsey 1972, 5; Fowler 1984). The diagnostic attribute of the record is that of variability: for Binford it takes the form of variability in assemblages of artefacts, in form, in function and in style (Binford 1983); for Hodder it takes the form of temporal, spatial, depositional and typological variability (Hodder 1986, 125). The diagnostic attributes of the resource, however, and the reason for its importance to archaeologists are that it is considered finite and consequently non-renewable (Darvill 1987, 1; McGimsey 1972, 24; but for contrary arguments see Carman 1996, 7–8; 2000, 8–9; Holtorf 2001). The use to which the record will be put is always that of research, whereas the resource will be preserved, either for future research or for public access (Chapter 7). Neither record nor resource is a natural category that exists independently of observation: both are the creation of the expectations made of them. Accordingly, the 'record' is governed by archaeological method and theory, meeting the requirements of researchers and their work (Patrik 1985). By contrast, the 'resource' is a creation of regulation and law, serving the purposes of archaeological policy (Cleere 1989, 10; Smith 2004, 76–8). In fulfilling its research role, the record constitutes evidence to be used in understanding the past (Barrett 1987, 6). The resource, however, is seen as just that – a resource to be used for a range of possible purposes, of which research is only one. In seeking the record, various techniques of survey are applied (Cleere 1984c, 126; see below), while the resource is subject to characterisation studies and processes of categorisation (Darvill 1993; Carman 1996). Once identified, components of the record are selected for use on the basis of their relevance to specific research projects (Binford 1977, 2), whereas components of the resource are selected on the basis of their ascribed significance or importance (Cleere 1984c, 127; Schaafsma 1989; Wester 1990; Chapter 5).

Table 4.2 is a preliminary attempt to categorise the kinds of material that comprise both record and resource. Each of the three columns covers a particular category, showing its distinctive characteristics and how it is generally treated. The left column concerns movable objects: no matter where they are or how long they stay there, they remain identifiable as particular kinds of object; and they will usually find their way into a collection or archive. Fragmentary objects – such as broken pottery sherds – are treated in exactly the same way: although not an intact object in the conventional sense, they nevertheless represent an object for archaeological purposes, and quite often are considered to stand for the entire

TABLE 4.2 *Archaeological objects*

	Object	Site and Monument	Landscape
Form	Mobile, but remains always 'itself': 'solid'	Fixed in space: 'bounded'	Extensive: 'unbounded'; changes over time
Treatment	Collection/archive	Preservation in situ	Conservation
Mutability		Unchanging	Subject to change

object of which they were once a part. The central column concerns sites and monuments: these are fixed in space and can be distinguished from their surroundings by having boundaries – physical or conceptual – placed around them; they are generally subject to preservation in place rather than removal elsewhere. The third column concerns landscapes, which are not single things which can have a boundary placed around them: they are extensive and fill the space between other things. That is why the landscape, in particular, is different from other categories of thing, and treated differently. Here I have used the term 'conservation' rather than preservation: it carries with it the idea of maintaining the general character of space while allowing changes to take place, such as the removal of one object from that space and the insertion of another. As I and others have argued elsewhere (Carman 1998; 2002, 30–57; Fairclough 2008; Turner and Fairclough 2007), a landscape may not, strictly speaking, constitute a *thing* at all. Objects and sites or monuments are discrete, separable and identifiable single things that are not considered appropriate for alteration: the landscape is, by contrast, the set of relationships that gives them their separateness. Accordingly, what matters is not the retention of individual features within a landscape but rather the overall sense of the place (its *genius loci*).

It is worth noting that there are certain categories of thing that do not fit this neat tripartite scheme. Among these are environmental and other data (such as chemical residues and radiocarbon dates) which exist at a level below that of the object: they cannot be picked up and carried around or conveniently identified except as attributes of something else that can usually be defined as some kind of object. Similarly, human remains constitute neither objects as artefacts nor yet something large and fixed enough to be considered a site: humans in our frameworks of thought are conveniently separated out from all other classes of object in the universe. Rock art – an area of increasing interest to archaeologists (Chippindale and

Taçon 1998) – can be treated as 'art', in which case it is usually ascribed some of the qualities of a movable object such as a painting. Others, however, treat it more as a 'site', in which case it is ascribed many of the attributes of a fixed monument. It cannot, however, be both at once. Gardens and certain other areas of land can be treated as having many of the attributes of fixed sites rather than unbounded landscapes. At one level they perhaps ought to be considered as landscapes, but are usually too bounded by physical or conceptual limits to truly merit membership of this category. These categories, therefore, must be treated with a certain caution. While each is 'real' in the sense that it is meaningful to us and sufficiently reflective of external reality to merit attention, they are also convenient fictions we use to make sense of the world around us. This is an essential issue to take into account in understanding an inventory: ultimately all categories are arbitrary, but all nevertheless fall within the remit of an archaeological inventory and are incorporated one way or another.

A number of commentators have criticised the concept of 'site' as it is used in archaeology, which is not a particularly simple one (e.g., Dunnell 1992). The focus of attention is most often placed on its internal structure, in the form of stratigraphy representing activities at the site separated by time, as revealed in the process of archaeological work (Harris 1979; Hodder 1999; Roskams 2001; Lucas 2001a). The notion of the site is, however, a particularly pertinent issue for ARM, since so many of the activities of ARM practitioners are directed towards the discovery, recording, preservation and presentation of such phenomena (see below and Chapters 5–7). The concept of a 'site', as used in archaeology, has two meanings, rarely separated in archaeological discourse and often conflated. The first relates to material as found in the present: this is the site as the object of attention of archaeologists and ARM practitioners today. The second relates to the past: this is the site as the location of human activity in that past. It is likely that the site of human activity in the past – an ancient field system, a settlement site, a ritual monument or a defensive structure – may become the focus of archaeological investigation in the present. It is also possible, however, that taphonomic phenomena may remove material from one location to another: material deposited in a stream, for example, may be moved downstream by water action and deposited on the stream bank, or material deposited on an ancient beach may be included in an eroding cliff face and fall out onto the modern beach surface. In the latter cases, although the focus of archaeological attention, the site is not that of the human activity represented by the material. Sites are usually not sites in and of themselves but are the site of something else: of some kind of activity, such as archaeology; of a former object or structure, such as a now ruined building; or of something still extant such as a monument. Sites do not therefore stand alone and cannot be understood or comprehended without taking into account this additional qualifying attribute: accordingly, a site is usually considered to be the site of something specific.

The notion of the site as a singular, bounded entity (Carman 2002, 44–51) is problematic because it defies the reality as experienced by archaeologists. As a number of commentators have pointed out (Foley 1981; Dunnell and Dancey 1983; Tainter and Bagley 2005), archaeological material presents itself not as a set of discrete clusters across a landscape with empty space between but as a continuous distribution through space, albeit in greater or lesser concentrations. This measure of the density of a particular concentration has been termed 'salience', referring to the degree of shallowness, extent and material richness displayed by that concentration (Tainter and Bagley 2005, 61). A concentration with a high level of salience will be treated as a discrete 'site' for both research and ARM purposes, further supporting the supposed reality of the concept. Accordingly, ARM records may well be structured in terms of the presence or absence of 'sites'. These may correspond to other phenomena, such as upstanding monuments or buildings, that share the attribute of a solid external boundary.

While it is obvious that all objects of archaeological enquiry – and all those that potentially might offer opportunities for archaeological research – will be included in an inventory, there are other categories that also have need to be accommodated if the record is to be considered complete. These comprise those activities that represent effects on the material residues of the past that in turn have consequences for that material. While individual objects, sites and landscapes can be categorised as physical phenomena – collectively to be referred to as 'objects' or 'monuments' or 'sites', whichever is most convenient – activities to be recorded are of a different order: these are frequently and conveniently referred to as 'events'. Such events would include: deliberate archaeological interventions, such as non-intrusive survey work and excavations; singular and accidental finds, such as the discovery and retrieval of individual objects; and agricultural and construction work that has led either to the discovery of archaeological material or to its loss or damage. Other kinds of such 'events' include non-archaeological research, such as geological prospection, that may have implications for archaeological survey, such as the mapping or identification of alluvial deposits overlying older land surfaces, or the mapping of palaeochannels and ancient river beds. The implications of many such events will be for understanding the likelihood of the survival of remains in that location, or the difficulty of identifying remains prior to development or other work taking place. The value of geological work is often also in predictive modelling where material of particular kinds may survive.

Chapter 3 outlined the various means by which laws relating to archaeology set out to define the archaeological resource, by enumeration, categorisation and classification. It also outlined how in some jurisdictions different classes of material are treated differently. From the point of view of constructing an inventory of archaeological material these purely legal distinctions are not meaningful. Instead, an archaeological inventory requires the inclusion of anything and everything that can be considered archaeological – from fragmentary remains of individual objects, through complete objects singly or in groups, to material scatters, to upstanding monuments and buildings in use, to the landscapes in which they are located. As indicated above, it also requires the inclusion of those events that have consequences for that material. As Fraser and Newman (2006, 24) point out for the UK, such requirements would also include coverage of collections of artefacts, especially in museums, although these are frequently left out of archaeological inventories. Efforts at definition of what needs to be covered by such inventories most commonly take the form of lists of standard terms for classes of object, site or monument: some such thesauri are relatively simple, but others aim to be more comprehensive and complete (e.g., RCHME 1998). These may include terms not only for types of object (e.g., polished flint axe, clovis point) and site (e.g., stone row, stone circle, standing stone) but also for their forms, distinguishing between sites identified by crop mark, soil mark, earthworks or as upstanding structures or buildings. These terms – and their permitted variations – are those that will be entered onto the inventory database to allow systematic searches.

Identifying the resource

A key difference between much ARM archaeology and research archaeology is that ARM seeks to know what is there and its condition in order to be able to make decisions about its future. Research archaeology, by contrast, investigates what is available in order to learn about the past. Having said this, the two are inevitably interconnected: research archaeology may well be one of the futures decided on by ARM work, while research will contribute to the knowledge base for future ARM decision-making. The practical processes of seeking information on the resource are also shared and are identical for both researchers and ARM archaeologists: both involve survey in its various forms. The difference between the two areas again emerges, however, when material is encountered: the researcher will seek to understand it, while the ARM archaeologist will attempt to classify it according to pre-existing frameworks as represented by laws or guidance; this is the process recognised as 'categorisation' in Table 4.1 and outlined above. Archaeologists themselves will prefer various forms of systematic survey that can be relied on to produce reliable data for inclusion in the inventory. These will consist of classic archaeological techniques such as fieldwalking, earthwork survey, various forms of geoarchaeological prospection and the use of aerial photographs and other forms of remote sensing. These can be – and frequently are – supplemented and sometimes replaced altogether by less systematic forms of survey work, carried out either by archaeologists or by others, which are equally useful in developing the inventory. The purpose of this book is not to outline how to conduct these types of survey, but rather to outline their place in the ARM process. In what follows, some of the similarities and differences will be highlighted, and the advantages and difficulties associated with them.

The retrieval of diagnostic but unstratified artefacts from the surface is often a good indicator of the presence of underlying archaeology. The systematic collection of such objects for classification and archiving as part of a programme of fieldwalking is both an ARM and a research activity, carried out usually either by or under the supervision of professional archaeologists, although it is also highly suited to amateur and avocational involvement (Fasham et al. 1980). In general, the choice of location for the activity will have been made on the basis of prior indications of the likelihood that material will be recovered; accordingly, often such activities will be undertaken on known sites or in their vicinity to establish their nature or period – to distinguish, for example, settlement from military sites or, for example, prehistoric from historic period sites – or their extent. Alternatively, it may be conducted in a previously unexamined area in order to gain an impression of the nature, extent and 'salience' of any sites that might be encountered. Fieldwalking alone, however systematically conducted, is unlikely to provide all the information needed about possible concentrations of material: sometimes material is too deep or simply of the wrong kind to be brought to the surface.

Although it may be denied by many archaeologists, the work of those who use metal-detectors to uncover material from the past is not entirely dissimilar to the activity of fieldwalking. Differences lie in the manner of conducting such metal-detecting surveys and the primary purpose: they will involve typically only one or a very few people, and be aimed at finding

interesting objects for private retention. They are also not carried out for a
public purpose and may be conducted clandestinely or even illegally.
Often, ethical rules about the retrieval only of unstratified objects from
the ploughsoil may be flouted, causing damage to underlying archaeology.
As I have written elsewhere, metal-detector users, treasure-hunters and
pot-hunters

> do not do 'good' excavation: they do not carry out prior survey, they do not
> record stratigraphy, they do not retrieve all classes of data, and they do
> not publish results. But from their point of view, they may do very good
> excavation: they find and retrieve only what is relevant to them, leaving
> the rest for others; they may do minimal damage from their perspective,
> leaving only small holes in the site; and they do not impede development
> or other work by their small-scale and possibly clandestine presence
> (Carman 2004, 49).

Where reasonable relations can be established between archaeologists, the
agencies that employ them and such enthusiasts, however, the finds made
can be incorporated into the inventory to indicate the presence of likely
archaeology, as in the UK through the Portable Antiquities Scheme (Savile
2006, 71–3; Thomas 2012). There will necessarily be limits to the usefulness
of such advice: some finds and find-spots will remain unreported and
consequently unrecorded; some reporting may be incomplete or inaccu-
rate in terms of location and the material recovered, leading to a poor
appreciation of the salience of any sites. On the other hand, where good
relations exist, full reporting may be much more likely, and there may even
be the opportunity to examine finds made to confirm or deny any claims
made: some branches of archaeology (e.g., the study of battlefields: Scott et
al. 2007; Foard and Morris 2012) habitually use the data produced by metal-
detectorists and actively co-operate with them, to produce valuable data for
analysis and interpretation.

A third and very valuable indicator is of chance finds. These may take a
number of forms: material appearing on the surface of fields after plough-
ing; items discovered on digging for entirely non-archaeological purposes,
such as pipe-trenches or in a garden; or material simply being picked up
from the surface of a path or road. Most will be unstratified, and some (such
as those retrieved on country walks) entirely without context: nevertheless,
their presence can be used to determine the possible presence of other such
material. The problems with such reports are similar to those made by
metal-detectorists: find-spots or the finds themselves may be inaccurately
reported, and not all will be reported. Nevertheless, where the responsible

agency – be it a national archaeological service, a local authority archaeological office or a museum – advertises a willingness to advise on and
identify such stray finds, most may find their way into the inventory.

Upstanding features represent a more obvious target of attention for
archaeologists, although they are not necessarily to be considered as more
important than the evidence of buried remains. The accurate survey of
such phenomena can be crucial to appreciating what they represent in
terms of period and possible function – in the case of a linear feature, the
boundary of a settlement or associated fields, a political or military boundary; in the case of a circular or rectangular bank or ditch, a domestic or
ritual enclosure – and, of course, their condition and any threats they may
face from damage or erosion. Like fieldwalking, it is an activity that may be
undertaken primarily by professionals, but is also amenable to trained
amateurs. Various forms of geophysical survey, by contrast, are more likely
to be available only to professionals: apart from the need to be trained and
experienced in the use of the necessary equipment, the equipment itself
is expensive and not readily available to amateurs and avocational archaeologists. The use of metal-detectors has been mentioned above, and while
these are readily available, they are usable only for the detection of certain
kinds of material, whereas other techniques – magnetometry, resistivity and
the use of ground-penetrating radar, for instance – are able to locate
and identify buried features otherwise invisible (see, e.g., Scollar et al.
1990; Gaffney et al. 2002).

Such features can also be identified from aerial and satellite photographs as crop or soil marks in appropriate conditions, or as upstanding
remains. Aerial photography, in particular, although pioneered in
Europe, has become widely used throughout the world (Bewley and
Rączkowski 2002; Kennedy and Bewley 2004). Other areas have bene-
fited from satellite imagery, such as South and Central America and East
and South Asia, which has allowed the recognition of previously
unknown sites in inaccessible areas, and with the use of infra-red and
other frequencies to identify previously invisible features and site attributes. It has also been used to produce detailed maps and three-
dimensional images of known sites, which, especially when compared
with similar images produced through time, can be used to monitor the
general condition of sites, the effects of erosion, the encroachment of
foliage and of development, and the effects of, for example, tourism. All
these techniques can also be used in conjunction with the ground-based
techniques mentioned above to provide a good appreciation of sites
(see, e.g., papers in Campana and Forte 2006).

Where work has already begun and the presence of archaeological remains may be suspected, an archaeologist on site may be able to retrieve at least some material and information about the site before it is lost. Such 'watching briefs' can be used to identify artefacts that are revealed by digging work, or features exposed on the surface or in the side of excavated trenches. In effect, the process is not dissimilar to that of an archaeological excavation, except that digging is not systematically designed to reveal archaeological material and allow its recording: any action to record the material will need to be undertaken swiftly and with a view to the dangers inherent in construction work. No such recording will be complete: it will depend in part on the chance encounter of what may be present and the ability of the recorder to identify material as it appears and to record it – by photograph, drawing or description – at speed while also looking out for further material being revealed. In territories where archaeological mate-rial is the property of the state and where its presence requires official investigation, a watching brief of this kind may result in a halt to work and a full programme of archaeological examination. However, such briefs are more usually undertaken where permissions that may be required for development have already been granted and the watching brief therefore represents an effort at mitigation.

A full-scale excavation will, of course, reveal a wide range of data (see, e.g., Barker 1982; Roskams 2001). While the processes of such fieldwork have been subject to critique and examination in their own right (see, e.g., Tilley 1989; Lucas 2001a; 2001b; Carver 2004; Edgeworth 2006), its place as the most recognised and typical archaeological technique remains certain.

Sources of information

Where advance decisions need to be made about the probable effect of development on any archaeology at a particular location, some kind of prior assessment of the archaeology likely to be encountered will be required. The most useful first step will always be to review already available informa-tion and use this as a guide to what can be expected to be encountered. Where such information is lacking or falls short of a complete record, further fieldwork can also be undertaken prior to allowing development work to proceed, and this may include a watching brief (as outlined above). Nevertheless, a preliminary study will prove highly valuable, and the sources for this are often incorporated into an inventory.

Maps – both current and historical – are an invaluable tool. Current topographic maps may indicate the presence of earthworks or other features

of known archaeological interest or suggest the presence of features
otherwise not shown, such as by street layout or the retention of old
names for places. Reference to earlier maps of the same area – likely to
have been produced for a range of different purposes – will record changes
in topography and land use. They may also indicate features now lost, such
as earthworks, lines of ditch or hedge, roadways or buildings. Such maps
need to be used with a degree of caution (see, e.g., Lape 2002 for a
discussion of the use of historic maps in studying colonial settlement and
trade in Indonesia), but nevertheless, when used in combination and with
other sources of data, they can provide useful suggestions as to the presence
of archaeological features. Similarly, the work of previous investigators –
in Europe, frequently antiquarian research; elsewhere, often the work of
Europeans who have conquered or settled in the lands of others; and in
all cases, early ethnographers – can provide much useful information
about the presence or absence of features. Such 'text-aided' (Little 1992)
or 'documentary' (Wilkie 2006) archaeology is used particularly for
the more recent periods, encompassing the period of European domina-
tion and capitalism, increasingly referred to internationally as 'historical
archaeology' (Funari et al. 1999; Hicks and Beaudry 2006; Little 2007)
rather than by more regional terms (e.g., 'post-Columbian' archaeology
in the Americas, 'post-contact' archaeology in Australasia or 'post-
medieval' archaeology in Europe), but it is also of value for much earlier
periods from which remains may have survived as ruins or earthworks
into historical times.

An equally valuable source is that of local knowledge. Some of this
may come from local collectors, pot-hunters, treasure-hunters or metal-
detectorists (depending on preferred nomenclatures) who choose to record
their finds and are willing to discuss the context of discovery. Similarly,
students of the local past, those who work outdoors and have developed an
affinity for changes in topography and soil and a capacity to identify non-
natural material, and long-lived residents who have noticed changes in
their surroundings may all have valuable insights and understanding of
relevance to archaeological investigation. This has been particularly recognised by the professional archaeological community in relation to traditional and Indigenous communities with long-term oral histories (Wilkie
2006, 19; McDonald et al. 1991). Valuable work to record and thereby offer
some protection to Indigenous heritage places has relied almost entirely on
such testimony (e.g., Smith et al. 1993); the role of the archaeologist in such
scenarios is entirely that of a recorder of information given, for addition to
an inventory (but see also Chapter 7).

Where information exists fully in the public domain – as published material or part of a publicly accessible archive – no issues of sensitivity arise. However, where the information comes from private archival material or from individual respondents, such issues may be crucial. Landowners or the finders of individual objects may be very sensitive to issues of access and unwilling for the information they provide to be made widely available. Similarly, advice from traditional or Indigenous cultures may represent 'secret' knowledges that must not be made available to outsiders, or which can only be made available to certain categories of person, such as either men or women (see, e.g., Smith et al. 1993). In such cases, any inventory will provide for the withholding of the details of sites so identified from the wider user community.

Content of records

Records will consist of multiple components rather than take a single form. These will include map-based data, which may also be delivered via a geographic information system, a basic data form providing a summary of all known material concerning the item recorded, relevant publications and other literature relating to the item, and a file (electronic or paper) in which other pertinent material, such as official notifications, will be kept.

Table 4.3 is an idealised and suggested 'average' format for an archaeological record form, allowing inclusion of all of the components of the record discussed above, whether a site or an intervention. Not all inventories will contain everything listed in Table 4.3, while others may exceed it significantly (see, e.g., Thornes and Bold 1998, 33–44); however, the essential content will be shared by all records. Such records may also include supporting documentation, such as maps and written records of survey and research. Many of the reports will consist of examples of the 'grey literature' referred to in Chapter 2 but nevertheless retained as part of the archive; others will be published literature which will also be available to those consulting the inventory. The content of the recording form is broken down into a number of specific fields, such as basic locational data, the specifics of the object being recorded, information relevant to decision-making and information useful in managing the site. Within these broader fields, specific information is entered; some of this may be unobtainable or apparently irrelevant, but the system will generally be designed so as to be as flexible and all-embracing as possible to accommodate future research needs. Searches of the system may be possible using any of the data fields.

TABLE 4.3 *Minimum content of an idealised archaeological record*

Basic data	Object / event specifics
Site name	Descriptor
Unique identifier (alphanumeric)	(standardised)
Geographical location	Period
(e.g., national grid reference, GPS	(standardised)
reference, latitude/longitude)	Membership of clusters/groups of sites or
Administrative location	monuments
Height above sea level	Related sites (by unique identifier)
Geology	Full description (free text)
Soil type	

Sources of data

Published sources: publications, reports, etc.
History of events: fieldwalking, stray finds, excavations, construction or agricultural activity

Management information

Designations: scientific importance, national monument, National Park, etc.
Current land use
Form: built structure, ruin, earthwork, crop mark, find-spot, excavation, etc.
Condition: degree of preservation (good/poor)
Vulnerability (good, poor)

Administrative information	System data
Owner	Initial date of entry in system
Occupier	Subsequent updates
Other interested parties/stakeholders	

A unique identifier for each entry is considered essential. While in some records the site or object name, its descriptor or its location may be enough to differentiate it clearly from all other records, there will be occasions where these are not enough: more than one site or event may exist at the same location and therefore bear the same name; similar objects may exist near by; or incomplete data or recording may confuse different records. The most common form will be a simple alphanumeric coding system for all records. Where a number of objects or events coincide at, for example, the same location, the same basic coding may be used for all, differentiated by suffixed letters or numbers: for example, entry number 00001a, b, c ,; or ABCi, ii, iii. The most convenient system – and the one most widely used – is perhaps that of sequential numbering, with the first entry as '1' and going as high as is necessary. More sophisticated structures can, however, be devised if necessary, based on site status or broad location, such as administrative district, but if any change takes place the identifier will also need to change to reflect this, thus complicating the system and requiring a further record system to allow cross-checks between changes in the record. Where the system is electronically based, the electronic system may itself allocate the identifier to avoid human error in duplication or data entry. Variations on the basic principle apply in a number of territories. The complex ArchéoDATA system devised in France (Arroyo-Bishop and Zarzosa 1992) creates codes that relate the site not only to its geographical location – within country and district and by site – but also to individual features and excavation units within the site.

Locational information is also essential. This will be connected to map-based information referring back to the data record. The more precise the locational data – preferably to within a few metres – the more accurate and the more useful the data. Where the site is large, it may be recorded either as a point at its centre or by a range of locations indicating its extent: where a point only is included, some indication of size may also be useful. Of course, the map will also indicate its extent, and any supporting reports or other information may include plans making this clear. Where the site overlaps with or overlies another site, because each will have its own unique identifier, confusion between the two can be avoided. Exactly how the information as to location is shown will vary from territory to territory: in countries such as the UK and Australia, which have their own national grid systems, it may be recorded in accordance with that grid; alternatively, detailed longitude and latitude may be used. Some GPS systems will provide readings equivalent to national grids, but where this is not the case, suitable adjustment will need to be made. Whatever the system used, however, it will need to be consistent across the inventory to avoid confusion. The administrative location will be useful both for searches and for management purposes, especially allocating responsibility for management of the site or object. The precise nature of this will, of course, depend on the administrative structure of the territory concerned, where such responsibilities are placed by laws and regulations, and the body responsible for the inventory. At whatever level it is kept, the administrative location will need to specify all lower levels of administration that apply. Accordingly, a national archive may specify states, provinces or regions as well as, for example, county, city or district. Where it is kept at supranational level, such as by an international agency or a continent-level authority such as the EU or Council of Europe, or the Organisations of African or American States, then it will specify countries also. Where, in a federal state, it is kept at state or provincial level, it will specify only such lower administrative levels as apply.

Information on the natural setting of the site will prove useful both for future researchers – who will not need to carry out their own analysis of underlying geology or soils, or measure the height relative to sea level – and also as predictive tools for those seeking similar sites elsewhere. Where a search of the records indicates that certain kinds of site – settlement, defensive, ritual, etc. – cluster in particular environments, then it can be inferred that the most likely place to find a new site will be in a location with similar characteristics. Similarly, the use of the record for the purposes of managing the archaeological resource will be enhanced by the inclusion of such information: it can be inferred that unexamined areas with similar geological profiles may contain sites of a similar nature. The fact is, however, that in many cases such information is not recorded, either owing to factors related to the recorder or because the information is not readily available: it is not likely that an Indigenous informant, an amateur detectorist or the locator of a chance find, for instance, will be interested in such information or knowledgeable about how to retrieve it.

Details of the site or object are, of course, integral to the record and will include not only a full description but also shorter, standardised information for use in searches. Accordingly, use of alternative terms for the same object-type will be avoided: instead, a standardised terminology will be employed, and variations within the broader category of type, function, period and style will be addressed in the fuller description. Other shorthand search terms may also be used to limit searches, so that a search for, say, Neolithic burial mounds in an area of Europe will avoid epi-Palaeolithic, Mesolithic, Bronze Age, Iron Age, Classical and medieval types. For events, a different set of standardised terms will be applied – differentiating excavation from various kinds of survey, chance finds, etc. The content of each record will be unique and specific to the site, object or event in question, but rarely do sites exist in isolation: they may form part of a related group of sites, located side by side or sequentially through time, or part of a cluster of monuments of similar kind located close together – such as a barrow-field or individual houses in a settlement. This set of relationships will also be described and the identifiers of related sites or structures listed to allow their identification. The free text description, which may be lifted directly from other sources, such as reports, will also include references to these related groups or clusters.

An earlier section outlined the various sources of data for records, and these too will be incorporated into an inventory system. For published sources, only sufficient information will be given to identify them and allow them to be found in a library or other repository. For unpublished sources, more information may be given in order for full understanding of the processes by which information was retrieved to be established. This will include as full a history of events affecting the site as possible, and these will cross-reference with records for those events. As indicated in the previous section, the kinds of events will cover not only specific archae-ological activity but also others that have had some impact on the acquisi-tion of archaeological knowledge. These data will feed directly into information needed for the site's management, and these final sets of data will require constant updating to keep abreast of changing circumstances.

Ideally all this information would be recorded in a manner that allows historical information also to be retrieved, so that a full site history from the time of first recording can be constructed. Depending on the laws and structures of management in place, the site may be subject to a range of different kinds of regime relating to its preservation (Chapter 6); these will be included to signify any particular rules regarding what may be done in, on or in relation to the site or object. While information on setting and context will have been noted earlier in the record, it is also useful to know to what use it is currently being put, since this will affect decisions made about it. Different uses may have different consequences for the object or place in question. Its form – single object, upstanding monument, ruin, buried feature, find-spot, etc. – may well be evident from the description but is useful to record in shorthand form, taking due account of standardised terms. Knowledge of its current state of preservation will be valuable for decision-making purposes and for any attempt at assessment in terms of its relative significance (Chapter 5), while an indication of likely threats that may cause damage will indicate how urgent any intervention may need to be.

Any intervention to ensure preservation will impact on others affected, especially those with an interest in the land where a site is located: they therefore also need to be recorded. This will include any owner where this is not the state agency responsible for managing the archaeological resource, the occupier of the site if different from the owner, and any others who may be affected. These 'stakeholders' (a term now widely used: Merriman 2004b; Carman 2005a, 84–5; Smith and Waterton 2009, 77–102) can be varied: from those with a direct economic concern through those who have other interests, such as intellectual or spiritual ones, to those who will be affected only indirectly or at a distance by any decision taken. Beyond Europe, the most likely stakeholders in an ancient site may be an Indigenous population, who may – and legitimately – claim a direct connection with the site through their ancestors (see, e.g., Layton 1989; Rubertone 2008a; Smith 2004); in some territories, such as the USA, their rights are enshrined in legislation (Smith 2004, 156–73; Ferguson 2009, 172–5). Decisions as to who may qualify as a stakeholder in any particular circumstance will depend on the particular circumstances, and are not easy to make: there will be those who consider themselves able to claim an interest who are not necessarily immediately apparent. Accordingly, in recording those with an interest, a reasonable degree of imagination may have to be applied.

The final set of information refers to the record itself and indicates when it was made, probably by whom, and will list any subsequent updates. Whether in paper or electronic form, past versions may well also be retained so that the full history of the site and its record can be retrieved. This will allow errors and omissions to be rectified – retrospectively, if necessary – to create as accurate a record as possible. The times of changes and updates to the record are vital to correlate with changes in the condition of the object recorded, the level of knowledge available at the time and any political or other factors that may have affected recording. It is a reminder that no record is truly objective, and even if objectivity and absolute accuracy are the aim, they are in practice impossible to achieve. Human error alone will render objectivity an unrealisable aim, and where archaeology is heavily politicised – as in many parts of the world, and inevitably so where it is tied to ideas of national or ethnic identity (e.g., Kohl and Fawcett 1995; Meskell 1998; Hamilakis and Duke 2007; Ickerodt 2010; Gomes 2010) – this will be even more questionable.

Inventory as a practice

Overall, an inventory entry provides a quick snapshot of the current knowledge and understanding of a particular site, object or archaeological activity. Such entries are not intended to be treated as definitive, since additional current material may await addition and because they need to be read in conjunction with the supporting reports and other materials referred to in the record. However, they are frequently relied on for planning, development and management purposes. This makes the record important: while exclusion from the inventory implies a lack of significance, inclusion – even if notionally merely to provide comprehensive coverage – will provide some status to the site, monument or event. Since such records are prepared and held in accordance with official regulation, this accordance of status to the items included is compounded: not only are they information to be taken note of in decision-making, but they are officially sanctioned and recognised and subject to official regulation. In the same way that the purpose of legislation in the field of archaeology is to make archaeology matter (Carman 1996), so entry of individual items on the inventory confirms their significance. Omission from the inventory will mean an individual item can be ignored for all official and decision-making purposes. This gives the inventory power in identifying those places and objects that are of relevance to those in authority: by selecting which categories of object are to be included and which excluded, the record can be used to define what constitutes 'heritage' in a particular context, creating what Smith (2006) has dubbed the 'authorised heritage discourse' for a particular territory (Harrison 2010).

Categorisation is really what inventory is all about. The use of standardised recording techniques and terminology will serve to reduce the uniqueness of each item in an inventory to something like anything else that is similar, reducing the specific experience of each excavation to a generalised category of 'dig', each survey to every other survey, every chance find to all others, all earthworks to all others, all upstanding buildings to all others and so on. This, however, is the purpose of an inventory: to make each entry fall into a recognisable category so that comparisons can be drawn and differences and similarities exposed. As I have argued elsewhere (Carman 1996, 161), placing an object into an inventory of objects that are deemed similar serves to change its identity: it ceases to be a singular, unique object or event and is stripped of its own specific identity; but it then can be allocated a new one that determines its subsequent career. To put it bluntly, an ancient pile of stones in a field ceases to be an agricultural nuisance or a convenient landmark and becomes an 'ancient monument' or 'archaeological site' with a new, enhanced status. All such items with the same designation can be made subject to the same systems of control and management, thereby legitimising the process by which they were designated and the function of the inventory in which they are included.

Table 4.4 presents a selected list of the categories of object that may be officially recognised in a number of different states across the world. Not all these are specifically archaeological: natural features, areas designated as 'National Parks' and human remains can be considered to constitute forms of 'natural' object, although inevitably overlain with cultural meanings (see, e.g., Lozny 2008; Sweeney and Hodder 2002). Intangible practices (the subject of one of the more recent UNESCO conventions: Ahmad 2006) are also not archaeological, although they may give rise to material

TABLE 4.4 *Categories of object given official recognition in different countries*

Country		Category of Object								
	Natural features	Archaeological sites	National Parks	Gardens, parks, battlefields	Intangible practices	Indigenous sites	Buildings and urban areas	Other monuments	Human remains and burial grounds	Cultural landscapes
Argentina		X	X				X			
Australia	X	X	X	X	X	X		X	X	X
Brazil	X	X	X			X	X			
Canada	X	X	X		X		X	X	X	X
China	X	X	X	X	X	X	X	X		X
Ghana	X	X	X					X		
India	X	X	X		X	X		X		X
Japan	X	X		X	X	X				
Mexico	X	X	X							
Nigeria	X		X			X		X	X	X
Peru	X	X								
Poland	X	X		X			X	X		

(continued)

TABLE 4.4 *(continued)*

Country	Natural features	Archaeological sites	National Parks	Gardens, parks, battlefields	Intangible practices	Indigenous sites	Buildings and urban areas	Other monuments	Human remains and burial grounds	Cultural landscapes
Russia	X	X		X	X		X			
South Africa	X	X	X	X			X		X	
Thailand	X	X	X		X	X	X			
United Kingdom	X	X	X	X			X	X		X
United States of America	X	X	X	X		X	X		X	X

source: Messenger and Smith 2010

creations that will be of archaeological interest and form a category that is arguably altering wider conceptions of what constitutes 'heritage' (Smith and Akagawa 2009; Waterton and Smith 2010). However, the majority of categories are material in form and constructed rather than being the product of processes considered 'natural' and therefore outside the human and cultural realm. This process of creating categories serves to legitimise and support the particular claims to expertise of archaeologists (and others) and thereby the processes of professionalisation covered in Chapter 2.

Inventory of one kind or another is frequently the first response when any particular components of the archaeological record are considered at risk. Stone (2005) reports being asked to provide to the British military assistance 'with the identification and protection of the archaeological cultural heritage in Iraq' (Stone 2011, 1) in advance of the allied invasion: in effect, a list of important sites to be avoided in military action, although, as Curtis (2011, 196) reports, this was not 'a very useful exercise' owing to lack of care by the military at a number of very significant sites. In the aftermath of that conflict lists were made of items looted from the Iraq Museum (Curtis 2011, 193), and since then a database of destruction to the Iraqi cultural heritage has also been created (Isakhan 2015) to allow the quantification of the consequences for the archaeology of Iraq of the conflict itself and subsequent pacification. A similar list – albeit less concerned with quantifying the value of sites (see Chapter 5) – was established following the Balkan conflicts of the 1990s (Reidlmayer 2002).

It will be noted that inventories of all kinds are limited to particular jurisdictions, reflecting the basis of ARM in legal processes (Chapter 3). In general, they operate at the level of the nation-state, and any one such list does not compare directly with that of another (Table 4.3 and Chapter 2). International lists – such as UNESCO's World Heritage List (Askew 2010) – reflect the choices made by national governments, albeit in accordance with internationally agreed guidelines, but are also intended to contain the best and most distinctive rather than the typical or common, and so are highly selective. Whereas national, regional or local lists are held to be complete and include everything that may be of any interest to archaeologists past, present and future, these 'global' lists represent the special and the unique. All such lists are nevertheless treated as if equivalent in some way: in discussion of archaeological resource management, the World Heritage List is frequently held up as 'typical' and possibly even ideal, despite the fact that it is not intended to be a complete catalogue of all classes of object (see, e.g., papers in White and Carman 2006 and the number of papers concerning world heritage to the exclusion of other categories in the

International Journal of Heritage Studies). While places listed on the World Heritage List remain the responsibility of the state in which they are located, and therefore represent that state, there are some efforts to internationalise the list by the creation of World Heritage Sites that cross borders: an example is the Roman Limes in Europe, which include Hadrian's Wall in Britain and the Roman Limes in Germany, together with sites in Austria, Hungary and the Balkans, and ultimately extending through territories in the Middle East and North Africa (http://whc.unesco.org/en/list/430). The consequences of this development for our appreciation of the World Heritage List will be interesting to see, although it is likely that it will make little difference to actual practice and individual components of these cross-border sites will remain the responsibility of individual countries, thus confirming the essentially 'nationalist' nature of the archaeological resource.

Byrne (2008, 159–60) argues that the action of inventory serves to commodify archaeological sites by its concentration on their physical attributes rather than the meanings and values associated with them (but see Chapter 5). He goes on to argue that the 'record may take on a greater reality' than the object it represents (Byrne 2008, 160), since it is the record that will be referred to in any decision-making processes affecting it, rather than direct contact with the place or object itself. As Byrne (2008, 160) puts it, 'the real place, the place [or object on] the ground, fades away as continuing references are made to the always more readily accessible inventory data'. This is a further consequence of inventory, and linked to the inevitable process of selection it entails and the reduction of its constituents to categories of object rather than unique elements that bear no relation to other things.

Conclusion

Inventory is a vital component of the ARM 'package', for without it none of the others can be achieved (Thornes and Bold 1998, 1; National Museum of Denmark 1992; Fraser and Newman 2006; Howard 2001, 196–8). The rhetoric of the field claims totality and objectivity for the records it contains, but in practice the process is essentially one of selection of particular kinds of things for particular kinds of treatment. Although the past is ubiquitously represented around us in natural, built and destroyed structures and in a range of ongoing cultural practices (Carman 2002), not all of these are recognised as coming to us from the past – especially those that represent our everyday encounters – and not all are deemed worthy of identification and recording. Any inventory therefore belies its rhetoric: it is not a complete record but a selective one, and because it is selective only those things that meet a set of criteria for entry will be included. Those items left out of it will remain unrecognised and will be deemed unworthy of status until they too are held to meet the requisite standards for entry.

Inventory is also an integral part of the role of ARM as a political activity: one that creates and supports structures of authority to which we are all expected to subscribe and in which archaeologists as specialist experts are deeply implicated (Smith 2004). In many countries qualified archaeologists are the only people entitled to carry out the kind of work that creates the information to be entered on an inventory of archaeological sites and objects. There may also be limitations placed on those who have access to the content of records. Where this is limited to those who have expert or official status, it will confirm the role of authority in constructing the sense of identity of those on whose behalf the inventory is notionally constructed – usually the citizens of a particular nation-state. Where access is more widely allowed, only parts of the record may be made available, to protect places considered especially vulnerable to threats from non-archaeological retrieval of material, or perhaps to protect other sensitive information such as the names of those identified as having an interest in the material on the record. The form in which the record is kept may also serve to limit access, whether intentionally or not: the location of a physical record, of paper and other material, may make it difficult for all those who cannot reach that location or who cannot do so at times when it is specifically made available; while a digital version may be more widely available via the internet, it may be in practice be less widely accessible because of problems with computer access or infrastructural issues, especially in countries with insufficient infrastructure or poor wireless access.

As a result of these factors, the contribution the inventory can make to outreach and 'public' archaeologies (Merriman 2004b; Skeates et al. 2012; Chapter 7) will depend on the degree of access the general public have to the content of the inventory. It nevertheless is a vital tool for both the management of archaeological resources – which is the entire topic of this book – and for research archaeology. The distinction made earlier between the 'record' as an object of research and the 'resource' as an object of management is therefore not as clear as this may suggest. As the material represented by the inventory, the record and the resource are identical. While the inventory provides raw material for researchers, new research provides additional material for the inventory: the two are not separated

quite so easily, although there is one difference that may be worth men-
tioning. Research is inevitably future-oriented: it seeks to find out new
things that were not known before; for researchers the inventory is a source
of past knowledge. For managers of the archaeological resource, who make
decisions in the present, the inventory contains material that is of current
value and relevance and is therefore always of the present. This takes us
back to the point made earlier in the chapter: that inventories represent no
more than the state of knowledge at a particular moment and are never
really complete or definitive. To treat them as complete and definitive,
which may be tempting to do, is to deny their inherently temporary and
contingent nature.

CHAPTER 5

Evaluation

If inventory is a vital first step in managing cultural resources, then giving a value to those resources is the central practice of ARM on which all subsequent practices depend. Debate concerning the ways in which values adhere to archaeological material and the kinds of values that are relevant is currently (late 2014) going through a period of revival. It is a topic to which archaeologists and others regularly return, but not constantly: it was a matter of considerable interest in the mid- to late 1980s, then dwindled until 1996, which saw a series of key publications (see, e.g., Bruier and Mathers 1996; Carman 1996; Carver 1996), with a revival of interest in 2005–6 (e.g., Mathers et al. 2005a; Clark 2001; 2006), followed by something of a hiatus until from 2010 a series of further publications (e.g., Smith et al. 2010) and the entry of economic ideas have maintained impetus (Carman forthcoming).

Within periods of interest concern alternates between practitioners, who seek or suggest methods of valuation, and academic commentators, who may suggest their own schemes, which are frequently at odds with those of practitioners. The primary difference between the kinds of valuation preferred or required by practitioners and those offered and discussed by academic commentators is that the former represent a value to be applied to particular components of the archaeological resource – individual sites, places or objects – to allow comparison and decision-making, and the latter represent more generalised concepts to be applied to the archaeological resource as a category. As a consequence the term 'evaluation' carries two distinct and separate meanings: for the academic commentator it refers to a primarily analytical process that seeks to under-stand the phenomena under scrutiny, especially in their capacity as 'archae-ological resource'; for the practitioner it is a primarily descriptive process that seeks to identify the specific characteristics of an individual site or other object. For the former, evaluation is a process worthy of study in its own right and concerned with the kinds of values being applied; for the latter it is a technique that provides data for the future management of particular places. Darvill (2005) conveniently labels these differences as the distinction between 'value' systems and 'importance' systems: the former are 'holistic, . . . have general orientation, largely relate to the production of archaeological resources [i.e., the initial selection of things as "archaeological"], and are conceptual, widespread within the population, and generated with reference to past experience', while the latter are 'atomistic, . . . have specific orientations, are generally pragmatic, relate to the consumption of the resource [i.e., future uses and treatment] . . . look to the future, have local relevance, and are created and administered by specialists' (Darvill 2005, 37).

As described by Loechl et al. (2009, 103), the process of evaluation as applied to historic military landscapes in the USA 'entails three major activities: defining significance, assessing integrity, and selecting boundaries': this is an 'importance' system in Darvill's (2005) terms. While significance is concerned with deciding how important an archaeological resource may be, especially in comparison with others (see, e.g., Barker 2009, 70–71), integrity concerns the physical attributes of the site and represent a measure of 'authenticity' (see, e.g., Mydland and Grahn 2012, 571), although, as will be discussed below, it also relates to issues of vulnerability and condition, while the selection of boundaries determines the extent of the area to be classed as 'archaeological'. By contrast, Briuer and Mathers's (1996) bibliographic survey of publications on significance also addressed issues related to research design, public involvement and the appropriate application of field techniques, thereby broadening the range of issues relating to evaluation. A narrower approach than either is advocated by Clark (2001), who limits the concerns to the establishment of significance by a study of physical fabric alone, although this is tempered by a concern to use this data 'place the site in its wider . . . context' and to assess 'its value in local, regional and national terms', including 'any amenity or social values associated with the site' (Clark 2001, 96–7).

This chapter is concerned with the first two of the processes outlined by Loechl et al. (2009): those of defining significance and assessing integrity. The third – boundary selection – is a topic for Chapter 6, on 'Preservation'. After a general discussion of the levels at which significance and importance can be attributed, discussion will focus on the methods and criteria offered for evaluation, and how these relate to decision-making processes.

A final section will consider the effects on the discipline and on the resource of such processes of evaluation.

Levels of importance and significance

In considering 'levels' of value applied to components of the archaeological resource, it needs to borne in mind that these operate in two linked but separate realms. The most obvious and most commonly applied is that where objects are directly compared to each other in terms of their importance: here the value scheme is a shared one to which all are made subject, and those objects deemed less worthy are granted a lower priority than those deemed of higher value. The other realm is where it is not objects are ranked, but the kind of value they may have. Most typically, levels of global, national or local value are placed in a hierarchical relation to one another: the consequence is that objects of global value are held to be more worthy than those of purely national importance, and those of national importance are given a higher rank than those valued merely locally. To complicate matters, and in contrast to the overarching idea of such a ranking, there may be levels of importance within each of these categories so that an object may be of more or less global, national or local value. Accordingly, in a truly universal scheme of relative value objects will be assessed simultaneously along two different 'dimensions': the result may be that an object with low global value may be outranked by an object with high local value despite the fact that the object valued locally has no global value. In general, however, this is not the case: global value will be held to outrank national value, and national value to outrank local value.

The terms in which these levels of value will be expressed will differ depending on the status to which they apply. For an object to qualify for 'World Heritage' status under the World Heritage Convention it needs to meet the standard of 'outstanding universal value', which is a deliberately vague formulation designed to capture a wide range of different characteristics and attributes, a characteristic also noted by Smith (2006, 97–8) and justified by Cleere (2001). It is modified in terms of ten 'selection criteria' which must be met, including, so far as they relate to cultural heritage (the remainder relate more properly to the 'natural' world):

- to represent a masterpiece of human creative genius;
- to exhibit an important interchange of human values, over a span of time or within a cultural area of the world, on developments in

architecture or technology, monumental arts, town planning or landscape design;
- to bear a unique, or at least exceptional, testimony to a cultural
  tradition or to a civilisation which is living or which has disappeared;
- to be an outstanding example of a type of building, architectural or
  technological ensemble or landscape which illustrates (a) significant
  stage(s) in human history;
- to be an outstanding example of a traditional human settlement,
  land use, or sea use which is representative of a culture (or cultures)
  or human interaction with the environment, especially when it
  has become vulnerable under the impact of irreversible change
  (www.unesco.org/en/criteria; the full list is also cited in Askew 2010).

These in turn are vague formulations that can only be interpreted in
subjective terms: what exactly will qualify, for instance, as 'a masterpiece
of human creative genius', and how it will be recognised? Would this book
and its contents count? The third criterion ('to bear … testimony to a
cultural tradition or to a civilisation') is also so general as to qualify any
cultural form for entry. Accordingly, assessment for entry into a 'global' list
is based on a breadth of approach that needs to accommodate significant
differences between very different offerings for inclusion. In practice, therefore, a set of other criteria is adopted to allow an assessment of heritage
value by UNESCO (Manders et al. 2012), in particular:

- the capacity to yield important information about the past
- historical significance
- scientific significance
- aesthetic significance
- social or spiritual value
- experiential significance
- economic significance (not to be confused with economic value,
  which is a measure of purely monetary worth)
- provenance
- representativeness
- rarity/uniqueness
- condition
- interpretive potential.

Together, these represent the kinds of values – singly or collectively – that
an item of significant heritage value should represent (compare Table 5.1
below). Not all will apply to all those items considered to be of significance,

TABLE 5.1 *Recommended assessment criteria for the significance/importance and representativeness of sites*

Country	Criteria		
USA (Briuer and Mathers 1996, 14)	Chronological periods		
	Quantity/diversity of material		
	Datable remains		
	Presence of architectural features		
	Archival records (documentation)		
	Site type		
	Site function		
	Site size		
	Physical integrity		
	Cultural/ethnic affiliations		
	Historic themes		
	Environmental habitat		
	Topographic setting		
	Severity/immediacy of threat		
UK (Darvill et al. 1987)	Characterisation criteria	Discrimination criteria	Assessment criteria
	Period (currency)	Survival	Condition
	Rarity	Group value (association)	Fragility
	Diversity (form)		Vulnerability
	Period (representivity)	Potential	Conservation value
		Documentation	
		Group value (clustering)	
		Diversity (features)	
		Amenity value	
Europe (Deeben et al. 1999)	Aesthetic value		
	Historical value		
	Integrity		
	Preservation		
	Rarity		
	Research potential		
	Group value		
	Representivity		

(continued)

TABLE 5.1 *(continued)*

Country	Criteria	
South Africa (Whitelaw 2005)	Sites with no oral or written history	Sites with written or oral history
	Organic preservation	Historical/cultural significance
	Length of sequences	Volume of written/ oral history
	Exceptional elements	Degree of preservation
	Research potential	Degree of research
	Previous archaeological investigation	Potential for public display
	Extent of previous archaeological investigation	Aesthetic appeal
	Potential for public display	Potential for management plan
	Aesthetic appeal	
	Potential for management plan	
Australia (Freestone et al. 2008, 159)	Place in the course of history	
	Uncommon, rare or endangered	
	Information potential	
	Demonstrates characteristics of a class of cultural place or environment	
	Representation of aesthetic values	
	Demonstrates creative or technical achievement	
	Close association with a particular cultural group	
	Association with an individual or individuals of historical importance	
	Part of an Indigenous tradition	

but it is expected that an item of high value will reflect a balance of all these values. Once entered on the World Heritage List, all places are deemed to have the single quality of 'outstanding universal value', so no direct comparison becomes possible and all are deemed to be equally important. It may also be assumed that they are all of greater value than objects of only 'national' or 'local' value. This effectively removes them from the realm of evaluation, since no other object can compete with them in terms of value.

It is usually at the national level that more complex forms of evaluation take place, whereby components of the archaeological resource are placed in direct competition with each other. Here criteria may be much more explicit, even if not specifically laid down by legal or other authority. Table 5.1 sets out some criteria for application at the national level. The list for the USA is derived by Briuer and Mathers (1996) from the criteria that tend to be applied by practitioners in seeking to meet the standard of 'scientific significance' laid down by US federal law, which is otherwise only loosely defined, and those for entry onto the US National Register of Historic Places (http://www.nps.gov/nr/about.htm; Hardesty and Little 2009). The list for the UK is not required strictly by legislation but was developed to meet the needs of a project conducted on behalf of the official agency for England (Darvill et al. 1987), and a reduced form is included in official advice to planning authorities. The European-wide criteria (Deeben et al. 1999) were developed explicitly for the Netherlands to meet legislative and administrative imperatives, but in themselves they have no legal force. The South African list (Whitelaw 2005) was created to meet the needs of legislation concerning the preservation of sites in the province of Kwa-Zulu Natal; it is one of few that makes an explicit distinction between sites with oral or written history and those without, which may be considered a distinction between 'historic' sites and 'purely archaeological' ones. The Australian list (Freestone et al. 2008) was also developed to meet the needs of legislation but has a wider concern than the purely archaeological, since it also covers cultural places in general and the natural environment. The specifics of criteria will be discussed below, but it is worth noting: (a) that in none of these schemes is any differential weighting applied to the various criteria, so the relative weight given to any of them will depend very much on the specifics of individual cases; and (b) that all include a concern for 'inherent' attributes such as the degree to which the object is representative of the class of object to which it belongs, for its current state of survival and for its future potential.

Startin (1993) discusses the manner in which judgements are made for assessing 'national importance' by practitioners: his points are particularly relevant to the UK context but will resonate with those working elsewhere. Although acknowledging that judgements are inevitably subjective (described by him as 'intuitive judgement' [Startin 1993, 186]), he nevertheless emphasises their basis in professional knowledge and the degree of consensus that exists among professionals for the application of common criteria. This is especially true for well-known and agreed categories of material (Startin 1993, 194), while such consensus has to be built for less familiar or newly emergent categories (Startin 1993, 195). While recognising the distinction made above between national and more local levels of value (Startin 1993, 193), he also acknowledges the complexities that arise from the nature of the resource itself, especially that of the physical scale at which assessment should take place. As he puts it:

> In general ... three levels can be recognised. Firstly, [places such as major] settlements may be judged as a whole ... Secondly individual monuments ... or component areas will be judged independently in their own right. Thirdly, specific areas will be subject to ... judgement [when they are placed directly under threat from, e.g., development] (Startin 1993, 196).

What constitutes 'national' for particular areas of the world will, of course, depend on the political form of that territory. As outlined in Chapter 3, there are key differences between federal and other kinds of territory. In countries organised along federal lines, it may be that individual provinces or states will have their own idea of their national status; but others may recognise the country of which they are a part as the 'nation' while they are merely a component region. Similarly, apparently unitary states such as the United Kingdom may nonetheless be divided into separate nations (see, e.g., Schofield et al. 2011, 6–7), so that there are no UK-wide national monuments, but there are English, Scottish, Welsh and Northern Irish sites of national status. A further complication arising as a result of the redrawing of national boundaries consequent on political changes is the claims that may be made by one state on sites in neighbouring territories (see, e.g., Silverman 2011). Accordingly, the precise meaning of the status of 'national' importance will always be contingent on the notion of 'nationality' to be applied, and this is a factor that lies beyond the realm of merely professional expertise.

Local value is a level of evaluation rarely directly considered, despite the fact that the one thing all archaeological resources have in common is their relationship to a particular locality, either by their fixity in space or, in the case of movable items, the fact of discovery at a particular location. In so far as this kind of value is discussed, there is a division between separate discourses: while some value schemes operate within the context of 'community engagement' so that local values are generally held to be those applied *by* a local community to a site or object, others relate to those *reflecting* value to that community as established by an agency external to that community. The former discourse is especially evident in relation to archaeological relations with descendant communities of various kinds – especially, but not exclusively, Indigenous communities – and relates especially to encouraging an understanding by archaeological professionals of the different kinds of values those communities associate with the places and objects that are particularly meaningful to them (see, e.g., Lilley and Williams 2005; Baugher 2005; Yu 2010; Bruning 2010). The latter discourse emerges most commonly in relation to World Heritage sites (e.g., Shen 2010; Graham 2010), where the enhanced status granted by the designation serves to detach the place from its inhabitants (Aranda 2010) and indeed in some instances has led to the removal from it of the very people who gave it its cultural value in the first place (e.g., Lee Long 2000, 318–20).

Archaeological relations with communities of various kinds are more properly a topic for Chapter 7, and much that is said there will resonate with and refer to what is briefly said here, but a brief discussion of the connection between community engagement and issues of value will serve to emphasise once more the interconnectedness of topics in ARM and the arbitrariness of separation. Lilley and Williams (2005) are at pains to point out the lack of what they term 'mutuality' between archaeological conceptions of significance deriving from the application of criteria such as those set out in Table 5.1 and Indigenous interests in places. In seeking to overcome this, they instigated a programme of research that provided a longitudinal study of place that brought the archaeology into contact with living memory, allowing a transfer of understanding that passed both ways between archaeologists and Indigenous people. Similar projects elsewhere in Australia (e.g., Smith et al. 1993) have also generated new information to augment that available from the purely material remains. In discussing North America, Swidler and Yeatts (2005) argue that 'when evaluating the significance of a place . . . it must be from the standpoint of the culture to which it is integral' (Swidler and Yeatts 2005, 283), which in turn requires the 'involvement of the groups who may have ties to the area under study' (Swidler and Yeatts 2005, 285). The question remains, however, of exactly what is actually happening in terms of assessing such 'community' values and – beyond that – what should be done in assessing them. A mere translation of non-archaeological values into archaeological terms so that they can be reported represents an effectual denial of the legitimacy of such values by the need to reduce them to other terms. On the other hand, to treat them as fundamentally different is to perpetuate the non-mutuality identified by Swidler and Yeatts (2005), but this goes far to explain the ongoing 'aspirational' approach taken in so much of the literature (see, e.g., Funari 2005 on Brazil; Yu 2010 on Peru; Aranda 2010 for Mexico; Baugher 2005 and Bruning 2010 for the USA), which looks to the future for a more 'mutual' way forward but does not describe any actual current practice.

It is far more widespread for decision-makers to decide on behalf of communities the values that are relevant to those communities. Graham's (2010) description of processes at Lunenburg, Canada, and Koper/Capodistria, Slovenia, emphasises the community consultation involved in the development of conservation plans for the sites but does not deny that it was the 'experts' involved in the project who made final decisions. It is also clear that the kinds of value considered relevant were more economic than strictly cultural: as he puts it, 'the strategies proposed [for the conservation plan] introduce expanded parameters to the business of heritage conservation' (Graham 2010, 276), which required the establishment of expert bodies to advise local authorities. Similarly, Shen's (2010) discussion of heritage values of World Heritage sites in China focuses on the economic values they represent, especially as tourist sites: as Shen puts it, promoting World Heritage status 'has played an important role in re-evaluating the cultural value of heritage by transforming it into economic value' (Shen 2010, 263–4) and thereby transforming local attitudes to their familiar and traditional material forms.

The connection between World Heritage status and local values closes the circle on the levels at which values are applied to the archaeological resource: World Heritage status at once provides the impetus for a consideration of local value and offers the capacity to transform local cultural values to practical economic benefits. Both local and World Heritage values effectively ignore and bypass the 'national' level of evaluation: they are constructed on entirely separate bases and operate quite independently of one another. Nevertheless, it is national imperatives that drive the designation of World Heritage sites, and it is primarily at the national level that objects, sites and places are deemed to be worthy of consideration as 'important'; hence the dearth of literature on strictly 'local' values.

Methods of assessment

Despite the intangibility of the values attached to archaeological resources, and their mutability (see, e.g., Leone and Potter 1992), the methods used to assess significance or importance frequently collapse to a more developed version of those generally applied simply to identify resources, such as those outlined in Chapter 4: 'classic archaeological techniques such as fieldwalking, earthwork survey, various forms of geoarchaeological prospection, and the use of aerial photographs and other forms of remote sensing', augmented by research of historic sources also as outlined in Chapter 4 (and see also Clark 2001, 73–95). The difference in their application lies in the broader context within which evaluation is carried out: while inventory requires only to record presence or absence, evaluation requires a knowledge and appreciation of the wider historical and cultural frameworks within which the object is located. Accordingly, Clark (2001, 96–7) recommends that 'Statements of significance should try to ... place the site in its wider academic or scientific context – whether historical, architectural, social, archaeological, ecological or technical' and urges that its 'various phases of alteration' should also be taken note of. As well as assessing its value 'in local, regional and national terms' on the basis of these factors, there is also the need to 'identify any amenity or social values associated with the site'. Together these provide four main phases to the evaluation process.

Placing a site, object or place in its wider temporal and social context is largely a product of the kind of recording covered in Chapter 4. They relate especially to the object in its original form or – for something already extant (such as a location) – its adoption as a place of significance to a particular community; subsequent changes are recorded separately. Mydland and Grahn (2012) in assessing sites for the Norwegian Directorate of Cultural Heritage take a pragmatic approach to the issue of original form and relate this directly to 'building materials and styles', which collapses to the amount of 'original substance' the object (usually a building) contains. They also address the issue of representativeness, defined in terms of 'rarity and frequency' (Mydland and Grahn 2012, 571). By contrast, and in considering perhaps more truly 'archaeological' material than upstanding buildings, Mathers et al. (2005b) emphasise that any assessment of representativeness will reflect the degree of inclusion in inventories and that how sites are defined – something that changes over time – will have a direct effect on evaluations, a point also noted by Barker (2009, 70–71). Accordingly, placing an object or site in its broader context of creation involves a good understanding of that wider context and the processes of identification current at the time of its initial identification and any subsequent recording. This is an explicitly comparative process – comparing one object or site against others of the same type, and types against other types.

A concern for the changes an object, site or place has gone through in its lifetime is integral to any assessment of the 'character' of an object. This is the aim of so-called 'characterisation' study (Fairclough 2006; 2008; Turner and Fairclough 2007), which is offered as a means of:

- managing change . . .
- defining essential 'character' as well as identifying hard archaeological values
- understanding the present (focusing of course on the historic dimension) as well as the past in itself
- identifying and promoting the benefits and uses that the archaeological resource affords (Fairclough 2006, 270).

Fairclough (2006) presents characterisation as an alternative to other forms of evaluation, especially what he (following British usage) terms 'assessment', which is the application of set criteria such as those listed in Table 5.1 to establish 'rigorous, transparent and consistent' judgements of value (Fairclough 2006, 255). Indeed, he goes further, claiming that characterisation describes 'character rather than [ascribing] relative values' (Fairclough 2006, 273), on the basis that 'there is no such thing as good or bad character' (Schofield et al. 2011, 112). Accordingly, characterisation – whether of the broader 'historic environment' ,which is Fairclough's (2006) concern, or of individual sites and structures (e.g., Barrett et al. 2007) – is necessarily less concerned with original form than with current condition and the processes that brought it to that state: it is a 'presentist' approach that specifically addresses issues of change over time. Characterisation is also necessarily not as detailed an approach as the application of criteria such as those set out in Table 5.1: it is concerned with the overall impression of a place or object, not with its very specific attributes, although these may contribute to the distinctiveness from other objects and places that characterisation aims to capture. There is no attempt to compare objects of characterisation with other objects, because it is assumed from the outset that the accumulated histories will inevitably make them distinctive from one another.

Both the previous processes have been concerned exclusively with the fabric of the object being assessed. When, however, it comes to evaluating value in terms of locality, these factors must be related to others that are extraneous to the object in question. Most obviously, and frequently most typically for archaeological sites, a direct comparison will be made between sites in terms of their type, their degree of preservation and the potential research value they can offer, following the kinds of criteria listed in Table 5.1. The literature abounds with discussion of this process and how it should be conducted: for instance, Schaafsma's (1989) call to reject the idea that sites not recognised as 'significant' in American legal terms should therefore be rendered 'insignificant' is echoed in Carver's (1996) argument that threatened sites in the UK that can be shown to have current research value should be excavated immediately, and all others (threatened or not) should be assumed to have potential value for future researchers and should be preserved. The issue as to whether a site should be considered of international, national or local importance based on its physical attributes alone will depend on a wider comparison of the kinds and numbers of sites at these different geographical scales, as discussed above (see also Sherfy and Luce 1979 for USA).

There are, however, factors other than the purely physical which will determine the level at which an object, site or place has significance. As Matthews (2008) argues, the concept of the site itself may need to be reconsidered in addressing the question of its value to those to whom it 'belongs': as he puts it, sites are 'places that capture both with their histories and their definition in the present the conflicting forces that lead people to ... connect with the past' (Matthews 2008, 89). From this perspective, the objects and places that are of interest to archaeologists represent not only the accumulation of physical traces that inform about processes in the past, but also associations of meaning to communities in the present. Such communities can be very diverse: as McManamon (1991) has listed them from his experience in the USA, they comprise: the (unspecified) general public; students and teachers; members of Congress and the executive branch; government attorneys, managers and archaeologists, and Native Americans. Put in more global terms, these become: an unidentified general public; those in education; legislators and politicians; officials and agents of government; and local or descendant communities. All or any of these groups may claim sites as of relevance to them and ascribe levels of importance to their definition as makers – and markers – of community cohesion. Dublin (2008), for example, examines the changing significance of part of the New Mexico landscape to its Native inhabitants and incoming European settlers and the ongoing presence of Zuni practices more than 400 years of Native–European interaction supporting Zuni claims to land. Politicians are likely to relate to sites at the level at which they operate: local officials will emphasise the significance to the locality, while national representatives will be more concerned with sites of national or international importance. The kind of criteria to be applied may include those relating to fabric but will also include others that relate to issues of identity and community creation (as discussed, for instance, in Smith and Waterton 2009); these are as likely to be exclusive as inclusive, since communities frequently wish to define their difference from others, and making claims on specific heritage objects (or types of objects) and places is a means to do this (see, e.g., contributions to Rubertone's [2008a] volume charting the diverse claims attaching to sites of meaning to Native Americans).

Briuer and Mathers (1996, 27, emphasis removed) chart the shift of focus in discussions of significance from the 1970s to the 1990s from a concern with 'contemporary archaeological research, to future research values, to the importance of archaeological resources to other (allied) disciplines, to the value of cultural resources to all disciplines and finally to, consideration of broader public and social values'. This latter concern is reflected in the USA especially in Leone and Potter's (1992) call for a 'dialogue among equals', where the values of non-archaeologists are included in the consideration, and Martin's (n.d.) call for sensitivity to others' perspectives on the basis that it can lead to better decision-making. Pressure from Indigenous communities has no doubt accelerated the process in countries such as the USA and Australia since the prehistoric archaeology of those lands is inevitably that of the Indigenous population, although the process was slower elsewhere, such as in African territories, where the separation of local populations from their past by the intervention of European colonisers has led to the detachment of people from their archaeological past (see, e.g., Segobye 2008). Nonetheless, efforts to seek an understanding of the values placed on archaeological resources by those communities who may lay claim to them are increasingly part of the evaluation process. Such efforts fall into two types of approach: one is to enquire of specific communities the kinds of interest they have in archaeological resources and establish the specifically community values placed upon them (see, e.g., Mydland and Grahn 2012); the other is to take a broader approach to 'social' or 'public' value, such as those espoused by the 'public value' scheme in the UK (Clark 2006).

The values that may concern communities in relation to archaeological resources may be considered to be those identified by Johnston (1994) in her consideration of what she termed 'social value'. These consist of:

- providing a sense of connection with the past
- tying the past affectionately to the present
- providing an essential reference point in a community's identity or sense of itself
- helping to give a disempowered group back its history
- providing a sense of collective attachment to place
- 'loom[ing] large in the daily comings and goings of life' and are 'places where people gather' (Johnston 1994, 7).

These can be identified mostly by asking people their opinion and by noting how they engage with such places and objects: examples are to be found in the work of Jones (2004) for a specific archaeological object, Smith (2006) for locales and Priede (2009) for landscapes. This is not to say that such an approach to value does not have its flaws. In particular, as is evident from any such study, there is a close reliance on anecdotal responses and on personal memory. This leads to a focus on the very recent past, even though issues may relate to an ancient place or object: it is the relationship of that place or object to the experience of those currently living which is assessed. This in turn leads to a tendency to place emphasis on places with positive values rather than those that are 'taboo' or which have left darker memories or been bypassed or ignored. Overall, in terms of understanding community, there is a tendency to seek evidence of community unity rather than disharmony. Like the approaches used to determine significance in terms of historical and other context (see above), this kind of investigation treats objects, sites and places as singular rather than engaging in direct comparison with others that are similar. It is clear that the kinds of values that are ascribed to such objects and places are multiple and can be conflicting: but at the same time none prevents the ascription of other values to the same object at the same time. Accordingly, community values can sit alongside intellectual and academic, popular, economic, recreational and tourist values.

Wider 'public' value schemes go beyond the responses of individuals and specific communities to delineate the values of archaeological resources to the world at large, although frequently in terms that specify the direct recipients of the benefits they offer. Accordingly, the 'public value' scheme advocated by the Heritage Lottery Fund in the UK (DEMOS 2004; Hewison and Holden 2006) adopted a tripartite approach to value: so-called 'intrinsic' values, which are those relating especially to fabric as discussed above; 'instrumental' values, relating to the benefits that can accrue from various uses to which the object or place can be put such as tourism, educational or amenity use; and 'institutional' values, which derive from the activities of those organisations involved in managing and using the resource. While 'intrinsic' value in this scheme represents the inclusion of specifically 'academic' values, the other types of value identified derive from an explicitly 'economic' approach to valuation which is concerned with the uses to which resources can be put. A specific interest in assessing sites for their 'instrumental' value may be that of addressing their tourist interest and value, and these concerns may be discussed explicitly in terms of marketing (e.g., Hausmann 2007) or in terms of how local communities relate to the use of their own culture as a tourist resource (e.g., Keitumetse 2009). Other kinds of values represented by this category include the health benefits of being able to walk safely in an area free of traffic or other pollution, the sense of community cohesion that derives from close association with a particular object or place (e.g., as reported by Jones 2004) or (as indicated by Johnston 1994) as a place where people can gather. 'Institutional' values are of a kind similar to instrumental values, but derive not from the object or place itself but from the organisations that arise because of its presence. These may include the development of a feeling of trust between community members and those charged with the care of the object or place, which in turn may lead to greater willingness of community members to become involved with such organisations and thereby enhance democratic engagement with policy-making. Alternatively, the establish-ment of a group concerned with archaeological resources may encourage the establishment of other groups for other purposes, creating opportunities for community involvement and thereby closer cohesion among the group. In focusing on such benefits, the 'Public Value' scheme concentrates on the practical benefits that derive from the existence and maintenance of archaeological (and other) resources.

All these approaches to evaluation – identifying academic and scien-tific value, changes over time and current condition, local and commu-nity values, and wider 'public' benefits – are generally assumed to depend on expertise for their recognition. Accordingly, it is a notable feature of the literature – academic and professional – that it never specifies exactly what needs to be *done* to assess the qualities under review. Criteria (such as those listed in Table 5.1) are listed, the types of value to be sought are identified, and there are discussions of which values are of greater or lesser relevance in particular contexts; but precisely how one goes about the business of comparing one object, site or place with another to achieve a result that can be used in decision-making is never made explicit (see, e.g., IfA 1994; Clark 2001; Mathers et al. 2005a; Loechl et al. 2009). Startin (1993) is explicit about the relationship between professional expertise and assessment, and the results of his comparison of evaluations made before and after the adoption of clear criteria confirm the common basis on which such judgements were made, which do not deviate very far from those made using the criteria. The overall conclusion is that such expert assessment is at least consistent from one expert to another and from one site to another and accordingly can be relied on to produce similar results that are directly comparable. It does, however, raise questions about the degree to which any evaluation truly reflects more widely held ideas about the importance of archaeological remains.

Criteria of evaluation

As can be seen in Table 5.1 and as mentioned above, the criteria that may be applied to assess archaeological remains for their significance reduce to a relatively short list, albeit couched in different terms in different territories. An attempt at grouping these is set out in Table 5.2, and the UNESCO criteria are also included for comparative purposes: note that some criteria fit under more than one generic heading, and not all criteria are addressed in all territories listed. The groups are necessarily somewhat arbitrary and intuitive, and some specific criteria may fit into more than one group, but it is the shortness of the list that is the point here: the diversity of specific criteria notwithstanding, and the diversity of archaeological materials represented within each territory, the criteria nevertheless reduce to no more than eight actual measures against which that material is assessed. It is notable that only one of the criteria listed at the national level does not find its way into the scheme: that of 'site size' (Briuer and Mathers 1996, 14) applies only in the USA and, as Bruier and Mathers (1996, 14) point out, it is only one item of the list they produce, all of which are contested. In fact, site size as a criterion appears in only one of the papers cited in their survey of the literature. Reed (1987) advocates the use of a range of variables – not just site size, but also the number of artefact classes identifiable at the site, surface and subsurface features and deposits, and a range of other factors, all to be compared with similar characteristics at other sites to determine the relative significance of individual sites. Their size may be a factor, but only in relation to other factors: a large empty site would represent a relatively low significance unless there are other factors also taken into account.

A concern shared by all the territories listed and UNESCO (albeit less obviously by UNESCO) is that of chronological period. Underlying this for all is a sense that the material has to reflect a particular period in the human past. There are possible reasons for this: because some periods are considered of more significance than others, or because some periods are more poorly represented than others. The primary issue in territories such as the USA, UK and Australia is one of clear identification: it relates to the ability to date remains, to identify which particular part of the past the remains belong to or to relate them to particular cultural groups whether archaeological or extant. For Australia and South Africa association with specific histories – of individuals or events – is also a factor, which is an extension to

TABLE 5.2 *Value criteria across territories*

Territory/criterion	UNESCO	USA	UK	Europe	South Africa	Australia
Chronology/period	Historical significance	Chronological periods Datable remains Site type Site function Cultural/ethnic affiliation Historic themes	Period (currency)	Historical value	(Sites with/without written history) Historical/cultural significance	Place in course of history Demonstrates creative or technical achievement Close association with a particular cultural group Association with individuals of historical importance
Quality of remains	Capacity to yield important information about the past Scientific significance Social or spiritual value Experiential significance Economic significance	Quantity/diversity of material Presence of architectural features Physical integrity Environmental habitat Topographic setting	Survival Group values Diversity	Integrity Preservation Group value	Organic preservation Length of sequences Degree of preservation	Demonstrates characteristics of a class of cultural place
Rarity	Rarity/uniqueness		Rarity	Rarity	Exceptional elements	Uncommon, rare or endangered
Representativeness	Representativeness	Datable remains Site type Site function Cultural/ethnic affiliation Historic themes	Period (representivity)	Representivity		Demonstrates characteristics of a class of cultural place Part of an Indigenous tradition

(continued)

TABLE 5.2 (continued)

Territory/criterion	UNESCO	USA	UK	Europe	South Africa	Australia
Vulnerability		Severity/immediacy of threat	Condition Fragility Vulnerability			
Documentation	Provenance	Archival records (documentation)	Documentation		Volume of written/oral history Previous archaeological investigation Extent of previous archaeological investigation Degree of research	
Aesthetics	Aesthetic significance			Aesthetic value	Aesthetic appeal	Representation of aesthetic values
Future value	Interpretive potential		Potential Conservation value	Research potential	Research potential Potential for public display Potential for management plan	Information potential

periods of European colonisation for a concern with cultural affiliation. The Australian interest in demonstration of particular achievements reflects a similar concern to the U.S. criterion of how the site or object represents historic themes: in both cases it serves to place the site or object within broader processes over time, which ameliorates the rather narrower focus of purely chronological placement. The UNESCO, European and South African criterion of historical value or significance is rather more vague: it can relate to any other concern in this field and others too. It can, however, be considered to be reflective of the other UNESCO criterion of a capacity to inform about the past, which ultimately underlies all the criteria in this field and indeed all criteria listed.

Similarly shared is some concern for the overall quality of the remains. The USA and South African criteria, and to a limited extent the UK criteria, are quite specifically concerned with technical archaeological issues by indicating the particular physical characteristics significant remains should have: architectural features (USA), organic preservation and lengthy stratigraphic sequences (South Africa) and diversity of features (UK). The degree of preservation – variously called survival, integrity or preservation – is a concern for the USA, UK, Europe and South Africa. Since the European criteria specify both integrity and preservation, however, the two terms may not be synonyms, and while preservation relates to the physical survival of particular elements, integrity may relate to the degree to which the site or object also maintains its contextual unity. Similarly, the U.S. criteria separate physical integrity from other contextual concerns, such as topographic and environmental setting, which reflect a concern for group values in the UK and Europe. These relate especially to the relationship of the site or object to other sites or objects, either of the same period and type or otherwise. The specific relationships identified will determine how the site or object is related to short- or long-term cultural forms, an idea also reflected in the Australian criterion relating to classes of cultural place.

The UNESCO criteria listed under this heading are all much more vague: they represent judgements based not on the physical fabric of the site or object but on its perception and its place in history as interpreted in relation to other – extraneous – factors. Social and spiritual value may relate to the site's or object's association with specific cultural groups, and experiential significance may relate to specific physical characteristics or to the site's integrity in its capacity to impart a particular sense of 'pastness' (see, e.g., Garden 2006; Holtorf 2013). Scientific and economic significance are measures related to the contribution to knowledge the site or object may impart – confirming, refining and reinforcing the criterion relating to the capacity to inform significantly about the past. Collectively they represent the attributes that are to be considered most relevant in assessing the overall value of the site or object.

The following two sets of criteria can be considered at once complementary and contradictory. Rarity suggests that very few of that class of object exists, or at least remain extant; but representativeness suggests that it is in some way typical of its class, period or geographical region. On the other hand, a comparatively rare class can nevertheless be definitive of its period or region by virtue of its distinctiveness from other classes of material. Mere rarity is a factor for UNESCO, the UK, Europe and Australia, indicating a concern for including all classes of material in any management programme. For South Africa it is the presence of exceptional elements that is key, perhaps reflecting UNESCO's interest in the unique: it is likely that the UNESCO pairing of rarity and uniqueness reflects a specific concern for the special to be offset against an interest in the typical. For Australia, rarity is combined with the uncommon and exceptional and with threat to survival, providing a range of criteria that can be deemed complementary or as alternatives. Representativeness is generally held to relate to chronological period, and this is certainly true for the USA, UK and Europe. For Australia and the USA, the ability of the site or object to represent a particular culture or ethnicity, and for Australia especially Indigenous peoples, is significant: representativeness here is deemed to be of particular histories defined by ethnic difference rather than of chronological periods.

The Australian connection of rarity with threat is not reflected in other territories for which vulnerability is an issue. Only the UK and USA show a specific concern for the threats to sites or objects. In the USA it is the immediacy of the threat that is taken into account with its severity. In the UK concern is for the current condition – which complements the concern noted above for survival – which operates alongside an interest in the fragility of the remains, and therefore its capacity to survive threats, and its vulnerability to threat as a measure of how imminent is any such threat.

Pre-existing information about the site or object which relates its biography is of concern to several territories. From a purely archaeological perspective the USA, UK and South Africa are primarily concerned with archival and historical records as well as previous archaeological research: while South Africa is quite explicit about separating historical evidence from archaeological investigation, the USA and UK criteria are more loosely phrased. Nonetheless, under the general heading of 'documentation' falls also a concern for the presence or absence of previous investigation, its quantity and the depth of research. By contrast, the UNESCO concern for 'provenance' reflects a different disciplinary base for its concern with site or object biography: it is a concept derived from a concern with the history of its origin and subsequent ownership (e.g., for books, Shaw 2005), making it a concern largely for authenticity and genuineness rather than the capacity of the site or object to inform about the past, standing in contrast to the criterion discussed above. Similarly, UNESCO values aesthetic significance, which is to be distinguished from aesthetic appeal. Like provenance, aesthetic value derives more from art-historical considerations than archaeology as such, locating the object in its place in the history of representation, although this criterion is also shared by Europe and Australia. While for UNESCO and Europe the latter is generalised, for Australia aesthetic qualities (like other attributes) must relate to specific cultural traditions. In contrast, the South African criteria expressly list aesthetic appeal, assuming a common capacity for appreciation by all peoples.

While all the previous criteria reflect a concern for the current state of the object or site, the final set looks explicitly to the future by indicating various kinds of potential. Use of the term 'potential' is interesting: it implies that there is no certainty that the potential will ever be realised and that there is no fixed term during which realisation will be sought. Of the territories considered here, only the UK offers a single, generalised 'potential' as a criterion, although this is generally understood to indicate a potential for providing information rather than any other kind; to emphasise the point, conservation value is distinguished. Other territories are more specific, UNESCO showing a concern for interpretive potential, Europe for research potential and Australia for informational potential. While classed for this purpose as 'future value', these criteria need not in fact relate to future use at all: they are a reflection of current understandings and appreciation of the site or object. Only two territories of these show an actual concern for the future of the site: the UK, with conservation value, relating to the capacity of the site or object to be conserved for future treatment; and South Africa, which looks beyond research potential also to potential for public display and for the development of a broader management plan (see Chapter 6).

There is an interesting paradox that emerges from this review of criteria. On the one hand, as the above indicates, there are in practice very few general criteria against which archaeological remains are assessed for their significance: a total of eight areas as listed in Table 5.2 (and see Carman

2002, 22–3, on the principles and practices of ARM, equally short lists). On the other, the specific criteria that are applied within each set derive from the particular context of their origin. In Europe and the UK the archaeological past operates at a national level so that all pasts are deemed equal and are not claimed by specific groups of people, but are held to relate to the population as a whole. Accordingly criteria are more general and make no distinction between periods or cultural affiliation. By contrast, in the USA, Australia, South Africa and other former colonial territories – where European colonisers have appropriated the pasts of an Indigenous populations – there is much more concern to distinguish pasts, separating them by ethnicity or cultural affiliation and drawing a distinction between prehistoric and historic periods. UNESCO – much less a territory than a particular kind of institution – takes a different approach again: its criteria are highly generalised and nevertheless divided by source academic discipline, distinguishing fine art considerations from those deriving from history or economics. The relevance of the divided history of ARM (see Chapters 1 and 2) is here made manifest despite the assumed unanimity of archaeology across the globe and the common agreement as to appropriate ARM theory and practice.

Valuation as a process

After listing the things that exist, the management process requires that archaeologists follow some procedure to make some kind of discrimination between them and to determine what future each component of the archaeological record may have. Whatever result is achieved in terms of valuation, it is entirely dependent on a series of prior decisions as to what to consider, the level at which to consider it and the criteria that therefore apply. Unlike mere inventory, which describes but does not discriminate, the evaluation process has real and immediate consequences for the material under review.

Nevertheless, in the same way that the literature offers little advice on how sites are assessed – other than to list the criteria against which sites should be measured – the literature of the field offers little in the way of how decisions are actually made once an assessment has been achieved. Although reviews of archaeological practice (such as, in the UK, Hey and Lacey 2001) are occasionally undertaken, they limit themselves to the styles of fieldwork employed rather than the actual decision-making that follows from it: this is assumed to be 'in-built' into the professional archaeological process and is ultimately left to individual judgement. In practice, it will

reduce to a simple determination of the presence or absence of archaeological remains that are considered worth looking at in greater detail.
Perhaps paradoxically, given the importance given to assessment of
remains – since all kinds of intervention are described as 'assessment' or
'evaluation' (see, e.g., Willems and Brandt 2004; guidelines from the IfA at
http://www.archaeologists.net/codes/ifa) – there is more in the literature in
terms of the alternatives available, often reduced to the triple alternatives of
simple abandonment, or preservation in situ or by record (see Chapter 6).

Since the purpose of evaluation is to enable decisions to be made about
the future of the site or object, it has real consequences for its objects. The
possibilities include abandonment to any fate that befalls, untrammelled
by official interference: this may include anything along a continuum
from deliberate acts of preservation by non-official agencies or merely
stasis caused by non-interference as a result of being ignored, to deliberate
acts of preservation by official agencies. This is where a concern for levels
of evaluation and criteria come together. Where criteria determine that a
site or object has major significance and is worthy of protective action, it
will depend on the level at which those criteria are applied as to which
agency or agencies become responsible and indeed whether action is
taken at all; significance at the purely local level may mean there is no
relevant action to be taken, as compared with significance at the national
or global levels. Preservation in all its forms is the topic of the
next chapter, but here we may consider two aspects: the manner in
which decisions are reached based on evaluation, and the alternatives to
preservation that may be considered.

A number of authors have commented on the consequences of a dichotomy based on assessment of sites and objects as either significant or not.
As mentioned above, Schaafsma (1989) challenges such a neat distinction
and argues that instead all sites should be treated as significant until demonstrated – by excavation or other investigative technique – not to be so.
Similarly Carver (1996) – also mentioned above – argues for sites recognised
as significant on the basis of current understanding to be investigated immediately and all others to be assumed to hold potential value for future
investigators. Earlier commentators also addressed this issue, especially
Tainter and Lucas (1983), who point out that an assessment process that
examines all sites – rather than limiting itself to sites in immediate danger –
may prematurely render sites with unrecognised potential prone to abandonment and therefore destruction. In a contrast with Startin (1993), mentioned
above, who argues that established criteria (at least in England) tended to
confirm the judgements of previous archaeologists, Noble (1987) argues that

rather than relying on fixed criteria, and since (per Tainter and Lucas 1983) 'significance' depends to such a large extent on context, reliance should be placed on the expertise of individual archaeologists. Nevertheless, as we have seen, established criteria are used in the assessment of archaeological remains in various territories across the world, and their use is likely to become more, rather than less, common as ARM practice as known in the West spreads its influence.

The debate about significance couched in terms of what it means for practice forces a consideration of the outcomes of significance rankings. A high value may mean the effective removal of the site or object from the possibility of archaeological intervention; a lower value may either make it available for investigation or render it subject to abandonment and dereliction, leaving it for others to decide its fate.

Conclusion

The evaluation of archaeological resources is a very particular process, incorporating distinctive characteristics. Although couched in terms that imply that each object, site or landscape to be assessed is approached as a unique example – assessment for its particular 'significance' (Briuer and Mathers 1996) or 'importance' (Darvill 1995) – it is in practice always a comparative process whereby one object of evaluation will be explicitly or implicitly compared to others in the same class, however that class may be defined. The result is the creation of a hierarchy of value whereby some things or places will be valued highly, some less highly and others not at all. This stands in direct contrast to the process of inventory (Chapter 4), which aims to include all material and places that may be relevant to archaeological purposes, whether of enquiry or otherwise. By the application of implicit or explicit criteria for the purposes of assessment, evaluation identifies the specific attributes and characteristics an archaeological object or site is required to have to be classed as 'archaeological'. Evaluation thereby goes one stage further than inventory in categorising material: from all those things identified as potentially of interest by the process of inventory, evaluation marks those deemed to be specifically of relevance. Underlying this idea of establishing the relevance of the material to archaeologists is a concern for the 'authenticity' of the remains as 'archaeological'. As Holtorf and Schadla-Hall (2000), among others, have outlined, 'authenticity' is an ascribed attribute rather than an inherent one: accordingly, Holtorf's (2013) notion of acquired 'pastness' applies as much to archaeological remains as it does to anything else in the world. It is by the processes of inventory and evaluation that material deposits acquire their specific identity as 'archaeological resources'.

Evaluation is presented as an aid to archaeological decision-making, especially with respect to the investigation or preservation of objects or sites. As such – and as presented in this book – it is one element of a larger archaeological process comprising the collection of data, its analysis and the resultant output in the form of reports or physical preservation. However, evaluation also frequently stands alone as an independent practice that is divorced from other activities. This divorce from other aspects of archaeological work is reflected both in publications and in other areas of debate (see, e.g., Briuer and Mathers 1996; Carman 1996; Mathers et al. 2005a; Clark 2001; 2006) and in archaeological practice (see, e.g., Loechl et al. 2009; Barrett et al. 2007; Hardesty and Little 2009). The consequence is that it becomes an end in itself: rather than being a tool to be used at the service of the archaeological resource and of archaeologists to aid understanding, it becomes the role of archaeological material to meet the standard required by evaluation criteria. Only by so doing can it be deemed worthy of further attention by archaeologists and thus qualify as 'archaeological'. In theory, it can be argued, all possibilities remain open for any material, whatever the result of assessment: evaluation is merely a tool to aid immediate decision-making. In practice, however, the fate of material will largely be determined by the outcome of assessment. Since archaeology is throughout the world subject to legal or other official regulation (Chapter 3 and as reflected in much of the literature cited in this chapter), evaluation becomes an integral component of an official process. Accordingly, if material satisfies the criteria, its fate will be to be investigated further or preserved for the future; if not, it will be relegated to abandonment to any future that may happen.

For components of the archaeological resource – and for those archaeologists reliant on a supply of material to investigate to remain in employment – evaluation and assessment is a serious matter for it determines futures. It is commonly assumed, including by professional archaeological institutions, that the purpose of assessment is to identify those resources worthy of preservation for the future. The next chapter will indicate that 'preservation' is itself no simple concept, but that evaluation is deeply implicated in whatever form such preservation may take and indeed in the fate of all archaeological resources. Hence the statement at the opening of this chapter that giving a value to archaeological resources is the central practice of ARM on which all subsequent practices depend. It is central to the archaeological project.

CHAPTER 6

Preservation

While there is a widespread assumption that the preferred option
for archaeological resources is their protection from degradation and
destruction, there is in reality very little in the literature of ARM to justify
this. It is of little help in understanding what this imperative to preserve
means and involves that a range of different terms are also used to describe
it: preservation (this volume; Carman 2002; Lozny 2008), conservation
(Clark 2001) and protection (Cleere 1984; Messenger and Smith 2010),
among others. In addition to this, there are the different forms of preservation that are offered: preservation in situ (Corfield et al. 1998), preservation
'by record' (Wainwright 1989, 168–9) and reconstruction, a very specific
form of archaeological presentation (Stone and Planel 1999), all of which
may have different names in different territories. The issue of preservation,
of course, also assumes its opposite, destruction, and it has long been held
that excavation is itself destructive (Wheeler 1954, 15). However, there are
now arguments being made by archaeologists that what we have thought
of as a bad thing is merely another form of transformation, something of
which we are guilty whatever we do to components of the archaeological
record (Lucas 2001b, 40). Holtorf (2005) and, elsewhere, I (Carman 2013,
750) argue that both preservation and destruction ultimately serve the
same purpose: that to preserve or to destroy something is respectively to
destroy or preserve something else, be it another object, an idea or a way
of life. In the case of preserving or destroying, the question is not about
the rightness of the action in itself, but about what thereby is being
preserved or destroyed instead.

These are the issues that this chapter will address from the perspective of
the role these various practices play in the archaeological project but also
the regulatory and institutional contexts in which they are located. The next
section will return us to concerns that first appeared in Chapter 3, with how

preservation is reflected in laws that govern archaeology. The following
section will examine how it relates to issues of ownership and custodianship, issues that underpin so much archaeological work. The section after
that will look at the practical means of preservation that may be applied,
and a final section will review the work that the preservationist project does
in the world, what it means that we preserve our material in these various
ways.

Legal mechanisms

As indicated in Chapter 3, every country in the world has laws that relate
to its archaeological resources, and these generally cover a range of topics
that relate to how these materials will be managed. A shared principle that
lies behind their existence is the belief that archaeological remains are
(a) important and (b) therefore the responsibility of public (usually equated
with state) institutions.

Table 6.1 provides a sample of territories and the state agencies to which
responsibility for archaeology is delegated under their laws, giving an idea
of the range of types of organisation to which such responsibility is given.
The level at which responsibility is placed depends on the type of state
concerned – federal or unitary – although there is no automatic or simple
correlation. It is perfectly feasible for a federal state such as India to retain
control over archaeological remains at the federal level and merely delegate operational activities to regional offices. By contrast others, such as
Brazil or Australia, delegate full responsibility to regional administrations
with no federal oversight, and others delegate responsibility but under a
common national framework, as applies in China. Some federal and all
unitary administrations retain full central control over archaeological
remains. More complex arrangements may, of course, also apply: a combination of state agencies and regional authority, such as exists in the USA
or Poland. Responsibility for different types of material may also be divided
between agencies, as for buried remains and upstanding remains in
Mauretania, or more recent and more ancient remains in Argentina, and
between terrestrial and maritime remains in Brazil. Such divisions may
also be made on the basis of function, as is the case with the various
agencies in India, which all operate under the auspices of the central
Indian Department of Culture.

In a number of places it is academic institutions – university departments
or museums – that carry the responsibility for archaeology; in others it is
branches of government that occupy this role; and in yet others authority

TABLE 6.1 *Agencies responsible for heritage protection*

Country	Responsible Agency
Argentina	Instituto Nacional de Antropología y Pensamiento Latinoamericano (National Institute of Anthropology and Latin American Thought); and Bernardino Rivadavia National Natural Sciences Museum (palaeontological remains)
Australia	Department of Environment and Heritage Australian Heritage Commission
Brazil	Regional administrations Brazilian Navy (underwater cultural heritage)
Canada	Parks Canada Provincial authorities
Centrafrique	University Centre for Research and Documentation of Centrafrican History and Archaeology (CURDHACA)
China	Municipal/County Heritage Protection Units
France	National Institute for Preventive Archaeology Research (INRAP)
Ghana	Ghana Museums and Monuments Board
India	Department of Culture, including its subordinate offices: <ul><li>Archaeological Survey of India (ASI)</li><li>National Research Laboratory of Conservation of Cultural Property (NRLC)</li><li>Indira Gandhi National Centre for the Arts (IGNCA)</li><li>National Mission on Monuments and Antiquities (NMMA)</li><li>National Cultural Fund (NCF)</li></ul>
Japan	Agency for Cultural Affairs
Mali	Institute of Human Sciences (ISH)
Mauretania	Mauretanian Institute for Scientific Research (IMRS) National Foundation for the Protection of Ancient Cities (FNSVA)
Mexico	National Institute of Anthropology and History (INAH)

(*continued*)

TABLE 6.1 *(continued)*

Country	Responsible Agency
Niger	Department of Art and Archaeology (DARA) of Institute for Research of Human Sciences (IRSH), University of Abdou Moumouni of Niamey
Nigeria	Commission for Museums and Monuments
Peru	Instituto Nacional de Cultura (INC)
Poland	State Service for the Protection of Ancient Monuments (PSOZ)
	Centre for Archaeological Rescue Excavations (ORBA)
	Provincial offices for monument protection
Russia	Institute of Archaeology (Russian Academy of Sciences)
Senegal	Commission for Historic Monuments and Indigenous Arts (CMHAI)
South Africa	National Monuments Council
	South African Heritage Resources Agency (SAHRA)
Thailand	The Office of Archaeology (Fine Arts Department)
UK	English Heritage/Historic Scotland/Cadw
	Local government officials
United States of America	National Parks Service
	State Historic Protection Officer (SHPO)

Sources: Messenger and Smith (2010); Naffé et al. (2008).

is delegated to bodies independent of direct government control but operating subject to government funding and regulation. However, where delegation is apparently to an independent body – such as a museum or university department or an academic institute – it needs to be borne in mind the status that these institutions may represent: while in anglophone countries universities and many museums will be entirely independent of direct government control, in others universities and museums operate only as state institutions and their staff are government employees: this is the tradition in many European states and has been maintained by their former colonies in South America, Asia and Africa. Where, therefore, a notionally academic institution has responsibility for archaeology, in practice it will represent full government control over that resource. In no country is the responsibility for archaeology entirely delegated beyond government control: the only possible exceptions are those territories where (laws notwithstanding) there may exist no administrative mechanisms for its management, as is suggested may be the case for countries requiring major infrastructure investment, such as Burkina Faso (Nao 2008), Togo, Benin (Aguigah 2008), Chad or Cameroon (de Maret et al. 2008); in the latter cases Chad is reported as having only one working archaeologist and Cameroon a mere six, plus some students (de Maret et al. 2008, 146), which places severe limits on their capacity to manage their archaeological resources. The provision of resources will always be a factor in the management of archaeological resources, and the recent world financial crisis has emphasised this (Schlanger and Aitchison 2010).

The role these institutions play will vary depending on what is expected of them. For some – such as the U.S. or Canadian National Parks services, the UK national heritage agencies and museums in any territory – it is primarily the custodianship of places and things for which the state takes direct responsibility. They may also, like the responsible agencies in other countries, act as repositories of expertise in the management and conservation of objects, sites and landscapes, and provide advice to others involved in the archaeological process. Where specific legal authority is given to such a body, its 'advice' will often have the force of regulation: to act outside their prescribed practice may have consequences for those to whom the advice is directed. Those agencies given overarching control of archaeology within their particular territory may operate in one of two ways: either by internalising all operations, so that they not only control all archaeological work but also carry it out through their own staff, or by acting as monitor for the work carried out by others – including, perhaps, private archaeological units operating on a commercial basis as contractors (Everill 2007), universities and museums – and ensuring that they adhere to recognised standards of good practice. Where the state takes direct responsibility for archaeological resources (usually also equated with state ownership of all such resources; see below), the responsible agency will frequently act as a monitor of activity on privately owned land as well, its staff having the legal authority to interfere with any activity that may threaten archaeological resources or to appropriate objects that have been held by individuals as if their own property. In many, if not most, cases such *dirigiste* regimes exercise such power in theory only: they rarely have the resources or will to truly operate in such a fashion and in practice only take action against the most flagrant legal breaches. It is also often the case that state activities affecting archaeological resources will be ignored, so that major infrastructure projects will be allowed to go ahead unhindered by archaeological intervention, despite a legal requirement for that intervention. As Endere

(2010, 15) points out in the case of Argentina, however, the 'inability of [legislators] and policymakers to achieve their goals is not exclusively the consequence of financial problems . . . Most current laws are not the result of a clear policy . . . but are the product of sporadic inclusion of archaeology on some legislators' agendas.' The role of political will to preserve the archaeological resource should perhaps not be underestimated in attempting to assess the efficacy of any particular system: each system in place will derive from the specific context of its development and will have been designed to operate within that context, rendering direct comparison between systems difficult and complex, as also suggested in Chapter 3.

There are territories across the world where the powers that may be exercised by the state in relation to archaeological remains are limited by the need to consult those with a particular interest in those remains. Debates within archaeology focus especially on engagements with Indigenous communities, a particular form of the wider category of 'descendant community' who can claim certain types of material from the past as theirs because it was the product of their ancestors' activities and not that of a now dominant but different population: examples include Australian Aboriginal peoples, Native Americans, New Zealand Maori and the Sami of far northern Europe, among others (Weissner 1999). Rubertone (2008b, 14) points out that 'Indigenous groups . . . may be, and indeed often are, ill served by historic preservation' by limiting preservation activity to those things that interest specialists and reflect non-Indigenous values. However, as she also points out on the same page, there is now an extensive global concern to engage with Indigenous peoples and recognise the very close relationship they have with their pasts, both material and intangible. This is reflected in growing international ARM practice. Weissner's (1999) useful (although now slightly outdated) survey of the status of Indigenous people across the world allows the construction of a list of territories that has granted such peoples practical legal rights of various kinds, some more limited than others and to greater or lesser effect, especially as they relate to the physical evidence of their past:

- Australia
- Bolivia
- Brazil
- Canada
- Chile
- Colombia
- Finland

- Japan
- New Zealand
- Norway
- Paraguay
- Peru
- Sweden
- USA
- Venezuela.

These states are not all those containing Indigenous peoples. Territories in Africa, Asia and the islands of the Pacific are notable by their absence, which in part is because the governments of those territories may not recognise the existence of Indigenous groups within their boundaries, as was the case of the Sami in northern Europe until relatively recently (Weissner 1999, 92). While it may be true that not all countries contain an Indigenous population deserving specific identification from the majority population (most countries of Europe, for instance, and much of Africa), it may be the case that all countries contain groups who may be treated as distinct in regard to their own archaeology. An issue that has clouded relations between archaeological resource managers and Indigenous peoples has been the division noted in Chapter 1 between 'culture' and 'nature', which relegates Indigenous populations to the latter category (as acknowledged for Australia especially by Burke and Smith 2010). There are countries missing from Weissner's list, however, which have taken further steps to engage with Indigenous heritage and granted them rights especially in respect to archaeological remains. Accordingly, and perhaps inspired by the US Native American Graves Protection and Repatriation Act (NAGPRA), which gives Native American groups a right to claim human remains and associated artefacts (Ferguson 2009, 172–5; Bruning 2010, 214–24), Argentina has also granted such rights to its native population (Endere 2010, 12).

Indigenous peoples are not the only examples of descendant communities, however. Particularly in those areas of the world colonised by Europeans who then brought in people from other places to provide logistical support – especially as slaves – to their growth and expansion, there are very diverse communities who may claim specific material as their own. The best-known examples come from the USA, with widespread discussion of engagement with African American communities about aspects of their past (e.g., McDavid 2000; 2002; La Roche 2011; Levin 2011), but there is also archaeological engagement with, for example,

Asian communities who occupied particular areas within otherwise
European-dominated cities (Karskens [2001] on nineteenth-century
Sydney) and with those who make 'alternative' claims on the past, such as
modern Druids on the ancient monuments of Britain on grounds of faith
(Chippindale et al. 1990). A parallel developing concern is increasingly
with issues of class and the emergence of the modern world. The especially
British development of an 'archaeology of the 20th century' (Buchli and
Lucas 2001; Graves-Brown 2000) has opened the possibility of revisiting
what we thought we knew about ourselves, and using archaeology's capacity to give a voice to those who leave no trace in the documentary record to
remind us of the presence of those who are silent and invisible in our own
world, as advocated by Harrison and Schofield (2010, 146). While some
students of contemporary archaeology focus on identifying and classifying
the material evidence of the working class (e.g., Shackel et al. 2011 and
associated papers in the same volume), others have related such issues
specifically to the management of the archaeological resource. Gould
(1999) focuses especially on the value of investigating late nineteenth-
and twentieth-century buildings for an understanding of the 'power relationships, new systems of control and the creation of a work ethic' (Gould
1999, 153) that were created by the particular forms of these structures. His
point is that systems designed to preserve ancient material assessed for its
'significance' (see Chapter 5) relegate more modern remains to a class of
material to be noted but on which further action does not need to be taken.
The kind of regime in place can therefore also, whether intentionally or
not, determine the kind of analysis archaeologists can undertake.

As outlined in Chapter 3, the law-based arrangements for managing
the archaeological resource cover a range of matters. These include the
kinds of bodies to which responsibility for the archaeological resource is
delegated – a wider range than perhaps might be thought as we look
from the narrow confines of our own particular context – and the roles
they perform in terms of actual management or the oversight of others'
work. What is perhaps less appreciated is that these legal arrangements also
serve to determine, or at least influence – directly in the case of descendant
community engagement, and more indirectly in respect of other kinds of
material – the research agendas of archaeologists in any particular territory.

Ownership and custodianship

As outlined in Chapter 3, there is a clear distinction between those territories that claim state ownership of all archaeological remains and those

that allow private ownership but apply systems of control on how they may be used. There are states that apply a mixture of the two systems – so that some kinds of material may be claimed by the state but others remain in the hands of private owners, or where a change in the status of the material (such as its removal from privately owned soil) leads to a transfer of ownership to the state – and others where the mechanisms of control applied in states where private ownership is allowed are also applied to material automatically claimed by the state. The wider application of 'preventive archaeology' under a 'polluter pays' principle has altered the picture internationally: the clear-cut distinction between 'state control' and 'semi-privatised' systems has become blurred. Whereas state ownership of material and a system whereby certain items are designated might both be thought to generally imply a regime whereby material is preserved in situ, and 'preventive archaeology' a system of preservation 'by record', this is not always the case, as will be illustrated below.

A discussion in Chapter 3 outlined the ways in which material may be defined under relevant legislation. A similar tripartite system exists in terms of the ways in which archaeological material is preserved, outlined in Table 6.2. Here each system of preservation – of automatic state ownership, of designation of certain materials and of preventive archaeology – is differentiated by reference to how items for coverage are defined and by the point at which the system applies to them. Accordingly, in general, both state ownership and preventive archaeology systems select the material for coverage simply by their inclusion in the relevant (often national) inventory: simple existence is all that is required to be taken note of. By contrast, a system whereby objects, sites and places are selected for specific treatment requires the evaluation of all entries in a relevant inventory: only those deemed sufficiently important or significant will then be designated. The three systems are to be most clearly differentiated by the point at which the relevant system applies: in most states where state ownership applies, it does so from the moment of discovery and sometimes before, so that even unknown material is deemed the property of the state; where designation applies, the application of law must wait until a decision as to the status of the material has been made by the relevant authority, based on the results of evaluation; but for preventive archaeology it is the existence of some kind of threat to the material – of removal, of destruction, of transfer of ownership or location – that triggers the involvement of archaeologists.

Table 6.3 outlines in simplified form the legal regimes in place in a range of territories, as derived from papers in Messenger and Smith (2010) and Naffé et al. (2008), drawing on the general discussion in Chapter 3 in terms

TABLE 6.2 *Preservation by different means*

System	Defined by:	Applies at point of:
State ownership	Inventory	Discovery
Designation	Evaluation	Decision
Preventive archaeology	Inventory	Threat

TABLE 6.3 *Legal regimes by country*

Country	Legal system	Ownership
Argentina	Federal	State
Australia	Federal	Private
Brazil	Federal	State
Burkina Faso	Unitary	Private
Canada	Federal	Private
Centrafrique	Unitary	State
China	Unitary	State
France	Unitary	State
Ghana	Unitary	State
India	Federal	Private
Japan	Unitary	Private
Mali	Unitary	Private
Mauretania	Unitary	State
Mexico	Unitary	State
Niger	Federal (devolved)	Private
Peru	Unitary	State
Poland	Unitary	Private
Russia	Unitary	State
Senegal	Unitary	Private
South Africa	Unitary	Private
Thailand	Unitary	State
USA	Federal	Private

of the kinds of legal regime they represent (federal or unitary) and allowing private ownership of material or imposing state ownership. As will be discussed below, none, however, is very easy to allocate to a system of direct state control, designation or preventive archaeology.

Of those listed here – and no selection of countries will be typical of the world as a whole – only two federal states of the seven represented assume legal ownership of archaeological remains. By contrast, a majority of the unitary states (i.e., states where there is no devolution of legal authority to administrations at a lower level) claim remains as belonging to the state. There is an almost even divide here between those that claim state ownership and those that allow private ownership, but this belies some further complexity and other differences: while for anglophone countries and those most closely influenced by them private property is overwhelmingly favoured against state appropriation, in states influenced by continental European approaches there is greater emphasis on centralised authority over remains. However, even where the preference would be for state ownership (such as in Mali: Sanogo 2008), this may be impossible for logistical reasons and the archaeological resource remains de facto in private hands. In other cases, while some classes of material are automatically state property, others are allowed to be privately owned; this is the case especially in Poland, where retrieved objects are automatically the property of the state but sites remain in the ownership of the landowner (Kobyliński 2010, 142). Elsewhere, especially in federal states, while material on federal land may be automatically the property of the state, it may be the responsibility of subordinate administrative authorities to decide on the ownership and management of material within their jurisdiction, so that some may acquire ownership and others allow private owners.

Elsewhere (Carman 2002, 194–9; 2005a, 73–7) I have considered how state ownership of archaeological remains constitutes an appropriation of that material for the benefit of the state as an institution, rather than for the benefit of archaeology. This is in part a critique of the nation-state as a dominant political form: the state subsumes all its population into a single category of 'citizen', thereby eroding cultural variety. The same is true in respect of archaeological remains that are the heritage of particular groups: Aranda (2010) makes it clear how state ownership in Mexico, exercised by the agency of the National Institute of Anthropology and History (INAH), denies Indigenous communities access to or control over remains that they consider to be ancestral. State ownership of material in Mexico – as elsewhere – is seen as a hindrance to commercial development, and so the discovery of objects or sites goes unreported to the authorities as required by law; while some communities take action to protect such material and are recognised by staff of INAH as their allies in preserving Mexico's past, the communities are rarely involved in future decision-making or gain any benefits, and may see the material they have cared for removed to a distant location (Aranda 2010). In a contrasting example, however, Nuttall (1997, 233) reports on how Indigenous Alaskan people are using ownership of their cultural heritage to develop a tourist industry. Such issues raise questions as to the arguments concerning who should have control over archaeological resources: the so-called 'stewardship' debate.

As I have written elsewhere:

> The State is a single body claiming to act for a collective entity, its citizens. Unlike the museum [or an individual], the State may not claim exclusive property rights, but will take to itself certain key powers of use and disposition which will allow it to act as the preserver of an object. The language then applied is that of stewardship and custodianship rather than of ownership, but in practice it will amount to the same thing. As steward or custodian, however, the State is denied one of the key rights attached to exclusive ownership – that of disposal. Accordingly, the role of steward is one held in perpetuity, so that the object itself is also deemed to be one to be preserved for ever. ... The heritage thus offered may be used by all as an educational and inspirational resource: this does not, however, mean the passage of ownership rights to the citizens themselves, but instead to the State acting as their Trustee (Carman 2005a, 55–6).

On a similar basis, it is a widespread and common claim made by agencies of all kinds – national agencies, museums, independent trusts and others – that they do not own the material for which they are responsible but merely act as stewards for a wider community. That wider community may be limited to a list of 'stakeholders', who are deemed to have a direct interest in the material which is being held on their behalf, but specific identification of such interests can be difficult and any such list will include not only differing kinds of interests but also those that conflict (e.g., Carman 2005a, 83–5; Groarke and Warrick 2006, 164–7). One alternative is a vague formulation such as 'the common heritage of [hu]mankind' which, as Dingli (2006) argues, has a number of advantages:

- it distributes responsibility globally
- it recognises the global and local nature of archaeology
- it emphasises its role in enhancing the quality of life
- it removes archaeology from the realm of narrow interests and political decision-making.

As emphasised by a number of commentators (e.g., Askew 2010; Omland 2006), however, the idea of 'global' interest collapses to the concerns of particular interests, especially that of nation-states, because they are the agencies most able to claim the ability to act in the name of collectivities, and the institution generally granted the legitimacy to do so (Green 1990). Other alternatives (conveniently outlined in Young 2006, 15–16) are ownership by individuals, by cultures and by the nation (defined not as the state but as a community of people). While Young (2006) is specifically concerned to examine the claim of cultural ownership – and the difficulties that arise of defining a specific 'culture' and its membership – Leaman (2006) in the same volume (Scarre and Scarre 2006) examines the ethics of collecting and the care for the collected material that is implied by the act of possession. On a broader note, Groarke and Warrick (2006) examine the specific injunction placed on members of the Society for American Archaeology to promote and practice 'stewardship of the archaeological record' (SAA 2000). They suggest that this vague formulation, which does not specify on whose behalf archaeologists are acting, should be replaced by a form of words that focuses on the relationships of archaeologists with those whose their work affects and recognises the authority of others to regulate archaeology in others' interests (Groarke and Warrick 2006, 176). They suggest this definition of what stewardship means – not control over material but a recognition of the duties owed to others – should be paired with an obligation to 'act in a way that adheres to reasonable standards of research and investigation' (Groarke and Warrick 2006, 177), and that this will override any particular duty to any specific interest group.

The idea that archaeologists act towards the archaeological resource as stewards on behalf of others has its attractions: in particular, it gives us reason to deny any claims of exclusive ownership. However, as Groarke and Warrick (2006) and Smith and Waterton (2009) both make clear in their discussions of how archaeologists interact with the world beyond them, archaeologists also constitute a community with interests of its own. As Zimmerman (1998; 2000, 72) has pointed out, the appointment of archaeologists as stewards of their material assumes that only they have valid expertise to deal with such material, thus privileging a particular form of professional knowledge and giving authority to it. In this sense archaeologists are agents of what Smith has termed the 'authorised heritage discourse' (Smith 2006) – indeed its primary agents (Smith and Waterton 2009, 43) – which serves effectively to deny to those for whom archaeologists notionally work direct access and knowledge of their own pasts. Accordingly, the idea of 'stewardship' or 'custodianship' of the past is in essence a lie: it serves to mask the fact of effective control over the material and – more crucially – the meanings of the past, limiting them to those sanctioned by archaeological consensus. The practical and material expression of this control is represented by the various means employed to preserve the past, all of which directly involve and indeed depend on archaeologists.

Approaches to preservation

As suggested above and in Table 6.2, there are three main ways in which material is 'preserved': by selection after a process of comparative evaluation – a system of designation; by maintaining it in place – preservation in situ; and by investigation in advance of destruction – preservation 'by record' or *archéologie preventive*. These are not necessarily mutually exclusive. Indeed, a process of designation usually implies a preference for preservation in situ, for selected sites at least; this preference may well extend to other sites where there is no pressing alternative. For those sites facing the threat of damage or destruction that are not specifically designated for preservation in situ, some kind of remedial action may be preferred: this is often a form of preservation 'by record'.

The process of designation serves to separate certain individual objects from others that are similar, declaring the chosen object to be in some way distinctive or special, and thereby potentially relegating all others in the same class to a lesser status (see Chapter 5; Schaafsma 1989). The usual result is the recategorisation of the object so that it can be preserved in some way, often as a 'national monument', which is the case in such territories as Argentina (Endere 2010), India (Ota 2010) and Japan (where the term *shiseki* is applied; Okamura and Matsuda 2010). In Britain nationally significant sites are placed on a list or schedule and are therefore described as 'scheduled monuments', while buildings in use are placed on a list and therefore described as 'listed buildings'; the latter are graded, but all scheduled monuments are deemed equally important (Carman 1996; Breeze 2006; Wood 2006). A more complex structure applies in China, where responsibility is divided among various levels of authority: abandoned sites are designated as national major heritage protection units, provincial major heritage protection units or municipal or county major heritage protection units, depending on how they are assessed, while historic centres are designated as 'cultural city, town or village with important historic and cultural values' and movable objects are graded on a scale of 1 to 3, with Grade 1 as the most significant (Shen and Chen 2010). In federal territories such as Brazil, Canada or Germany, except where the federal authorities take specific responsibility for sites, that responsibility will fall onto subordinate authorities, and while some may designate, others may take ownership of all material, and others may do little or nothing in regard to their archaeology (see, e.g., DeBlasis 2010; Pokotylo and Mason 2010, 57–60; Reichstein 1984). In the USA, while states carry authority within their own borders (Crass 2009, 278), federal authority over archaeological resources is further affected by the emphasis placed on private property (Davis 2010, 197).

The point of a protective regime through the designatory approach is that not all material is given automatic protection: only that deemed worthy against appropriate criteria (see Chapter 5). The purpose is that such material is then made unavailable for any destructive or damaging use. Where such rules are effective, it will mean that sites and other material appropriately designated cannot be altered in any way that is deemed detrimental to them. As Kobyliński (2010, 147) outlines, for archaeologists this means creating 'optimal conditions for the site's long term endurance', leaving 'undisturbed the original context of the site' and intervening 'only in cases of emerging threats'. While this means that sites and structures cannot be bulldozed out of existence, and although it may also mean that natural processes of decay continue unaffected without monitoring (see papers in Corfield et al. 1998; Nixon 2004), it frequently also means that they are unavailable for archaeological investigation. This is the criticism levelled at the assumption of in situ preservation that applies in the UK: that sites that are deemed of national importance are then effectively removed from any possibility of actual study (e.g., Carver 1996). While the justification given for this is frequently that the site will be available for research by future archaeologists using more advanced techniques, if (the counter-argument goes) all the sites that are held to be interesting are preserved so that no archaeologist can touch them, these future archaeologists and new techniques will have no sites at which they can be developed (Carver 1996).

In those territories which have Indigenous populations a further reason for the designation of sites can be to separate those sites of special concern to the Indigenous population from others that may be of archaeological concern. As mentioned above, a number of territories across the world identify peoples that represent 'original' inhabitants of an area subsequently colonised, mostly by those of European stock, especially the Americas and Australasia, but also South Africa and far northern Europe (Weissner 1999). Several of these make specific provision for those categories of material or places that are significant to those populations: although not designation in the sense discussed above, the effect for archaeology can be the same in that the material is thereby made unavailable for archaeological investigation. The US NAGPRA legislation (Ferguson 2009, 172–5; Bruning 2010, 214–24) and laws never put into effect in Argentina (Endere 2010, 12) provide for the restitution to Indigenous groups of human remains and associated artefacts. Elsewhere, such as in Canada (Pokotylo and Mason 2010), Australia (Burke and Smith 2010) and the USA (Morgan 2010), more recent initiatives relate to setting aside areas of land, and thereby any archaeology it contains, that are claimed by Indigenous groups. In many cases these are arrangements that exist outside of legal regulation and provide mechanisms for management that meet a range of ethical needs: by ensuring control is in the hands of those with an interest in preserving the material, both preservation and recognition of rights of 'ownership' by descendants are recognised (for the USA see, e.g., King 2003; 2007).

A problem persists in territories that govern minority populations – especially those whose presence pre-dates the emergence of the polity in whose territory they dwell – but do not recognise them as a distinct population with claims on particular pasts and therefore particular material. Such territories may include China, Mexico, Peru, Russia, several territories in Africa, the UK and most countries of continental Europe (Willems 2010), whose very diverse populations are all treated as part of a single modern nation. In these states all archaeology is deemed to be that of a unified national past. However, with growing international pressure to recognise the status of minority groups, countries such as these too may need to find means to accommodate demands on particular pasts.

It is, of course, true that a process whereby certain sites are designated for specific protection does not necessarily imply that all others are irredeemably lost. So long as sites face no particular or immediate threat, then their preservation will be the default position adopted, requiring no particular action on the part of archaeologists. By merely failing to take action the site will remain in its current condition, although that condition may itself not be a stable one (see, e.g., discussions of archaeology in wetland environments: Cox et al. 1996; Kobyliński 2003) and as Kobyliński (2010, 147) points out, sites will need constant monitoring to ensure that they maintain their integrity. Work to this effect in the UK is reported in Corfield et al. (1998) and Nixon (2004), following from the principle adopted in the 1990s that, wherever possible, sites should be preserved in situ since there is general agreement that we understand only poorly the processes affecting archaeological material that has remained buried (and for a U.S. perspective on the processes affecting archaeological remains see Schiffer 1987). Accordingly, even the application of a principle of preservation in situ should not be understood to mean that material is entirely untouched.

The alternative – or complement – to preservation, whether by designation or by a system of state ownership and control of all archaeological material, is a process of ensuring that remains reveal their information content before they are lost. This goes by various names – 'rescue or salvage archaeology', 'preservation by record' or 'preventive archaeology' are three, with variations in different languages – and the chosen name reflects differences in underlying philosophy for each. In general, the idea of 'rescue' or 'salvage' archaeology – with its connotations of desperation and panic – has been abandoned in favour of terms implying more care and a pre-emptive rather than a reactive stance on behalf of archaeologists. Similarly, preservation 'by record' has been recognised as no preservation at all, since it entails the destruction of the material, either by its archaeological excavation or by the building or other activity that requires recording to take place. Accordingly, 'preventive archaeology' is now a preferred option. It is proactive rather than reactive and implies the existence of a wider range of responses than an immediate call for destructive investigation such as excavation and removal of material from its location. As listed by the U.S. Advisory Council on Historic Preservation (2007) these may include:

- preserving some sites while allowing others to be lost
- burying sites or including them in newly built structures
- using available funds to produce synthetic bodies of existing data rather than seeking new data from sites
- constructing barriers to divert traffic away from sites
- using available funds to produce educational material that otherwise would not be available
- 'mitigation banking' – trading the permanent preservation of sites against non-interference in others (cited in Chandler 2009, 121).

There are three foundational principles to preventive archaeology:

1. That archaeology is a public good whose loss should be mitigated by the beneficiary of that loss, such as a developer. This is an extension into archaeology of the more general principle that anyone who causes damage should pay to repair it; most commonly it is seen in the idea that a polluter (e.g., of a river or the air) should be responsible for decontamination.
2. That archaeology is only one among a range of factors affecting the suitability of any development work and, in the absence of any overriding archaeological imperative, other factors may require the loss of archaeology.

3. That the primary value of archaeology is as a store of information about the past. In case of impending loss, that information should be retrieved.

The purpose of such a system is not to interfere with development – as a system of automatic state ownership of the material may do, for instance, by placing the responsibility for the material and its control away from those who own the land and thereby preventing any further activity. Instead, it places the responsibility on those undertaking development by making the costs of archaeological work part of the costs of the project, and those archaeological costs can be expected to be low in comparison with the overall cost and with the returns expected of the project. Where it differs, in particular, from a state control model, which is based on reactions to discoveries, is in attempting to identify in advance the likely presence of significant remains and thereby including any archaeological investigation in the development project itself. Ideally, archaeologists effectively work as part of the construction team, undertaking a specific task in relation to the project as a whole, included in its costings and in its planning as any other specialists are. Indeed, the model for such an approach lies in Western attitudes towards the natural environment, and archaeological survey in advance of development work can conveniently be included in any wider Environmental Impact Analysis, and as Fleming and Campbell (2010, 244–7) point out, this is an integral part of any development sponsored by the World Bank.

Having first emerged especially in Britain in the late 1980s, the idea of preventive archaeology is now spreading across the world. As Willems (2010, 219) and others (see, e.g., chapters in Hamilakis and Duke 2007) emphasise, placing the responsibility for archaeology on those whose projects will lead to its destruction has the effect of removing archaeology from the realm of public concern and towards its 'privatisation'. This is certainly the case in the UK, USA and Australia, where archaeology is increasingly practised by commercial archaeological units and consultants employed by developers (Everill 2007, 119–21; Davis 2009, 32; Smith and Burke 2007, 3–19). In Britain the various roles that can take in such a system are frequently described as the 'four Cs': curator, contractor, consultant and client, of which three are archaeological (Schofield et al. 2011, 100–5). Of these, only the curator is a public official, usually employed by a local authority, and charged with oversight of the archaeological process. The consultant will be employed by a developer to advise on the treatment of archaeological remains and act as their representative in engaging with other archaeologists. The contractor will be employed by the developer to investigate archaeological remains and will report on their status for decision-making by the relevant authority as advised by the curator. The client of both the consultant and contractor is the developer.

However, preventive archaeology is not entirely irrelevant to territories where the assumption of state ownership and responsibility for archaeological remains is the rule. The French Institut National de Recherches Archéologiques Préventives (INRAP) is a state monopoly charged with ensuring the proper identification and treatment of archaeological remains by co-operating with regional and local archaeological services and private contractors (Demoule 2008, 188). Established in 2001, and deriving from imperatives contained in the European Convention on the Protection of the Archaeological Heritage as revised in Malta in 1992 (see Chapter 3), INRAP has contributed to a shift in French archaeological practice from a single state-controlled activity to one potentially divided between academic research and a professionalised commercial service, as perhaps seen in Italy and the USA (Demoule 2008, 190), which would represent a significant shift in the way archaeology is done and perceived in France. However, as Demoule (2008, 191–2) argues, the principle of 'polluter pays', which lies at the heart of preventive archaeology, offers the countries of the south, who face problems of looting to feed the international tourist and art markets and also a need to build infrastructure to support economic growth, a means to finance archaeological work without placing a burden on the state. The scope for its extension to (especially francophone) African countries is explored in the product of a conference held at Nouakchott, Mauretania, in 2007 (Naffé et al. 2008), where both practical and ideological barriers to its adoption are considered as well as its potential advantages. It is, however, also the mode of approach favoured in Japan (Okamura and Matsuda 2010, 102) and is emerging as an important aspect of archaeological practice in Poland (Kobyliński 2010, 146). However, preventive archaeology has a way to go before it achieves widespread adoption across the world: where an ideal of archaeological material as national patrimony and state property persists supported by strong state organisations, it is unlikely to make headway, as in India (Ota 2010, 74) or Russia (Petrov 2010, 157).

As this section has outlined, there are different ways of preserving archaeological material, not all of which represent preservation of the material itself but focus more on the information about the past it can provide. The chosen approach – and they are by no means mutually exclusive – will involve particular kinds of institutions and particular sets of relationships between institutions: state agencies, private contractors, commercial developers and others also involved in the process, as controllers and controlled or partners in a joint enterprise. Depending on the relative importance granted to archaeological remains, a concern for preservation will override other factors or be subordinate to them: where other factors are considered vital, archaeology may not enter into the equation at all, as for countries in Africa with more pressing urgencies, such as Burkina Faso (Nao 2008), Niger (Ide 2008) or Togo (Aguigah 2008).

The meaning of preservation

The purpose of previous stages in the ARM process has been to assist in making decisions concerning the future of archaeological remains. Accordingly, inventory records what is known and evaluation assesses it for its worthiness for investigation or continued existence. Legal measures provide the framework within which this is done and lay down the basis on which preservation is to be achieved. Issues of state custodianship versus state ownership vary from territory to territory, and the focus on preservation in situ versus forms of preservation by record varies similarly. However, the recent emergence of preventive archaeology combined with the professionalisation and commercialisation of archaeological organisation, allowing the rise of private consultants and contractors, is causing widespread change in terms of what the purpose of ARM is seen to be.

As Willems (2010, 216–17) outlines it for Europe, there is a shift away from a concern with the continued existence of individual sites and monuments and towards a concern for a 'historic environment' as a whole: that historic environment comprising not only archaeological remains but also their wider contexts and the meanings they represent. Olivier and Clark (2001) conveniently set out the widespread shifts they see having taken place in European ARM practice and thinking. These comprise, among other things:

- a changing role for archaeology in society
- increased democracy in decision-making, coupled with
- increased professionalisation of the discipline
- greater public access
- a shift in the kinds of values taken into consideration (see Chapter 5) and
- movement towards a more integrated and holistic management (Olivier and Clark 2001, 94–6).

Willems (2010) and Kristiansen (2012) agree: as Kristiansen (2012, 465) sums it up, the last thirty years have seen shifts of emphasis in European ARM:

- from assessment in quantified terms to qualitative terms
- from attempts at objectivity to a recognition of inevitable subjectivity
- from national to local histories.

Such changes imply that archaeologists are becoming more concerned for the publics and audiences for whom they claim to work than with their own status. They also imply a shift away from a concern with the construction of unitary pasts at the service of the nation-state towards one recognising the cultural and ethnic diversity of modern states – especially former colonial powers who attract to their borders people from those former colonies. In preserving a historic environment rather than archaeological remains, archaeologists have become part of a broader movement that has made having a claim to a particular past 'a human right ... granted to all people and nations', thereby achieving for themselves 'a new progressive status' (Kristiansen 2012, 465).

The trend is nevertheless away from the physical preservation of material to its incorporation in wider frameworks of meaning. Schaafsma's (1989) and Carver's (1996) criticisms of systems of designation have in fact, and paradoxically, been met by the emergence of a system of preventive archaeology – the emergence of which they were equally hostile to – by that system's focus on archaeological remains as stores of information worthy of investigation. Designatory systems tended to have the effect of removing material from all those with an interest: if a site is intended for preservation, then by definition archaeologists are denied access in the same way that others are. The principle of preserving sites for future archaeologists can only be met if in fact there is a mechanism whereby future archaeologists can gain access, but strict legal impediments do not provide for that: the site remains a place of inaction. A system whereby identified threats require archaeological intervention, however, places the site in the realm of current action. Table 6.4 summarises the differences between the approaches. While a focus on static preservation is oriented towards an unspecified future that may never arise, a dynamic preventive approach requires action in the present; and while preservation results in nothing, a preventive approach produces archaeological data.

The fact that the act of preservation – whatever form it may take – follows a process of evaluation suggests that objects are preserved because they are valued (as in Chapter 5). However, as indicated in Chapter 3, drawing on discussions in Carman (1996), it may be the fact that certain things are

TABLE 6.4 *Preservation versus prevention*

Framework	Focus	Time	Access	Realm	Outputs
Preservation	Statics	Future	None	Inaction	None
Prevention	Dynamics	Present	Archaeological	Action	Data

treated in certain ways that gives those things value. Accordingly, the process of working to ensure the preservation of archaeological remains serves to give those remains a status they would otherwise not be able to claim. Rather than archaeological remains having an innate significance which evaluation identifies and confirms, the ARM process itself is the mechanism by which the material comes to have value. The fact that particular types of people – archaeologists – show concern for particular kinds of object or place puts them in a category of 'interesting thing' which then requires a certain response, such as preservation. This process is perhaps not unlike the emergence of interest groups whenever archaeologists go to work on a body of material, as recorded by, for example, Boyd et al. (2005), giving rise to a community of concern that ensure its protection from harm.

It is also interesting that, in moving away from the 'traditional' forms of preservationist ARM, the archaeologist is still central to the process and indeed uses the new mechanisms to gain access to material to investigate. Although a strict preservationist framework denies archaeologists the opportunity actively to investigate material, it relies on them to identify and evaluate that material in advance of its preservation, and to monitor its survival thereafter: in Britain this is exemplified by work on the so-called Monuments Protection Programme (English Heritage 1997; 2000), which was designed to produce 'a more ambitious and theoretically informed ARM' (Fairclough 2006) by a close examination of the resource as then known, and especially the condition of sites and monuments protected by law. Even where a preventive archaeology approach – as is now taken in the UK – is notionally designed to identify sites for preservation, in practice it results in work for the archaeologist as a contractor to a developer (English Heritage 1992). The focus of the francophone version of preventive archaeology (Naffé et al. 2008) is largely on research in advance of development projects (e.g., Bordes et al. 2008; Depaepe 2008), although it may also incorporate an element of touristic development as well (Gill et al. 2008). There is also a very strong focus on strategic planning and the incorporation of archaeology into larger development plans, as in Nîmes (Breuil 2008).

All of these are functions requiring archaeological expertise and place the archaeologist as central to the 'preservation' of the material remains of the past.

This raises the question of what – exactly – is being preserved by the ARM process of preserving archaeological remains. In some instances it is the material itself – selected by processes of evaluation leading to its designation as worthy of passing to the future; in others it is the store of information that material contains – investigated before its destruction as part of a development process. However, in no case is it likely that all remains of the past will continue into the future, so as a preservationist project of material ARM has its weaknesses. Having said this, in all cases it is the role of the archaeologist that is preserved as an expert in identifying and deciding on the future of the archaeological resource: regardless of the framework in place and the means applied, it is archaeologists who work within those frameworks and who apply those means. Beyond that, it is the role of archaeology as an integral part of the modern way of doing things that is also preserved. As a number of commentators have outlined (e.g., Thomas 2004; Kehoe 2007), archaeology developed as part of the modernist project and is integrally bound up with it: accordingly it serves to support the mechanisms that promote concepts such as progress, the drive for economic growth and modernisation across the world. By devising mechanisms for the preservation of archaeological remains, archaeologists also provide the means to preserve themselves and their field of endeavour.

Conclusion

This chapter has treated preservation as the product of previous stages in the wider ARM process. Grounded in legislative regulation, preservation of material is the cumulative result of inventory to identify remains and its evaluation to decide on its future. Preservation is the outcome for material of appropriate quality, although that may not mean its physical survival. The increasingly common trend towards preventive archaeology across the globe may mean that material is investigated rather than kept, in order that development may proceed without undue interference from state authorities. This in turn increasingly places archaeology outside the realm of the state and into that of private commerce, which is a trend noted in both anglophone and non-anglophone territories: in the former, the cultural preference for private ownership eases the move away from state control of archaeology; in the latter it seems to be a product of the

devolution of authority that is inbuilt into a preventive system by application of the 'polluter pays' principle. The trend towards preventive archaeology is most strongly resisted in those territories with a firm commitment to
state ownership and control, where granting any kind of decision-making
authority to non-state agencies is perceived as a denial of the nation's
overriding commitment to the remains of its past. Further resistance to
the preventive framework can be made in claims made by subordinate
groups – especially Indigenous communities – for control over their own
pasts: rather than wishing to allow archaeologists access to material for
potentially destructive investigation, the greater desire is more commonly
to ensure the physical preservation of material.

The diversity of ARM practices and the underlying philosophies they
represent become particularly evident in considering preservation.
Although preservation is represented as a common aim across the globe,
this serves to mask key differences over issues of ownership and custodianship, the kinds of institutions and organisations granted authority over
archaeological remains, and the role that such material is deemed to
perform in particular societies. It is difficult to identify common trends:
states who claim ownership of material are as likely as not to subscribe to
either designatory or preventive frameworks; unitary and federal states are
as likely as not to allow commercial involvement in the archaeological
process. However, it is also true that the rule in ARM that only a few
variations are available to choose from (Table 6.5): states can opt for total
control over all material, usually by claiming direct ownership of all
material before or on discovery; or states may select the material they
choose to protect by a system of designation; or states may abandon efforts
to preserve and instead institute a system of preventive archaeology which
responds to threats to material from development; or they may choose

TABLE 6.5 *Options for preservation*

Choice	Framework option
1	State ownership of all material and automatic preservation
2	Preservation of designated material
3	State ownership of all material and preventive intervention to avoid interference with development projects
4	Preservation of designated material and preventive intervention in all other cases
5	Preventive intervention in all development projects

either ownership or designation and combine it with a framework of preventive archaeology.

All of these models have the capacity to be effective in regulating the effects of development on archaeological remains. Recent experience in those countries able to implement it, however, suggests that a preventive approach is likely to gain support from those affected by it. The principle of 'polluter pays' is based on equity and is reflected in approaches to the conservation of non-archaeological material, such as the natural environment. By incorporating archaeology into the development process itself, the fear that finding remains will serve to prevent further work – causing loss to those involved – is removed, and by placing archaeological investigation early in the process (e.g., at the point where approvals are given) removes uncertainty. It therefore has significant advantages over a strict regime. It also serves, however, to remove or reduce the authority of state institutions over archaeology and place greater responsibility on local and regional authorities and, where they emerge, private contractors employed directly by developers. The principle that archaeology belongs to the nation and its people is therefore eroded.

Preservation is – at least notionally – the end result of the ARM process, although, as will be seen in Chapter 7, some remains have an ongoing existence as material displayed to the public. Historically this has tended to be the purpose of preservation – the remains of the past acting as guides to behaviour in the present and signals for a future (see Chapter 1). With the development of archaeology as a field of enquiry, however, preservation for the purpose of providing materials for archaeologists to investigate became a more common concern. If commentators are to be believed (e.g., Olivier and Clark 2001; Willems 2010; Kristiansen 2012), the trend is back towards the preservation of material for the purposes of a wider public rather than a narrow intellectual and professional elite. The public display of material is therefore emerging as an imperative towards preservation: as we shall see in Chapter 7, this applies as much to material recovered from preservation by record as material preserved in situ.

CHAPTER 7

Presentation

It will be obvious that only those sites that have been preserved – whether deliberately through archaeological intervention or simply because neither humanity nor nature has caused them damage – can be offered for presentation to audiences of various kinds. It can be considered a duty of archaeologists to make their material available to others, since they claim to perform their work on behalf of those others. Not all archaeological material is, however, considered appropriate for this purpose, and this may say more about us as archaeologists than it does about the material or its potential audience, an issue to be developed throughout this chapter. The institutions through which material is made available also vary in terms of type across the world, reflecting the structure of archaeological organisation in each territory, although some types of institution, such as the museum, are represented universally. The forms that presentation can take will also vary, depending on the material itself, the institution responsible for it and its intended audience, among other factors. This chapter is titled 'Presentation' because that is the form of public engagement which most involves the archaeological resource itself: other forms of engagement are much more about the people involved (Carman 2002, 118–44; see also papers in *World Archaeology* 2002; Skeates at al. 2012; Jones 2013). To limit the concern of the chapter to matters of museum display and outreach – the major forms of presentation – will be to deny the increasing trend towards engagement and the democratisation of archaeology noted by commentators cited in Chapter 6 (especially Oliver and Clark 2001; Willems 2010; Kristiansen 2012), and on which there is a growing international literature.

The concluding chapter to Cleere's (1984a) seminal collection of papers on archaeological heritage management deriving from his overseas travels makes it clear that the educational and interpretive purposes of archaeology – the subject of this chapter – are central to the purpose of ARM, even if frequently inadequately supported (Cleere 1984c, 128–9). Interestingly, it makes less of an appearance in the One World Archaeology volume of five years later (Cleere 1989) and even less in Messenger and Smith's (2010) more recent collection. Instead, the engagement of archaeologists with others has become the topic of a separate branch of the literature, generally described as 'public archaeology' (Merriman 2004b; Skeates et al. 2012; Dalglish 2013) or 'community archaeology' (Moshenska and Dhanjal 2011) because of its focus on relations between categories of person using archaeology as the topic of discussion, rather than placing a focus on the material of archaeology itself. It can be argued, however, that the purpose of archaeology is to provide the material for debates about a range of issues, using the past to inform the present rather than limiting ourselves to a mere antiquarian interest. As previously noted in Chapters 2 and 6, Harrison and Schofield (2010, 146) take a particular view of the role of archaeology in the modern world. Similarly, Carol McDavid writes of her work in the USA:

> Making archaeology matter . . . has been the focus of [my] work, so I have become very involved in the recent activist archaeology discourse which sees civic engagement as a primary reason for doing archaeological work in the first place . . . In the context of African American archaeology, being an activist archaeologist means using [the] work to deconstruct racism and white privilege in the present, even as we try to understand how these things occurred in the past . . . We use [critical race theory] to theorise about race and white privilege even as we try to think carefully and intentionally about how knowledge is created and controlled, and then act upon what we learn (McDavid 2009, 246–7).

For these archaeologists, presenting the results of their work is central to their purpose, and so mere preservation of sites (the topic of Chapter 5) is not enough. Instead, archaeological practice as they see it is at the service of a wider community and a wider agenda than the mere study of the past.

This chapter will relate these present-focused aspects of archaeology to the preservationist creed that has driven ARM since its emergence in the late nineteenth century (see Chapter 1), emphasising how archaeological engagement with others operates as a complement and alternative to legal approaches (Chapter 3), and refers back to material introduced in Chapter 2. An opening section will discuss the practicalities of making material available and the institutions involved in doing so, taking us into a discussion of 'outreach' in the form of educational activity and engagements in tourism, a discussion of archaeological engagements with others and, finally, how archaeology is implicated in the creation and definition of particular kinds of person.

Objects and audiences

The ICOMOS Charter for the Interpretation and Presentation of Cultural Heritage Sites (the Ename Charter) places the public interpretation of material at the heart of the ARM process: the first principle espoused by the charter is that 'presentation programs ... should facilitate physical and intellectual access by the public' (ICOMOS 2006). For the purposes of the charter, 'interpretation' is taken to mean 'the full range of potential activities intended to heighten public awareness and enhance understanding of ... sites' while 'presentation' is taken to mean 'the carefully planned communication of interpretive content' at a site (ICOMOS 2006). The charter then offers a series of further principles on which presentation should be based:

- soundness of information sources
- attention to setting and context
- preservation of authenticity
- planning for sustainability
- concern for inclusiveness
- importance of research, evaluation and training (ICOMOS 2006).

These all emphasise the role of the professional interpreter of the past and therefore place significant responsibility on the archaeologist. In discussing the charter and its implications, however, Jameson (2008, 436–8) makes clear that not all these principles are so clear-cut. 'Authenticity' is, for instance, an ascribed value (Holtorf and Schadla-Hall 2000; Gustafsson and Karlsson 2012, 479–81) and does not inhere in the material itself. Sustainability is an ill-defined concept for archaeology (Howard 2013) and may not simply collapse to issues of site 'integrity' (see Chapter 5), as the charter implies. The principle of 'inclusiveness' may serve to weaken or undermine the role of the archaeological expert by the inclusion of non-archaeological understandings (as advocated, however, by some: see, e.g., Prangnell et al. 2011), while a focus on the generation of revenue from such sites may place the emphasis on paying tourists to the exclusion of others. As a consequence, the Ename Charter, although designed to act as a global standard for the presentation of sites, relies on its interpretation in individual territories, and, depending on local understanding of

TABLE 7.1 *Types of access*

Type of access	Description	Example
Direct physical	Physical contact, using all the senses	Site visit
Indirect physical	Limited use of the senses, such as sight only	Viewpoint Museum display with object under glass
Direct intellectual	Full cognitive appreciation	Full academic knowledge
Indirect intellectual	Limited cognitive appreciation	Mere knowledge of existence
Emotional	A feeling of individual close connection	Nostalgia

concepts such as 'setting', 'authenticity', 'sustainability', or 'inclusiveness', may be interpreted and therefore applied differently in different territories.

The result is that, while any territory may claim that its archaeological remains are accessible to its people, as all those covered in Messenger and Smith (2010) do, it does not mean that they share the same understanding of what 'access' means. There are, indeed, several different types of access, as set out in Table 7.1, although physical, intellectual and emotional access may be combined in various ways. Although direct physical access may be possible, this does not necessarily equate to full intellectual understanding of what is being encountered, and there may be little or no emotional attachment. By contrast, full physical access may combine with full understanding and a strong emotional tie to create a holistic experience of direct connection; without the emotional tie a merely cerebral experience may be the result. Indirect physical access may combine with a full intellectual understanding, so that mere sight is enough to satisfy academic curiosity, but it may also combine with limited knowledge to result in limited overall appreciation. It is most likely that a strong emotional tie will relate to a reasonably full cognitive appreciation even if physical access is limited: however, that greater knowledge need not be of an archaeological kind and could relate to religious, spiritual or various 'alternative' understandings (Schadla-Hall 2004).

Recent literature has focused very strongly on providing a fuller experience of the encounter with archaeology for those who are not dedicated archaeologists (see, e.g., Smith and Waterton 2009; chapters in Skeates et al. 2012; Dalglish 2013). However, there is a distinction that must be made between the material of archaeology – the objects, sites and places which can inform us about the past and which may be selected for preservation – and the practice of archaeology itself. While the former and their interpretation can be seen as the 'products' of archaeological work, the work itself takes the form of a craft which is actively performed in the world (Shanks and McGuire 1996; Edgeworth 2006). Both material and practice are amenable to public access, but not necessarily in the same manner. While one concerns static objects – preserved either in a museum or in situ – the other concerns physical activities performed with a number of others; while one may be a solitary experience, the other is inevitably a communal experience and shared; while one is inevitably an encounter only with things, the other is an encounter both with things and other people; and finally, while one is (because the inanimate nature of the objects) a one-way relationship, the other is a complex set of mutually discursive relationships. There are therefore clear differences in the types of experience to be had.

Priede's (2009) study of the influences that shape perceptions of highland landscapes indicates that the conventional professional concern with attributes related to physical form (as emphasised in many evaluation schemes: see Chapter 5) does not reflect the attitudes of the wider public. Instead, her work indicates that responses are related to what she terms the 'socialised self', which is itself conditioned by three complex elements which she describes as 'identity', 'culture' and 'time' (Priede 2009, 88–9). Those aspects of identity she found to be most influential on attitudes were age, personal interests and occupation, and familiarity with place. Those aspects of culture most relevant were ideas about beauty and 'wildness' coupled with assumptions of a timeless, unchanging form particularly associated with rural upland open spaces and perhaps deriving from the continuing influence of the Picturesque and Romantic traditions of aesthetics. Time was evident particularly in differences of appreciation between those of different ages and raises the possibility that attitudes of individuals may change with age: this is, as she points out, however, a matter for further research. The relevance of this research for archaeology lies in what it says about how people engage with material.

We may assume that familiarity with the kind of material being presented will play a part in its reception: those who are more familiar with a particular kind of object, site or place will respond to it differently from someone who is less familiar; similarly, personal interests will influence their approach. Accordingly (and drawing here on my own experience of watching people at historic sites), a person unfamiliar with the (typically

ruined) European medieval castle may need guidance as to how to investigate it: the standard tropes of finding the remains of structures such as
kitchens and their ovens, gazing down the central well and walking around
the walls – all learned at an early age in countries such as Britain – will not
be immediately obvious to someone from another part of the world;
similarly, a Greek visitor to northern Europe may not be able to 'see' the
presence of large-scale prehistoric structures since they are covered in grass
with all the appearance of a natural rise and fall of ground; but for someone
familiar with such sites they may represent a form of childhood playground
rather than the product of a past culture. Cultural factors affecting response
may have less to do with ideas about Romanticism – although these too may
play their part – than perhaps the assignment of a quality of 'age' to material:
as noted in my own work (Carman 1996, 190–91) and discussed by Holtorf
and Schadla-Hall (2000) and Holtorf (2001; 2013), the inherent quality of
age is not the key factor in appreciating archaeological material, but rather,
as Holtorf (2013) puts it, the quality of 'pastness' it represents. In so far as
measured time plays a part, it is perhaps in the identification of degrees of
age – as the familiar but 'old', the vaguely familiar but 'very old', and
material from so long ago that it is to all intents and purposes alien.

Displaying material

Movable objects are most likely to be placed on display as part of museum
exhibitions (see Chapter 4, Table 4.1). As part of museum collections they
are placed in relation to other objects of similar kind or deriving from
similar contexts to present an interpretation of a period of the past or a way
of life. All such displays have an aim reflected in their form, and both the
purpose and form are selected by the curator responsible for the display. It
will be designed to evoke a particular kind of response from the audience
and may also assume a particular kind of audience (Table 7.2).

As Pearce (2006, 335–6) explains, however, different

> exhibition layouts stimulate different kinds of understanding. [Those
> which move] the visitor along a predetermined route, present knowledge
> as if it were the map of well-known terrain where all the relationships are
> well understood, while exhibitions with looser structures and a variety of
> circulation routes show [archaeological] knowledge as a proposition,
> stimulating further, or different, propositions.

By contrast, however, some exhibitions are at root about the material on
display and – while also seeking a particular outcome in terms of visitor

TABLE 7.2 *Purposes and forms of display*

Visitor-centred	Object-centred
Didactic/educational	Systematic
Entertaining	Thematic
Emotive	Participatory
– aesthetic	
– evocative/romantic	
Responsive	
– to viewer's presence	
Interactive	
– with visitor's wishes	

Source: Belcher (1991).

response – are more concerned with the proper ordering of that material than with the proper ordering of visitors: these are 'object-centred' displays. A systematic display seeks to place similar kinds of object in relation to one another: whether in terms of some developmental sequence, such as from simpler to more complex (however defined), or in chronological sequence. A thematic display will place together objects that are to be found or used in groups or as assemblages; they may be ordered in terms of functional utility or ritual association, for example. A participatory display is one in which visitors are encouraged to take part – either by visitors providing the objects to be put on show, or perhaps by handling them and talking about them. The trend in European museums – at least according to some commentators (e.g., Kaitavuori 2010) – is towards the greater 'usability' of museum collections and therefore greater participation by 'users', by encouraging users to donate or lend material for display, or by a more active engagement with the interpretation of material and thus a direct involvement in setting the agenda for the exhibition.

Earthbound sites are at once each unique and yet fall into categories defined by form, location and historic period – 'hillfort', 'castle', 'monastic building', 'temple', burial mound', 'cemetery' – which may also imply a function in modern terms, whether securely known or otherwise. They tend to be solitary objects, unless a number of different sites cluster around the same location, and although a site may contain different areas within it, each specialising in a particular function – those for habitation, defence, storage, ritual practice, etc. (assuming they can be identified as such) – the site itself operates as a single unit, defying any simple effort to place it in relation to other sites. Accordingly, visitors to a site will tend to see it in isolation and understand it accordingly: theirs will be a passive reading if presented with a pre-digested set of interpretations. Copeland (2004, 140, citing Moscardo 1996) lists an alternative approach, consisting of offering the visitor:

- a variety of experience
- greater controls over their experience
- connections with personal experience
- a questioning attitude.

Gustafsson and Karlsson (2006) are keen to point out that traditional interpretive signing – by information boards – creates a dichotomy: of 'expert' and active producer of signs; and of non-expert and passive reader of them. In a later article (Gustafsson and Karlsson 2012) they go further to point out that signs explaining the preservation process and why some sites may not be made directly accessible to visitors serve to exacerbate this division between the 'expert' and others: as a result 'visitors [to sites] are viewed more as a problem than as an asset' (Gustafsson and Karlsson 2012, 490). A particularly British response to overcoming the alien nature of archaeological sites from their audiences – or any site from the past, come to that – is the suggestion of 'hot' interpretation, designed specifically to engage visitors' emotions by overcoming such factors as distance in time and space, unfamiliarity with the material and the imposition of under-standing by interpretive material (Uzzell and Ballantyne 2008). Although prone to abuse as a form of exploitation, such an approach to site visitors seeks to close the gap between the modern observer and the ancient material under observation.

Such concerns relate directly to the site as a place of experience rather than as a place that represents a particular narrative. The alternative to an experience-based approach is therefore to provide a story located in the site, as argued for by a number of writers, including McCarthy (2008), and experimented with by several others, especially in the USA (see, e.g., Ferguson 1992; Spector 1993; Yentsch 1994; Shrire 1995; Gibbs 2008). McCarthy (2008, 540–42), suggests that the construction of narratives not about things but about the people who engaged with them in the past serves to address three key issues for archaeological practice:

- constructing an image of the past that is relevant and meaningful to a public audience, and therefore the practice of archaeology itself;
- creating new criteria for assessing archaeological significance (see Chapter 6); and
- notions of archaeological 'truth', by forcing archaeologists to think about the implications of their interpretations for current audiences.

Beyond this are specific attempts to emphasise the role of archaeology in creating the past, such as were employed at Annapolis in the 1980s and 1990s (Leone et al. 1987; Potter 1994; Potter and Leone 1986; 1987; 1992). Using a series of devices to focus visitor attention – a twenty-minute audio-visual presentation, interpretive on-site signs, a guided tour of archaeological activity and a self-guided tour of the city led by a handbook – the aim was to reveal how 'many aspects of contemporary ... life [in a capitalist economy] that are taken for granted are neither natural nor inevitable' (Potter 1997, 36). 'Archaeology in Annapolis' was accordingly and expressly an attempt to create 'a critical archaeology [that could] inspire enlightenment [and] lead to emancipatory social action' (Potter 1997, 36). The tours themselves were led always by active members of the site teams rather than by specialist presenters, although advised by a performance artist (Potter 1997, 40–43).

Landscapes – the third type of object recognised in Chapter 4 – perhaps present themselves to us more than being presented to us by others. Following the definition of landscape given in Chapter 4 – as the 'set of relationships that gives [objects contained within it] their separateness' – a landscape becomes a space to move through. As Tilley (1994) puts it:

> Looking at the two-dimensional plane of the modern topographic map ... it is quite impossible to envisage the landscape in which these places are embedded. The representation fails, and cannot substitute for being there, being *in place*. [The] process of observation requires time and a feeling for the place (Tilley 1994, 75, emphasis in original).

Tilley's mention of observation as the key activity in respect of a landscape is not accidental: landscapes are very often primarily considered as something to look at from a distance rather than experienced from within (see, e.g., Urry 1990 on the 'tourist gaze'; Cosgrove 1984 and 2000 on the iconography of landscapes). As Johnson (2007) argues, the all-encompassing Romantic gaze, as exemplified by poets such as Wordsworth (Johnson 2007, 18–21), was transformed by academic students of landscape – including archaeologists – into other forms: particularly, the map, the aerial photograph and the 'hachured plan' (Johnson 2007, 85–95). Indeed, the most common methods adopted to present extensive spaces to those otherwise unfamiliar to them is through sight.

There is, perhaps surprisingly, very little discussion of the presentation of landscapes in the literature of archaeology except in terms of archaeological representation. In the days before widespread public transport a common form was the painted panorama, such as that of the Dutch coast near The Hague by Mesdag (Sillevis 1981). While few of these survive (Sillevis 1981, 769, suggests no more than twenty worldwide), in their aim to represent the extent of large spaces they reflect the Romantic ideal of the 'aerial, superhuman ... view that comprehended all the region "at once"' (Johnson 2007, 21). The same is true of those concerned less with scenery than with action: the panorama of the Battle of Sedan housed in Sedan fortress, France, aims to represent all the action of that widespread event in a single glance; in doing so it refers back in aim to earlier representations of conflict, such as the battle tapestries at Blenheim Palace, England, which encompass sequential events as if taking place simultaneously. Such constructed visions are represented as if seen from a particular point in space, real or imagined, and reflect the placement of tourist view spots in real space, designed to offer what may be considered the best points of vantage to apprehend the landscape as a whole. These viewpoints – usually placed at some distance away from the specific object of view – are frequently marked by an indicator of some kind, very often an information board that gives the viewer a briefing as to what specifically they can see from that location, and perhaps also what they should be looking out for. At Naseby battlefield, England, a monument and signboard placed on high ground overlooking the space of the fight invites the visitor to gaze down into it (Carman and Carman 2006, 72–5), which is the most typical manner of presenting such extensive areas of ground.

This distancing of the observer can be contrasted with the most common alternative, which locates the visitor within the landscape. Typically this may take the form of a constructed pathway – or several alternative pathways – through the space, taking the visitor to and through locations of interest designed to give an overall impression of the terrain and its contents in the form of distinctive built and natural features. The landscape at Roystone Grange, Derbyshire, England, is explored as a landscape by the paths that lead the visitor through the space, exploiting the presence of upstanding buildings, buried remains and reconstructed features representing different periods of use (http://www.derbyshireheritage.co.uk/Menu/A rchaeology/Buildings/Roystone-Grange-Hall.php). Similarly, the historic battlefield of Tewkesbury, England, is marked by a dedicated 'battlefield walk' indicated by signposts taking visitors through the sites of action and remnants of the medieval landscape in the form of archaeological sites and ancient field systems (Carman and Carman 2006, 110–14).

Conclusion

Different styles of display and presentation reflect at once the characteristics of different types of object, the different audiences to which they are addressed and the different aims of those responsible for the presentation. The next section will specifically address two of these alternative purposes, but in closing this section it is perhaps worth considering the relationships between the audiences for different types of object.

There is evidence that those with an interest in visiting museums are also those who visit other kinds of heritage place, such as archaeological sites or historic buildings (Merriman 1991), and may also be those with an interest in landscape-based pursuits (Derry 2011). Derry (2011, drawing on a survey in the USA reported in Cordell 2004), refers to them respectively as 'back country actives', 'outdoor avids' and 'water bugs': the first are 'slightly more male than female ... and are predominately white [and rural]'; the second are 'primarily young, male, white, and in the upper income bracket'; the third are 'nearly two-thirds women and disproportionately [for the USA] white ... middle-aged, upper income ... [and] mostly urban' (Derry 2011). The emphasis on income levels and ethnicity reflects the results of Merriman's (1991) national survey in the UK, which also emphasises income levels and educational attainment. Overall, as a result, the actual audience for archaeology represents much less than half the population, at least in anglophone countries – a total of 29.4 per cent comprising potential visitors in the USA (per Derry 2011) and only 17 per cent of the sample representing 'frequent visitors' to museums in the UK (Merriman 1991, 49). In other words, our audience is relatively small and relatively homogeneous – representing essentially people like ourselves (and see Carman 2011).

Education and tourism

It is a truism that archaeological sites are of interest to a wider audience than just other archaeologists (see, e.g., Holtorf 2010). What is perhaps not so clear is what archaeologists should make of this interest: are we offering mere entertainment, or do we have a more serious educational role? While we can argue for the educational benefits of presenting our material and the results of our researchers to the wider world, the nagging thought must remain that, whatever our intention, it is not matched by that of our audiences.

Archaeology and education

The past few years has seen a number of publications concerned with connecting archaeology with education: while some have been concerned with how archaeology should be taught (e.g., Bender and Smith 2000; Burke and Smith 2007), others have focused more on what is – or possibly is not – taught (Stone and Mackenzie 1990b; Corbishley 2011). A more recent turn has been to consider the wider educative role of archaeology, contrasting the role of archaeologists as educators who aim to serve the purposes of archaeology with those who aim to serve wider social purposes. Perhaps representing the former, McManamon (2000) wishes the public at large to acquire knowledge of various kinds of value the archaeological past can have, especially its associative and commemorative value and its educational and information value. Accordingly he argues for particular kinds of messages to be directed at the archaeological public (as set out in Table 7.3) and for the adoption of a particular set of guidelines on doing so (McManamon 2000, 13–15). These messages all work to the particular advantage of archaeologists and archaeology by emphasising the distinctive nature of archaeological resources and the role of the trained archaeologist in their care. This is a position supported by archaeological organisations such as the Society for American Archaeology, whose Principles of Archaeological Ethics require the enlistment of public support for ARM practices (SAA 2000).

Taking a more critical approach, Franklin and Moe (2012, 570–72) emphasise the widespread attempts to create 'archaeological literacy', which is usually composed of an understanding of five aspects of the discipline:

TABLE 7.3 *Archaeological messages for the public (after McManamon 2000, 13–14)*

A local focus: archaeology is about local pasts
The value of archaeological resources
The need for care in study and conservation
The archaeological resource as non-renewable
The distinction between scientific archaeology and looting

- stewardship and preservation of archaeological sites, which is assumed to contribute to the development of 'good citizenship';
- the fundamental concepts of archaeology, which is deemed to provide an understanding of how the past is constructed out of its material remains, the importance of contextual data and so on;
- the various uses to which archaeology can be put, including the generation of 'critical thinking';
- access to archaeology, thereby making others direct participants in the work of archaeology; and
- the specific content of archaeological interpretations, providing information about how people lived in the past (Franklin and Moe 2012, 572–6).

As an alternative to these five rather narrow and self-serving perspectives, none of which can be shown to lead to the results expected, Franklin and Moe (2012, 577, emphasis in original) offer four *big ideas or enduring understandings* as the aim of an 'archaeological literacy':

1. understanding the past is essential to understand the present and future;
2. learning about diverse cultures is essential to living in a pluralistic world;
3. archaeology is a systematic way to learn about past cultures; and
4. stewardship of archaeological material is everyone's responsibility.

Taking a similar line, an interesting distinction recently made has been between *teaching about archaeology* and *teaching through archaeology* (Bartoy 2012). While the former represents the kind of approach advocated by McManamon (2000), the latter develops the ideas of Franklin and Moe (2012) concerning citizenship. Bartoy (2012, 557–8) argues that teaching through (rather than about) archaeology – that is, using the insights of archaeology as a means to engage with others and to help them develop their own understandings – inculcates two vital skills: critical thinking and thereby an understanding of the 'important distinction between evidence and conclusions . . . between the real world and our interpretations of that world'; and 'developing a sense of cultural relativism – of [the] importance of viewing cultures in their own terms' (Bartoy 2012, 557). These two goals of teaching, he argues, provide 'a powerful tool for change within a democratic society' (Bartoy 2012, 558).

Others have sought to place discussions of archaeological educational practice into wider contexts. Kehoe (2012) charts the rise of programmes to educate people about the past through material remains from the emergence of archaeology in the nineteenth century, although formal programmes of public education only grew alongside the development of and explicitly recognised ARM from the 1970s. As she points out, however, the creation of a Public Education Committee of the Society for American Archaeology in the 1990s resulted in the powerful gendering of this aspect of archaeological work by the recruitment of women and the reduction of ideas of archaeological education to school-level teaching: as she adds, 'women predominate, too, in museum education departments . . . The gender bias . . . will not go away, holding down rewards, both pecuniary and prestige, for archaeologists willing to work with schoolteachers' (Kehoe 2012, 543). She also emphasises the 'incongruity of the American past revealed by anthropological anthropology with the national legitimizing myth' (Kehoe 2012, 549), which links with Jeppson's concern for archaeology's role (or lack thereof) in the ongoing 'culture wars' over values between those labelled 'secular progressive' and those labelled 'traditional' (Jeppson 2012, 583). In particular, she is concerned for the removal from formal curricula of such subjects as 'social studies', broadly concerned to consider 'social relationships and the functioning of society' (Jeppson 2012, 584). Social studies, she argues, stood against a 'traditional history curriculum that is more narrowly focused [on the stories of famous, dead, white males]' (Jeppson 2012, 585). She offers historical archaeology as a counterpoint to this traditional version of the past, building (as per Bartoy and Franklin and Moe above) on its capacity to offer a critical engagement with the past and 'to challenge traditional conservative meta-narratives with competing narratives' (Jeppson 2012, 588).

In many ways these debates concerning the role of archaeology in the USA reflect those of an earlier decade. Stone and MacKenzie's international perspective on 'the excluded past' in education across the world (1990b) identifies five reasons for the absence of certain pasts, or those of Indigenous or other minority groups in particular, from history curricula:

- already overcrowded curricula
- ignorance among educators
- poor coverage in textbooks (mostly written by historians rather than archaeologists) of earlier periods
- a perception of certain pasts as irrelevant to modern life
- overtly political reasons based in ideology (Stone and MacKenzie 1990a, 3–4).

As Singh (1994, 209) has discussed from the perspective of political change in South Africa, university academics can be both the 'legitimators and deligitimators of state power' through the varying interpretations of the past that they offer, and can thereby be agents of, or challengers to, such exclusions. They nonetheless represent a particular interest group in themselves, who are constituent of and subject to the exclusions that operate in a particular society, reflected in those topics that find their way into, or are excluded from, educational curricula. Singh points out that those intellectuals excluded from academia by social and political forces may take prominent positions in other fields – such as literature, art or journalism – and thereby make significant contributions to society, but not through education in its narrow sense (Singh 1994, 209); she therefore argues for a broad alliance of intellectuals and others who will be jointly 'participating in the . . . task of opening up a space for critical engagement in the reconstructive project for the citizenry as a whole' (Singh 1994, 219).

Archaeology as a tourist resource

Lipe (2009, 61), discussing the various values that archaeology represents (see also Chapter 5), argues that 'the lure of the aesthetic and the authentic enhances direct public engagement with archaeological values . . . Archaeological tourism can make . . . a significant contribution to public appreciation of archaeology.' From this perspective the purpose of making sites available for visitors is to serve the interests of archaeology, but he usefully also points out the potential disadvantages of doing so: destruction 'due to unwise overuse or overdevelopment, the creation of false or "hyped" histories, [and] the promotion of looting at unprotected sites' (Lipe 2009, 61). In similar vein, Okamura (2010, 57) raises the issue of the 'ranking' of sites by the promotion of tourism, which renders what he terms 'minor' and 'invisible' sites prone to risk. Taking a different perspective, Silberman (2010, 69) emphasises that the promotion of sites for tourism, and the necessary ancillary provision of parking and visitor centre, leads to an 'increasingly standardised experience . . . [a] patterned behaviour of visita-tion that this spatial arrangement creates'. He goes on to point out that the consequence is that the scope for presenting challenging or alternative interpretations becomes more limited, and that archaeology thereby runs the risk of becoming reduced to a branch of the entertainment industry.

The behaviours of tourists themselves are a valid area for investigation. Palmer (2009) makes a strong case for the use of 'covert' observation strategies involving watching how people behave at and interact with the places they visit. She supplements this observational data with data collected by inter-views carried out as conversations with subjects to discover aspects of their role as tourists not directly identifiable from observation alone. McClanahan's (2007) work at the Heart of Neolithic Orkney World Heritage Site established some clear sets of attitudes displayed by visitors:

- that the sites were understood to be 'untamed' and 'unmanaged', especially because major monuments are free to enter and the entire WHS lies in a remote location (at least as perceived from the major cities of Britain);
- that the sites are seen as 'authentic', possibly linked to the idea they are 'unmanaged' because of no obvious presence;
- that the sites are understood by the local community to be 'contested' because as WHS they 'belong' to the world rather than Orkney, and they represent an era before Orkney was absorbed into Scotland (McClanahan 2007, 36).

For the managers of the sites she also identified key issues to be taken into account for their preservation:

- visitors will take particular routes around sites, and this is related to the type of visitor they are;
- most visitors will enter the site by a particular route, constrained by the provision of parking and drop points, which will lead to excessive wear over that ground; but
- people are also concerned for conservation issues and this governs their behaviour at sites in an effort to engage 'in appropriate visitor behaviour'; this includes a tendency to follow what appear to be established paths – whether made by a site's management or other-wise – because they see the trails made by previous visitors as 'the right way to go' even if in fact damaging to the site (McClanahan 2007, 37).

McClanahan's work also identified the need for managers of sites marked as tourist destinations to take due account of local sensitivities and culture. She cites, in particular, the need for 'outsiders' to Orkney to establish a bond of trust before Orkney people will engage with them (McClanahan 2007, 36–7), a factor also noted in relation to other engagements of archae-ologists with communities (see, e.g., papers in *World Archaeology* 2002).

A review of sections related to tourism in the *Encyclopaedia of Global Archaeology* (Smith 2013) indicates that in so far as archaeologists consider archaeological material as a tourist resource, this tends to be under the rubric of 'heritage' rather than 'archaeology'. Chapter 4 set out the distinc-tion between the archaeological record (the object of archaeological research) and the archaeological resource (the topic of this book, the object of management). Table 7.4 sets out the differences between the record and the heritage, based on the principle that the latter is what we choose to make available to the wider public at large.

TABLE 7.4 *The archaeological record and the archaeological heritage*

Characteristic	The Archaeological ...	
	Record	Heritage
Serves the purposes of	researchers	the public
Key attribute	variability	representativeness
Used for	research	preservation for access
Creation of	archaeological theory/ method	regulation
Considered as	evidence	source
Identified by	survey	categorisation
Selected for	relevance	importance

Direction of travel ⟶

of material from record to heritage

But this is also a realm of transformation from one type of archaeological object to

another, because both categories are made of the same material

⟷

Since these phenomena represent different 'versions' of the same body of material, they are capable of transformation from one to another, back and forth. Indeed, the creation of the heritage as a category is little more than a process of the designation and changes in accepted treatment of particular kinds of material. This is frequently represented in archaeology by the sequence record – resource – heritage (a combination of Table 4.1 and 7.4: see also Carman 2002, 18), which also represents the normal 'direction of travel' of a body of archaeological material from discovery onwards (cf. Schiffer 1972; Carman 1990). On first discovery, archaeological remains are part of the archaeological record and are considered and treated as such. Once discovered, however, they may also become part of the archaeological resource, to be kept for the future benefit of archaeology as a discipline. Beyond this, the material may be considered as appropriate for a more public audience and will become part of the heritage that is of concern to the world as a whole. This trajectory from record through resource to heritage is normal because rarely – if indeed ever – will something be classed as 'heritage' on immediate discovery and subsequently transformed to 'mere' record. Material as 'heritage' therefore represents the final stage in its life: it is unlikely to lose its status as a tourist resource.

Conclusion

The link between the status of material – as record, as resource or as (tourist) heritage – and its audience is thereby a crucial one, and in many ways it is the status that determines what that audience will be. For researchers, archaeological material is a record to be analysed. As an educational tool, archaeology is much more of a resource: it is there to be used for purposes of learning and teaching, frequently about archaeology for the purposes of promoting the field, but also as a tool to introduce more complex ideas about how the world works and challenging convenient assumptions about the inevitability of the current state of things. It also makes archaeologists involved in education a resource, as the providers of the material on which these educational programmes are based. As heritage, archaeological material is removed from the strictly archaeological frame of reference altogether and given to others to manipulate and use as they will. Archaeologists remain as providers – of discoveries, of information and of interpretations – but our direct involvement in the process of tourist development becomes less direct. Arguably, and this may explain the focus on 'heritage' as the tourist version of archaeology, it ceases to be anything archaeological at all: returning us to Lipe's (2009) concern that archaeology as a tourist resource reduces it to a branch of the entertainment industry.

Nonetheless, in engaging with others, archaeologists also attempt to include others directly in the work of archaeology, in recognition – as reflected moreover in discussions of archaeological education – that the material we seek to understand and manage is not entirely ours alone but belongs to the community at large. This is the concern of the remaining sections.

Archaeologists and communities

Community archaeology projects of all kinds usually proceed on the basis of a number of assumptions, among them:

- that the community with which archaeologists are engaging pre-exists the arrival of the archaeologist;

- that such communities have an established sense of identity; and
- that that identity is grounded in what they perceive as their past as represented by certain kinds of material.

All these assumptions can, however, be challenged on the basis of experience.

Archaeological interest as a catalyst for community creation

The application of ideas about cognitive ownership (Boyd et al. 2005; Boyd 2012) has led researchers to see the process of value formation as one closely tied to academic and professional interest in a site or place; in other words, it has led them to see that by treating objects in certain ways they gained an increasing and more complex set of values. This is a model of value I have applied elsewhere, derived from especially the *Rubbish Theory* work of Michael Thompson (1979; Schwarz and Thompson 1990). As I put it then: you start with a socially induced predilection that leads you to favour the sort of social arrangements promised by protecting particular classes of material; having chosen, you then look around for ways to value that class of material over others (Carman 1996, 31). This is the process that leads in particular – but not exclusively – to the legal protection of ancient remains and its management as a 'public' good. Archaeological material achieves this public status not out of some inherent quality in the object itself, but by dint of becoming an object of attention.

In a similar process, in a series of case studies Boyd et al. (2005, 98–107) indicate the processes by which professional interest in sites in Australia engendered the development of local interests and values built around differing attributes. Accordingly, they show how local Aboriginal interests mostly focused on sites representing Indigenous and traditional attitudes to land and environment, or to the history of their engagement with incoming colonisers. European Australians also recognised such claims and the sometimes spiritual dimension that these indicate. Others, however, were more concerned with current social and economic uses – as tourist sites, recreational space or thoroughfares – although not all of these conflicted with Aboriginal conceptions: the attitude of skateboarders to a rock art site, for instance, could be seen as another example of significance to a particular subculture (Boyd et al. 2005, 107). However, these values did not attach to the site until it became the focus of attention by researchers: it was by raising questions about such places that values were ascribed and that their importance to inhabitants of the locality and beyond was marked.

The same set of processes was evident at the Hilton of Cadboll site in Scotland (Jones 2004). Here excavation of the lower portion of an inscribed Pictish stone and its reconstruction ignited controversy over the ownership and placement of the reunited object, which was claimed both by the national museum in Edinburgh and the locality. Investigation of the contexts within which contemporary meanings for the stone are created identified a complex set of interlocking values. Academic and intellectual values included those of archaeology, art history, folklore and oral history (Jones 2004, 27–33). In parallel to these, there was a more symbolic sense of the stone's identity, as a living part of the community, and as an object 'born' into the locality (Jones 2004, 33–7). As such, it at once belongs to the community, is part of it and also constitutive of it: 'as well as being conceived of as a living member of the community, the monument is also simultaneously an icon for the [community] as a whole' (Jones 2004, 37). This extends into the monument's role in the construction of a sense of place, and indeed of reforging a 'lost' sense of community cohesion (Jones 2004, 39) that could be 'healed' (at least symbolically) by reuniting the two original pieces of the monument.

In both these cases (and see also Levin 2011 on the excavation of the first US president's house), 'community' interest did not pre-exist scholarly attention to a particular site or monument. It was the presence and interest of scholars that incited such interest.

A pre-existing identity?

A critique of ideas of 'community' (at least as perceived within policy and archaeological circles) has been outlined by Smith and Waterton (2009). For them, communities are not '"good", "safe" and "comfortable"' (Smith and Waterton 2009, 13) but 'contested, fraught and dissonant' (Smith and Waterton 2009, 138). They point out that to ask 'why the "socially excluded" should visit stately homes and art galleries' misses the point: why not ask instead 'why the middle classes aren't visiting ... museums that commemorate working-class life in industrial regions, or ... [those] that address less comforting aspects of history, such as slavery' (Smith and Waterton 2009, 12). However, as indicated above, an interest in archaeology and related matters is known to be a predominately middle-class trait; by contrast, a closer concern with family histories and genealogy is usually associated with those of lower social status (Merriman 1991). Accordingly, it will be the middle classes (as Smith and Waterton call them) who visit both stately homes and art galleries and also museums of working-class life and slavery. Their 'socially excluded' will be equally excluded (or choose to exclude themselves) from both types of exhibition.

In both the Castleton (Smith 2006, 237–75) and Hilton of Cadboll (Jones 2004) cases, there was a myth of 'lost' community regained by connection with heritage – a recently lost mining heritage in the former, a more ancient one in the latter. But what was really happening was the active creation of a new community that had not existed previously. The same was true in Oudenaarde during the commemoration of the 1708 battle: here, despite the nearby presence of a dedicated heritage consultancy which ran its own visitor-friendly archaeological site at Ename (http://www.ename974. org/Eng/pagina/center_overzicht.html), the main focus was on tourism rather than local associations. Efforts to promote the commemoration of the battle resulted not in the recruitment of an existing community of interest but in the creation of an entirely new one.

The communities that emerge from the practice of heritage and public archaeology are formed out of diverse interests. These are frequently described as 'stakeholders', partly to reflect current political terminology (especially in the UK; see, e.g., Merriman 2004a, 12–15) but also to emphasise the tangible connection between people and what they perceive as 'their' past. Merriman (2004a, 12) discusses stakeholding of heritage in terms of rights of ownership and interpretation, but this is to underestimate the complexity of 'stakeholding' as a phenomenon. As has been noted elsewhere (e.g., Carman 2005a, 84–98), stakeholders inevitably represent a range of diverse and potentially conflicting interests – some of them in material and matters other than the specific object of attention but which will be affected by decisions concerning it. Accordingly, reaching understanding and accommodation between these diverse concerns will inevitably mean the creation of new sets of relations that will in turn cause a redefinition of how the 'community' sees itself. No community formed around archaeology will have a pre-existing sense of itself: it will be created in response to the circumstances of its creation.

The link of identity with the past

Russell has challenged what he calls 'arborescent' models of the link between identity and the past (Russell 2010) whereby both derive from identical pre-existing 'roots'. Rather than being the fruit of pre-existing phenomena, he argues that 'Neither a [link with the past nor identity] is *a priori*' but that both are created together in the processes of social interaction (Russell 2010, 34). This idea connects to Laurajane Smith's (2006) notion of 'heritage' as an experience of performance – as an act of making, rather than what is thereby made – and to Higginbottom and Tonner's more recent argument about 'geographies of value', that 'it is the identity of the people that is co-performed in the production of the heritage site' (Higginbottom and Tonner 2010, 302). If we accept that neither heritage nor identity are 'givens', but that they are created in particular sets of circumstances, then it follows that one does not derive from the other: there is no causal link between them.

Those items classed as heritage acquire a new status and a new set of meanings. As anthropologist Mary Douglas and economist Baron Isherwood said of such things, they acquire 'an "otherworldly morality"' since they represent group investment, and such groups outlive their individual members (Douglas and Isherwood 1979, 37). In acquiring such meanings – and their 'otherworldly' status – they assert a particular, and new, form of identity to which subscription can be made. However, the process of creating this identity through the creation of heritage is inevitably as much an exclusionary process as it is an inclusionary one: as Smith notes, 'all identity construction is to a certain extent exclusionary as it defines who you are not, as much as who you are' (Smith 2006, 301). While Smith limits this 'exclusionary' process to subscription to her 'authorised heritage discourse', the point surely is that all claims to a past are inevitably exclusionary: as a white, middle-class, educated southern English person, any claim I might make to a connection with an Australian Indigenous past or to a northern English mining past would be as resisted as a Native American claim might be to English country-house culture. There are limits on those pasts to which we can claim affiliation and therefore to those identities we can construct for ourselves. In creating links with the past we thereby also create identity – but it is not a process whereby others are incorporated, but rather a mechanism by which we exclude those who are deemed 'different'.

Conclusion

The ultimate – and possibly depressing – conclusion is that in conducting public archaeology (whether we call it 'outreach' or 'community participation' or 'democratic archaeology' or any of the other terms identified by commentators: see, e.g., Carman 2005a, 86; Smith and Waterton 2009, 15–16) we are always and inevitably – and despite any desire to the contrary – dealing with people like ourselves. This, of course, is neither what we imagine we are doing nor what we would prefer to do: what we intend is to 'reach out' to those who would otherwise not have access to us and our work. But in the end all we can do is talk to those who already speak in our language and share our values. Moreover, and equally inevitably, the process by which we create the community with which we engage is grounded not in processes of inclusion (which we would like) but in processes of exclusion.

Because of who we are – as archaeologists – we focus our activities on material from the past. Our attention is therefore on two things: the past, and specific kinds of material. Those who have no interest in or claim on, or who can make no connection with, either the past or that body of material will inevitably be excluded from our activities. Whether this exclusion operates along lines of class, gender, age, educational attainment, ethnicity or any other factor, those who do not or cannot attach themselves to the material that is our concern will be excluded from our activities. It is a tragedy in the true sense. For us to alter our behaviour to accommodate the excluded – by changing what we do – will mean that we will cease to be archaeologists. For them to change to accommodate us will mean they lose their own sense of who they are. We perhaps need to recognise that as archaeologists we can do nothing about this because we would cease to be archaeologists if we did.

Inventing categories of person

Archaeologists are in practice very good at designating other categories of person, as McManamon (1991) has done for 'the public'. His five categories, drawn from his own experience, were: the general public (at large); students and teachers (i.e., those in education); members of Congress and the executive branch (legislators); government attorneys, managers and archaeologists (professionals); and Native Americans (Indigenous peoples). Referring to wider studies of the general public and their attitudes to science in the USA and elsewhere, he suggests that only up to 5 per cent of the US population can be considered 'archaeologically literate' – that is, well informed about archaeology and what archaeologists do. A further 25 per cent can be considered informed about and interested in scientific topics generally, including archaeology. The remaining 70 per cent are not at all well informed of scientific topics and largely uninterested in learning more; but they also show themselves to be generally supportive of scientific endeavours, including archaeology (McManamon 1991, 123). These categories are clearly not intended to be exclusive: the public at large must also include the other four categories; and there is no reason why a professional archaeologist in government service may not also be a student or teacher, a manager or a Native American, although McManamon treats them each as quite distinct. All of the categories save that of Native American will have a correlate in any other country of the world, since they can all be expected to have educators and students, legislators and government employees. Not all countries have an Indigenous population that can be considered in some way separate from the majority dominant population: in European countries the dominant population will generally be considered as the Indigenous population, and it is more recent incomers who will be in the minority. In this context it is interesting that McManamon does not distinguish African Americans, whose interest in archaeology and the past may be considered to be different from that of the dominant European American population. Although the differences between the situation and status of African Americans in the USA and incomer populations in Europe are many, such a distinction would allow an extension of McManamon's categories beyond the confines of the USA, at least in broad terms.

We identify others too who are not archaeologists, including those who examine sites of archaeological interest but not in the manner we do. In particular, pot-hunters, treasure-hunters, Italian *tombaroli* and amateur metal-detecting enthusiasts do not treat sites as archaeologists do. As mentioned in Chapter 4, from an archaeological perspective they do not do 'good' excavation because they do not do all the things archaeologists do; but from theirs they interfere very little with the evidence in the ground. These aspects apart, however, the significant point is that pot-hunters, treasure-hunters and metal-detectorists come with a different purpose. If an archaeologist were to encounter someone digging like a pot-hunter on one of their sites, they would castigate the pot-hunter for doing bad archaeology. In fact, they may be doing good pot-hunting – but of course they are doing it in an inappropriate context. It is on that basis that we judge them, not on the 'objective' quality of their handling of a trowel. The archaeological condemnation of pot-hunting technique is accordingly not an objective judgement and nor is it a subjective judgement, but it is instead a contextual one dependent on the particular purpose for which digging is done. As archaeologists, however, we claim the right to determine who is carrying our 'proper' investigation of a site and who is not.

A further group we identify as 'not us' includes those who have an interest in places and cultures we regard as fictional or imaginary. Among these are those who search for Ley lines: this is a particularly English phenomenon, representing to their believers either the ancient trackways by which early peoples traversed the landscape or lines of magnetic force connecting sites of significance, or both (e.g., Watkins 1925; Nye 1987; Sullivan 2000). Others include those who seek lost lands such as Atlantis, Lyonesse or Mu, or who look for evidence of mythical figures in the material record (e.g., Berlitz 1969; Hancock 2002). We may also seek to deny those of our own discipline who decide to investigate possible connections between cultures divided by space and time, such as the expeditions of Thor Heyerdahl in the Pacific and Atlantic (Heyerdahl 1950; 1958; 1970). The various strands of these so-called 'fringe' or 'alternative' archaeologies are neatly summed up by Schadla-Hall (2004, 257–8) as a concern with origins and hyperdiffusion, lost ancient knowledge and power, and confirming religious and mythological 'truths'. He also identifies the tropes by which they attract others to their cause especially by making associations between widely divergent phenomena based on apparent similarities, and by selective quotation of text from scholarly works which is divorced from its context (Schadla-Hall 2004, 258–61). Of course, the proponents of these approaches to the past consider themselves not as 'fringe' or 'alternative' but as contributors to the wider understanding of the human past, as we archaeologists do. It is we as professional experts in studying the past who designate these others as 'on the fringe' or 'alternative' to our very heavily sanctioned practices and approaches.

In our dealings with others, we inevitably allocate them a role in relation to our own. In so far as they differ from us in professional skill, in approach to the past or in the techniques they apply, we consider them insufficiently like us to qualify as part of the same community. This 'deficit' model is one we tend to apply more widely to the public at large (Merriman 2004a, 5–6), and it is out of this deficit model that we build a vision of ourselves as knowledgeable, skilled and qualified to speak on matters relating to the material past – and from this derives the professional expertise we apply in managing the archaeological resource on behalf of the wider world. In promoting ourselves and the work we do, we necessarily and unconsciously render those on whose behalf we work as inferior to us.

Conclusion

A concern for preservation (the subject of Chapter 6) has been the main driver for ARM practice over past decades, but, once preserved, sites also become available for public scrutiny and visiting. This inevitably implicates archaeologists with wider publics and raises issues relating to the definition of what it is to be an archaeologist and what it is not, how the distinction is defined and how it is managed. Answers will determine how we engage with others and their relationships with the material that is our particular concern. Ultimately we confront the question of distinguishing between kinds of public – as a body of people with deficient knowledge of the past requiring education, as tourists who are more or less knowledgeable, as consultees about the future of sites, as equal collaborators or as owners of the past who determine what our role should be. It also raises questions as to for whose benefit archaeological work in the public domain is carried out: that of the wider community, or that of archaeology and archaeologists.

As a result of the issues summarised above, the content of this chapter has turned from a focus on the presentation of material to a wider public towards a focus on the image of archaeology itself, and especially how archaeologists relate to other categories of person. A particular emphasis has been on the role of archaeologists in the creation of communities and thereby the definition of other categories of person. The latter issues are aspects frequently omitted from professional discussions of ARM in a strict sense, and most often relegated to the literature of public archaeology, which is treated as a separate arm of the discipline: within the ARM community we tend to assume our established professional status as over-riding other considerations, despite the critiques of our work emerging from the field of heritage studies (e.g., Carman 2002; Smith 2004; Waterton and Smith 2010). The suggestion of this chapter is therefore that these are issues we need to take seriously as part of our work: our concern is not only with the material that comes from the past but also with those human engagements in the present that derive from that work. This is material that will be discussed further in the next and final chapter.

PART III

CONCLUSIONS

CHAPTER 8

Archaeology in the world

The practices of ARM are the primary form of engagement between archaeology and the wider world. This is reflected in the earliest use of the term 'Public Archaeology' (McGimsey 1972) to mean what is now referred to as ARM, CRM or CHM, defined as a professional preservationist agenda grounded in law. In attempting to take an international perspective on these practices – an approach that contrasts with the more conventional approaches which describe the specific practices of ARM in individual countries (e.g., Cleere 1984a; Hunter and Ralston 1993; 2006; Smith and Burke 2007; Messenger and Smith 2010; Schofield et al. 2011) – this book ultimately emphasises two key aspects of archaeology. While neither is entirely absent from consideration in the literature, they are rarely considered together and given the status they perhaps deserve as distinguishing features of the discipline.

The first is that archaeology is a practice that takes place in the present. Although related to the past – as an effort to identify and understand material evidence of past lifeways – archaeology is nonetheless a set of activities and ideas that are rooted in modernity (Thomas 2004) and take place in the present, as reflected in discussions of archaeology as a 'craft' activity (Shanks and McGuire 1996). An opening focus on the historical development of ARM systems led to the main focus of the book – discussion of the universally recognised core activities of ARM practitioners. In doing so, consideration was given to the kinds of institutions involved in ARM and, by implication, the different kinds of power relations inherent in such professionalised practice, an issue that came to the fore in discussing our relations with various categories of 'other'. As a contemporary phenomenon, archaeology is deeply implicated in the workings of the modern world, with 'modernity' defined as:

a shorthand term for . . . industrial civilization. Portrayed in more detail, it is associated with (1) a certain set of attitudes towards the world, the idea of the world as open to transformation, by human intervention; (2) a complex of economic institutions, especially industrial production and a market economy; (3) a certain range of political institutions, including the nation-state and mass democracy (Giddens 1998, 94).

Archaeology reflects these by: providing resources – to the state and its institutions, to educators who mould understandings and to others to construct their own world views – that allow the transformation of the world; offering a systematic and professionalised means for investigating the past; and its status as a state-authorised activity.

The second is archaeology's status as a global activity. As indicated in Chapter 3, there is no country in the world that does not have some law relating to its archaeological heritage. Archaeological institutions operate at both the national and the global level: state-sponsored institutions such as UNESCO and its subsidiary committees such as ICOM, ICOMOS and ICAHM provide a global standard against which regional and local resource management practices are assessed; international bodies such as the International Union of Pre- and Proto-Historic Societies (IUPPS), the World Archaeological Congress (WAC), the Society for American Archaeology (SAA) and the European Association of Archaeologists (EAA) provide fora where archaeologists can meet and discuss issues of common interest and concern, including representatives of state agencies responsible for managing the archaeological resource. Archaeology is one of the few humanities subjects – possibly the only one – in which international practitioners can meet and meaningfully engage in discussion, regardless of the material or period that is their individual specialism. Archaeology is to be found everywhere where humans have been, however hostile to human existence – including under the deep oceans (Bass 2005), in the freezing and (largely) uninhabited continent of Antarctica (Harrowfield 2005) and in airless outer space (Spennemann 2006). Archaeologists too may be found in every country – albeit sometimes in small numbers, as in Chad or Cameroon (de Maret et al. 2008, 146) – but they are present nonetheless.

This chapter will focus on these two attributes of the field to locate ARM within its wider context and emphasise its status as a specifically archae-ological activity, an aspect sometimes forgotten by those who emphasise the research aspects of the field. In doing so, it will also include some discussion of debates in archaeological theory – a further omission from the general bulk of literature in ARM.

Archaeology as a contemporary activity

Lewis Binford wrote of the subject matter of archaeology that it 'is simply artifacts. We observe all those modifications of natural materials ... that humans and hominids produce as a result of their lifeways ... [We] do not study the past' (Binford 1989, 3). His then placing his focus on how we interpret the past through a process of inference serves to emphasise the place of archaeology as a contemporary activity. It also places emphasis on the status of the archaeological record and resource – identical in physical form but conceptually different (see Chapter 4) – as an entity we encounter in the present, however ancient its specific contents. The debate between Binford and Schiffer over the so-called 'Pompeii premise' (Binford 1981) addressed this issue directly. Schiffer's emphasis on reconstructing the original form of what was left to us in the present by a close examination of site formation processes and applying a particular 'middle range theory' (Schiffer 1972; 1987) was criticised by Binford (1981) as envisaging the archaeological record as an imperfect set of 'little Pompeiis' which required restoration to their pristine form. Whoever was more in the right – and, since the debate has moved on and one of the protagonists has since died, it may no longer matter – they were nonetheless both concerned ultimately with the material with which archaeologists deal as a phenomenon *in the present*: both agreed that to use it to make statements about the past required the application of some additional process.

Archaeology – and therefore the husbanding of its resource – is of course always conducted for current purposes. As Chapter 1 demonstrated (and see Carman 2012), those processes that have been identified as early instances of ARM in medieval Italy, early modern Scandinavia and Britain, and indeed later modern Europe, represented purposes of their time, not ours: they gave support, in particular, to rulers and the emergence of systems of rule that would be deemed inappropriate for a modern democracy; they were not formally trained or professionalised in the manner of modern archaeologists; and there was no hint of activity for a generalised 'public good' such as we would recognise for our own work. Even those developed systems of inventory and preservation that were created in India and which can be legitimately understood as instances of ARM as we understand it today were created for the purposes of Imperial rule over a subjugated population: the fact that such systems influenced similar practices in Britain and elsewhere not only indicates their effectiveness but also suggests a similar purpose with regard to the British population on behalf of those who advocated their adoption. While we may not choose to subscribe to such purposes today, they nevertheless represent a part of the legacy of our discipline: to fail to acknowledge it is to denigrate our precursors and also to deny the role of our discipline in creating the world in which we live.

The professionalisation of archaeology – a theme first broached in Chapter 2 but which also runs through the rest of the book – is a recent development that has significant implications for the field as an activity carried out in the present. As professionals, we are inevitably bound by current ideas of ethical practice, however contested (see, e.g., Tarlow 2001; Scarre and Scarre 2006). Our professional bodies are governed by sets of rules created to operate in the current context, including the dominance of capitalist ideals (Hamilakis and Duke 2007) and the competitive market, which places archaeologists in the status of contractors or employees (Everill 2009; Aitchison and Edwards 2008). Indeed the status of 'professional' is itself one with a relatively short history, one that can only exist within the conditions of late modernity and which carries with it ideals of trained expertise selection for entry and promotion on the basis of merit (Perkin 1989). Professionalisation assumes a vision of the ideal citizen as one who recognises and exhibits technical expertise organised in a hierarchy based on levels of expertise as demonstrated (Perkin 1989, 3–4). It also seeks recognition for the particular expertise as a *necessary* service and thereby status and power (reflecting Smith's [2006] concept of the authorised heritage discourse; Perkin 1989, 6), and the device used to achieve this is control of the market by limiting entry to the field only by those suitably – usually formally – qualified (Perkin 1989, 7).

The status of professional with which the archaeologist is endowed is what allows us to emerge as a community of interest in our own right: as Smith and Waterton (2009, 138) put it, archaeologists 'are just another community within this engagement' of communities with other communities. As argued in the previous chapter, however, that status also gives us the authority to define for the world at large the status of others who are not archaeologists, at least in their relations to the material for which we claim responsibility. In doing so, we determine not only how such material should be treated and who can so treat it, but also exactly what kind of material falls within our purview. It is perhaps no accident that the scope of archaeology has become so extensive over recent years: not only now are we concerned with material more than several thousand years old and which pre-dates written records, but we increasingly impose on periods previously the exclusive concern of others, such as the historian (Hicks and Beaudry 2006; Little 2007) and the sociologist, by turning our attention on to our own age (Harrison and Schofield 2010), and including material that is not strictly 'material' at all, such as music (Schofield et al. 2012, 312–15). However, the power to determine our own areas of concern also has unforeseen consequences: as Mourad (2007, 152–3) argues, by virtue of their specialist knowledge archaeologists can find themselves losing their status of 'civilian' by being called on to assist military forces in their engagement with archaeological material. As a result, our claim to stand as a disinterested party in disputes about cultural material is eroded and the critique offered by Smith and Waterton (2009) is given weight.

Professionalisation also provides the disciplinary authority to teach others what it is to be an archaeologist, as discussed in the previous chapter. In doing so we address some very diverse audiences: school-age children, as part of a wider curriculum (Cracknell and Corbishley 1986; Smardz and Smith 2000), young adults in specialist academic courses at university (Burke and Smith 2007), other adults in specifically vocational training (e.g., Chitty 1999) and the general public (Aston 2012). Each of these aims for a different outcome and adopts a particular kind of delivery for a different audience, who have particular sorts of relationships with their tutors (Table 8.1). In particular, while most of our audience is self-selecting – which limits our engagement to those who already largely value archaeology (as argued on different grounds in the previous chapter and elsewhere: Carman 2011) – only those of school age are captive, which may provide a case for ensuring the place of archaeology in school curricula. In terms of delivery, we reserve direct engagement with the real material of archaeology as an object of investigation (as opposed to mere observation) to those we hope will join us as fellow professionals: university students and vocational trainees. The rest must be content with looking at sites and, especially for the young, with exercises that replicate the practice of digging but without its purpose or any of its accompanying rigour in recording and interpretation. Otherwise, archaeology is presented as a specialist activity with a narrow role for a particular audience, and our role as educators (as argued in the previous chapter) becomes a self-serving one.

Archaeology is inevitably an activity in the present which relates to the past but is not itself *of* the past. Instead, it represents an intervention in the present for particular purposes. As a system for *managing* a particular body of material, which is what ARM represents, archaeology asserts its authority and status through a range of practices that

TABLE 8.1 *Archaeological education*

Educational level	Type	Audience	What is taught	Delivery	Outcome sought
School	Formal, part of broader curriculum	Children: captive	'The past'	Formal lessons, site visits, 'practice' excavations	An interest in the past
University	Formal, specialised	Young adults: self-selecting	'The past' and techniques of investigation	Lectures, seminars, field trips, field training	Intellectual skills
Vocational	Formal, specialised	Adults: self-selecting	Techniques of investigation	Field training, field trips, formal lessons	Practical skills
General	Informal, recreational	Mixed: self-selecting	'The past' and techniques of investigation	Site tours, popular media	The value of archaeology to society

- define that material, separating it from all other material in the world;
- categorise the material as specifically 'archaeological' and therefore the province of those recognised as archaeologists; and thereby
- give the material a particular set of values that support the enhanced status of the professional student of the material past (see also Carman 1996).

In this manner the functions of ARM serve to promote the interests of archaeology as a field of endeavour and archaeologists as a particular category of person in the contemporary world.

Archaeology as a global activity

As indicated above, archaeology and archaeologists are to be found throughout the globe. This is not accidental: the specifically European approaches to investigating and recording the past developed from the late medieval period (see Chapter 1; Schnapp 1996) were transported to the rest of the world as part of the package of modernising principles that travelled with European colonisers of other peoples' territories. Trigger (1989; 2006) conveniently outlines the processes by which archaeology spread to colonised territories and the impact of archaeological ideas on the peoples of those regions: the same processes saw the museums of Europe fill with exotic items and the discovery by Europeans of new cultures and civilisations. In identifying various modes of archaeology – nationalist, colonialist, imperialist – Trigger (1984) may also have charted without acknowledging it the specific processes by which archaeology became a global activity. The European colonial and Imperial project is already mentioned: the subsequent process by which colonised territories became independent nation-states (the nation-state being, of course, another successful European export: Gellner 1983; Hobsbawm 1990) also played its part, since all nations need a foundational myth rooted in a past, and archaeology can provide the evidence out of which to construct one (Kohl and Fawcett 1995; Atkinson et al. 1996; Diaz-Andreu and Champion 1996). The consequence has been not only the identification of archaeological remains all over the world and beyond but also the spread of archaeological practices.

The global unity of archaeology expresses itself in a number of ways. A significant factor is the identification of material of diverse kinds in diverse contexts as 'archaeology': the archaeological resource, especially in its guise of 'record' (see Chapters 4 and 7), is deemed to be a universal category. Accordingly, debates such as those between Binford and Schiffer over the 'Pompeii premise' (Binford 1981) are deemed to be of global relevance, even if the specific terms are challenged by those from other territories. It is true that the universal relevance of the anglophone processualist/post-processualist (or processualist/interpretive) division (Hodder et al. 1995) has been widely challenged as an irrelevance to francophone and Iberian-language archaeologies, among others, which have their own theoretical traditions (Hodder 1991; Ucko 1995). Nevertheless, the influence of anglophone archaeology is widespread and growing, to the extent that English is offered as the lingua franca for archaeology throughout Europe and is the language of choice for almost all international archaeological conferences. This allows the increasing recognition and adoption of anglophone concepts as well as practices by archaeologists in very diverse regions, so that the understanding of the archaeological record that holds sway in English-speaking territories is the norm across the world. Despite the very wide differences of material traces found across the globe and diverse excavation practices (Carver 2004), archaeologist everywhere are deemed to be engaged in an identical project and engaging with a universal phenomenon.

It is this assumption that archaeologists across the world are doing the same thing that has led to the recent spread of 'preventive archaeology' across the world, as discussed in Chapter 6 (see also Kobylínski 2010, 147–8; Naffé et al. 2008), from its origin in the anglophone tradition (Hunter and Ralston 1993; 2006; Olivier and Clark 2001; Sebastian and Lipe 2009). The notion of archaeology as a form of public service – offering the citizens of the nation-state an officially recognised past to which they can attach themselves, usually with pride – is in itself a Western idea and, like archaeology itself (see above), was spread by colonising forces and subsequently by the establishment of nation states on the Western model all across the globe. This is the case even in those (mostly) non-Western countries which find it hard to find resources for the most basic of public amenities: de Maret et al. (2008) make it very clear how sparse are the resources for archaeology in some African countries, but they nevertheless are able to employ a few people in the field; and although there remains a significant lack of coverage of countries in the southern continents (see, e.g., countries omitted from consideration in Cleere 1984a; 1989; Messenger and Smith 2010; McManamon and Hatton 2000), all can boast at least some effort towards a national patrimony based on archaeology. All in all, the idea of archaeology as a necessary adjunct of the state and as a general public good has been a highly successful export from Europe.

The spread of anglophone archaeology has been assisted by the rise of international bodies that represent archaeology to the world. The split of the World Archaeological Congress (WAC) from the International Union of Pre-and Proto-Historical Sciences (IUPPS) documented by Ucko (1986), Day (2006) and Stone (2006) gave birth to a highly successful organisation whose conferences have travelled to parts of the world where major international conferences in the field are unfamiliar: Venezuela in 1990, India in 1994 and South Africa in 1999. Despite problems encountered with organisation in the first two of these and a return for the next two conferences to Western countries (Stone 2006, 58–9), WAC has since visited Jordan (2013) and is next due to go to Japan. All of WAC's conferences are conducted in English (although use of other languages is permitted), which inevitably promotes an anglophone understanding of archaeology. The work of WAC beyond conferences also serves to promote the anglophone style: its publication series – all contributions in English and produced by British or American publishers since their establishment – has been hailed as changing the face of archaeology (Fox 1993); initiatives such as Archaeologists without Borders serve to offer training to archaeologists from economically disadvantaged countries by those from less economically disadvantaged, especially Britain and the USA; and the Global Libraries scheme offers books and other publications to economically disadvantaged institutions across the globe, most of which come from anglophone publishers (http://www.worldarch aeologicalcongress.org/activities). There is no harm as such in any of these activities, much that is good, and involvement in WAC encourages exchanges between individuals who might otherwise never meet. However, and however unwillingly, it is an anglophone discourse that dominates these exchanges not only in terms of language but also inevitably and as a consequence their underlying ideology.

WAC was one of the first archaeological bodies to specifically incorporate ARM into its concerns: the European Association of Archaeologists, founded in 1995, followed suit, and most recently the IUPPS – up to then a very conservative institution focusing on the interpretation of the past and largely ignoring archaeology's role in the present – has incorporated such debates in its own conferences. As a consequence, ARM has become part of the 'mainstream' of global archaeological debate, although the distinction between the study of the past and the public face of archaeology, as discussed in Chapter 2, remains in place. This is despite the relevance of mainstream archaeological theory to ARM. Binford (1983, 241) laid the charge against Schiffer's model of the archaeological record, and especially the place of 'Middle Range Theory' in that model (Schiffer 1972; 1988), that it suited proponents of ARM since it allowed sites to be written off as 'insignificant' if they could not be reconstructed into some pristine original form as 'prepackaged Pompeiis' (Binford 1983, 241). Since one of the central roles of ARM is to identify those sites that are 'significant' (Chapter 5) so that they can be treated in particular ways, especially by preservation (Chapter 6), an understanding of the material with which we deal as a 'record' of past activity has implications for how we make such decisions. A contrasting approach – as taken by, for example, Barrett (1987; 2001) – challenges the idea of a 'record' by instead offering material as the evidential base of which archaeologists construct interpretations. As Andrews et al. (2000, 530) put it, an 'excavation programme [should be] dedicated to the creation of an historical understanding [of the site] from the outset rather than the collation of an archive, and it is thus directed towards a product which has a recognizable value for everyone'. They do this by producing the written report as 'free text which forms a series of narratives in which structures and deposits are linked by reference to the processes of human inhabitation' (Andrews et al. 2000, 530), contrasting with the kind of 'significance statement' recommended by, for example, Clark (2001, 96–7).

As indicated earlier, and despite its evident relevance to ARM, archaeological theory is rarely to be found in the literature of ARM (see, e.g., its absence from the indexes to Cleere 1984a; 1989; Cooper et al. 1995; Messenger and Smith 2010). There is a chapter dedicated to the relationship between theory and (ARM) practice in Hunter and Ralston (2006) by Lucas (2006), but that is a treatment that stands entirely alone in the volume, with only one other reference to its content, which, like all other index entries for 'theory', is limited to a concern for research issues as distinct from those of ARM (Baker and Smith 2006, 143; Grenville 2006, 166–7, 173, 175). Where the implications of theory for ARM – and of ARM practice for theory – are to be found is in the literature of Heritage Studies (e.g., Smith 2004) or some of the earlier works promoting alternatives to processual archaeology (e.g., Shanks and Tilley 1987) or concerned with distinguishing ARM from other branches of the field, such as Embree (1990). These are universally scathing about the connection, usually to the detriment of ARM: for Smith (2004) processual approaches have contributed to the creation of a class of professional which serves to separate the past from those whose legacy it is; as noted in Chapter 2, for Shanks and Tilley (1987, 24) ARM and especially the process of evaluation that is central to it are simply 'a pricing of the past'; for Embree (1990, 31) ARM is simply 'applied archaeology'.

Whose archaeology?

These considerations relate especially to the role of ARM as a public service. As indicated in the previous chapter and above, there is a perceived division between the bureaucratic practices of ARM and what is considered public archaeology 'proper' in terms of engagement with other categories of person. As discussed by myself (Carman 2002, 96–114) and Merriman (2004a), in particular, this division serves to separate the treatment of archaeological material as a generalised 'public good' from the people who are its supposed owners. This is the final point made in the last sentence of the previous chapter – that although ARM practice notionally concerns the interaction of a body of professionals with a particular body of material, its real consequence is directed towards, and its real context is located in, human interactions in the present. This is the aspect of ARM least considered in the literature, but one that emerges very clearly from taking the wider view proposed in this book. Throughout we have been confronted by the highly political nature of archaeology in the public realm. Chapter 1 emphasised the specific cultural and historic contexts in which ARM practices developed and Chapter 3 the differences of ideology that underlie varying legislative mechanisms across the globe. Chapters 4 and 5 highlighted the processes of selection and hierarchisation inherent in ARM practice: that not all material finds its way into notionally 'complete' inventories, and that material that does is then ranked. Whatever the practical justifications for this – and there are many, all valid in strictly pragmatic terms – the outcome is to determine for an entire community, if not the world, what material can be considered to matter.

This branch of archaeology can as a consequence never be said to be politically neutral, and this in turn connects with one of the wider concerns within the discipline that periodically arises, although frequently considered a pointless and rather sterile distinction: that is, whether archaeology should be considered an art or a science discipline. The early processualist drive to establish archaeology as at least a scientific discipline, if not an actual 'hard' science (but see Watson et al. 1971; Salmon 1982; Watson 1991 for bids to do just that), led nowhere except to the post-processual challenge (e.g., Shanks and Tilley 1987; Hodder et al. 1995) and ultimately to the current search for consensus or at least accommodation as argued by Johnson (1999, 176–87). The place of ARM in these debates was always marginal: rather than being central to the project that is archaeology, ARM has existed on the fringe of debates about theory and method in the discipline. In so treating it, we have forgotten the essential role of the development of ARM-like practices in the foundation of the discipline (see Chapter 1). We have also forgotten that the original aim of many of those who founded archaeology as a separate discipline and a profession in the nineteenth and early twentieth centuries was for a public purpose.

Clark's (1939) discussion of archaeology and society, mentioned in Chapter 2, has been dismissed by Bruce Trigger as an argument that 'the ultimate goal of archaeologists should be to interpret their data in terms of social history' (Trigger 2006, 356), and therefore to define successive 'cultures' in the past. In reality, the book and its later editions (e.g., Clark 1947) are much more than that. They are an argument for state funding and support of archaeology because of the benefits archaeology beings to society. Clark is keen to distinguish the 'social value' of archaeology (Clark 1939, viii) from its political value – partly in response to the then overt use of archaeology for political purposes in Nazi Germany and the USSR. Nonetheless, he emphasises how valuable archaeology has been in creating a sense of identity in the new European nations created after the First World War and how a sense of a deep past – and its difference from the present – can serve to heal wounds and overcome difference. Ultimately his call is for archaeology to be conducted as a 'social enterprise supported by the community' (Clark 1939, 211). The message is largely reiterated in 1947 and thereafter:

> Archaeology may contribute to the integration of society not only by strengthening local ties and fostering patriotic sentiment, but ... by promoting a fuller realization of the underlying solidarity upon which the possibility of a world order ultimately rests (Clark 1947, 203).
> [T]he State ought to share the burden of maintaining civilization by subsidising the arts and fields of study ... such as archaeology ... while refraining from restrictive control (Clark 1947, 214).

It is clear from this that Clark allied archaeology with the arts and humanities rather than the natural sciences, despite his own crucial role in developing economic approaches based on environmental data. He also recognised its crucial role at the service of the public good: for him, although such terms as ARM, AHM, CRM had not yet emerged, ARM and archaeology as a study of the past are a single endeavour sharing a single ultimate purpose. Clark's statements serve to emphasise once again the essentially political nature of ARM by claiming a purpose for archaeology that goes beyond the mere application of technique to understand the past in neutral terms.

Clark is rarely – if ever – claimed as a proponent of 'activist' archaeology (see Chapter 7), and yet this is the role he proposes for archaeology in his work. This is in his terms admittedly a conservative activism – at the service of creating a unified sense of identity at the level of the nation-state, and a shared sense of service of humanity between nation-states – rather than the more radical approach taken by those who claim the status of activist today, but it provides the link that is so often missing in discussions of ARM between the two forms of public archaeology represented by ARM. The power of the idea that ARM is necessarily detached from individual engagement with archaeology was emphasised to me recently during a seminar where I was discussing, among other things, Boyd's idea of 'cognitive ownership' of sites (Boyd et al. 2005; Boyd 2012). A listener enquired if there was any 'legal basis' for the idea and how it could be applied without legislation, but that is the point behind the idea: it offers both the preservation of material and the chance for people to partake of the material remnants of their past without recourse to official mechanisms (Carman 2005a, 111–16). In the same way as Clark's (1939; 1947) approach, application of the cognitive ownership idea offers a link between the dual aspects of ARM that overcomes the divide.

Conclusion: where next?

ARM is the branch of archaeology that engages with the wider world. In doing so it is a 'public' endeavour in two senses: as a service industry that operates through official agencies to provide a generalised public good that supports the project of modernity as defined by cultural commentators such as Giddens (1998, 94) and outlined above, and as a means of acquainting specific individuals and communities with aspects of their local, regional and global pasts. It is a practice conducted throughout the globe based on the essential procedures of inventory and evaluation leading to preservation in situ or by record. Preservation may in turn allow a measure of public access to sites and their interpretation, and the education of non-archaeologists in an appreciation of the past and the means of its study has lain at the core of archaeological activity since the modern discipline first emerged in the nineteenth century. However the fundamental purpose of archaeology and of ARM is rarely overtly discussed: as archaeologists we know our work to be valuable and that archaeological remains matter; as a result it becomes self-evident that archaeology should be given support by legislation and sanctioned by political authority. I do not question the value of archaeology as a set of practices in the modern world, but it is also incumbent on us to be aware of the consequences for the world of what we do and what we are.

The global professionalisation and standardisation of archaeological organisation and practice offer advantages and threats. Although a genuinely international discourse in ARM has yet to develop – and this book offers only a tentative beginning – an increasing similarity of approach across the world would allow such a discourse to emerge, rather than the set of parallel regional and national discourses that we offer at present (e.g., in Cleere 1984a; Messenger and Smith 2010; and other works cited in this volume). This in turn would allow the ready transfer of experience and concepts from one part of the world to another and serve to internationalise (and thus de-'nationalise') ARM: at present because of key differences in ideology and practice, ARM remains a highly localised branch of archaeology in contrast to the discipline as a whole. Attempts to develop shared approaches across territorial boundaries can at present be seen less as ways of developing and improving practice than as a form of neo-colonialism: it is very rare to see ideas transfer from economically disadvantaged countries to economically advantaged ones, and so European and American styles of ARM tend to predominate. This is certainly true of the spread of 'preventive archaeology' (Chapter 6), which has its origin in the anglophone world – especially in the UK (Schofield et al. 2011), although variations also apply in the USA (Sebastian and Lipe 2009) and Australia (Smith and Burke 2007) – but which has been spread to African states via its adoption in France (Naffé et al. 2008).

A single universal approach to ARM is a challenge to – indeed a denial of – the great diversity of archaeology. As outlined in Chapter 4, the remains of past human activity found in one part of the world can differ markedly from those in another. In addition, what is recognised as archaeology in any territory will depend on the specific tradition of archaeology that has been developed in that region: there is nothing that is 'naturally' archaeological but depends on an archaeologist to recognise it as such (Edgeworth 2003), and this will depend on past experience, education and training, all of which are specific to particular areas. A system of preventive archaeology, in particular, assumes a sufficient supply of trained archaeologists to conduct work on large-scale projects, and while economically disadvantaged areas may never be able to meet that need owing to other priorities, even in richer countries the vagaries of economic fluctuation can have severe effects on the sector (Schlanger and Aitchison 2010). Whatever overall system is in place, however, archaeologists operate differently in different traditions, in choice of tool (e.g., trowel or hoe), styles of excavation (test-pitting, box-trench or open area), systems of recording and on-site organisation. Adoption of methods, organisation and approaches from elsewhere – and particularly of a single universal standard – will necessarily reduce this diversity, and this will have an effect on what is understood and recognised to constitute archaeology among the adoptees. As a consequence, archaeology as a global but diverse field of activity will suffer.

Such considerations leave us with choices to make. We need to decide whether we wish to continue developing a common approach to ARM – whether a 'preventive archaeology' or otherwise – or to recognise that diversity in approaches, taking full account of regional and local archaeological traditions, offers advantages that are too valuable to lose. We also need to examine the consequences for our discipline, for ourselves and for the wider world which we inhabit of the approaches to ARM that we take: whether we are happier as agents of the nation-state or in some other guise. We finally need to consider how best to accommodate the claims made on us and our work by those on whose behalf we work: whether to retain the division between ARM as a bureaucratic exercise and 'public archaeology' as an engagement with individuals and communities or to find ways to overcome that divide. We need to consider these issues as a whole, and to take into account the consequences of one choice on all the others. Further, we need to recognise that our choices have consequences for others beyond ourselves and our discipline. ARM is where archaeology meets the world: in choosing how to conduct ARM, we owe a duty to that world.

BIBLIOGRAPHY

Aberg, F. A. and Leech, R. H. 1992. The National Archaeological Record in England: past, present and future. In National Museum of Denmark. *Sites and Monuments: National Archaeological Records*. Copenhagen, National Museum of Denmark, pp. 157–70.

Advisory Council on Historic Preservation (ACHP) 2007. *Section 106 Archaeology Guidance*. Washington, DC, AHCP.

d'Agostino, B. 1984. Italy. In Cleere, H. F. (ed.) *Approaches to the Archaeological Heritage*. Cambridge, Cambridge, University Press, pp. 73–81.

Aguigah, A. D. 2008. Preventive archaeology: an urgency for the past of Togo and of West Africa. In Naffé, B. O. M., Lanfranchi, R. and Schlanger, N. (eds) *L'Archéologie préventive en Afrique: enjeux et perspectives*. Saint-Maur-des-Fossés, Éditions Sepia, pp. 127–34.

Ahmad, Y. 2006. The scope and definitions of heritage: from tangible to intangible. *International Journal of Heritage Studies* 12 (3), pp. 292–300.

Aitchison, K. and Edwards, R. 2008. *Archaeology Labour Market Intelligence: Profiling the Profession 2007/8*. Reading, Institute of Field Archaeologists.

Anderson, B. R. O'G. 1983. *Imagined Communities: Reflections on the Origin and Spread of Nationalism*. London, Verso.

Andrews, G., Barrett, J. C. and Lewis, J. S. C. 2000. Interpretation not record: the practice of archaeology. *Antiquity* 74, pp. 525–30.

Aranda, L. L. 2010. Heritage values and Mexican cultural policies: dispossession of the 'other's' culture by the Mexican archaeological system. In Smith, G., Messenger, P. M. and Soderland, H. A. (eds) *Heritage Values in Contemporary Society*. Walnut Creek, CA, Left Coast Press, pp. 225–38.

Arroyo-Bishop, D. and Lantada Zarzosa, M. T. 1992. The ArchéoDATA System: a method for structuring an European archaeological information system (AIS). In National Museum of Denmark. *Sites and Monuments: National Archaeological Records*. Copenhagen, National Museum of Denmark, pp. 133–56.

Askew, M. 2010. The magic list of global status: UNESCO, world heritage and the agendas of states. In Labadi, S. and Long, C. (eds) *Heritage and Globalisation. Key Issues in Cultural Heritage*. London, Routledge, pp. 19–44.

Aston. M. 2012. Publicising archaeology in Britain in the late twentieth century: a personal view. In Skeates, R., McDavid, C. and Carman, J. (eds) *The Oxford Handbook of Public Archaeology*. Oxford, Oxford University Press, pp. 443–60.

Atkinson, J. A., Banks, I. and O'Sullivan, B. (eds) 1996. *Nationalism and Archaeology: Scottish Archaeological Forum*. Glasgow, Cruithne Press.

Baker, D. and Smith, K. 2006. Local authority opportunities. In Hunter, J. and Ralston, I. (eds) *Archaeological Resource Management in the UK: An Introduction*. 2nd edition (revised). Stroud, Sutton, pp. 131–46.

Bankowski, Z. and MacCormick, D. N. 1991. Statutory interpretation in the United Kingdom. In MacCormick, D. N. and Summers, R. S. (eds) *Interpreting Statutes: A Comparative Study*. Aldershot, Dartmouth Publishing, pp. 359–406.

Barker, G. (ed.) 1999. *Companion Encyclopedia of Archaeology*. London, Routledge.

Barker, P. 1982. *Techniques of Archaeological Excavation*. London, Batsford.

Barker, P. 2009. The process made me do it: or, would a reasonably intelligent person agree that CRM is reasonably intelligent? In Sebastian, L. and Lipe, W. D. (eds) *Archaeology and Cultural Resource Management: Visions for the Future*. School for Advanced Research Seminar Series. Santa Fé, NM, SAR Press, pp. 65–90.

Barrett, G. R., Gaffney, V. G., Huckerby, C., Fitch, S. and Dingwall, L. 2007. *Heritage Management at Fort Hood, Texas: Experiments in Historic Landscape Characterisation*. British Archaeological Reports. Oxford, Archaeopress.

Barrett, J. 1987. Fields of discourse: reconstituting a social archaeology. *Critique of Anthropology* 7 (3), pp. 5–16.

Barrett, J. C. 2001. Agency, the duality of structure and the problem of the archaeological record. In Hodder, I. (ed.) *Archaeological Theory Today*. Cambridge, Polity Press, pp. 141–64.

Bartoy, K. M. 2012. Teaching *through* rather than *about* archaeology: education in the context of public archaeology. In Skeates, R., McDavid, C. and Carman, J. (eds) *The Oxford Handbook of Public Archaeology*. Oxford, Oxford University Press, pp. 552–65.

Bass, G. F. 2005. *Beneath the Seven Seas: Adventures with the Institute of Nautical Archaeology*. London, Thames & Hudson.

Baugher, S. 2005. Sacredness, sensitivity, and significance: the controversy over Native American sacred sites. In Mathers, C., Darvill, T. and Little, B. (eds) *Heritage of Value, Archaeology of Renown: Reshaping Archaeological Assessment and Significance*. Gainesville, FL, University Press of Florida, pp. 248–75.

Beales, D. and Biagini, E. F. 2002. *The Risorgimento and the Unification of Italy*. 2nd edition. Harlow, Pearson.

Belcher, M. 1991. *Exhibitions in Museums*. Leicester, Leicester University Press.

Bernbeck, R. and Pollock, S. 2007. 'Grabe, wo du stehst!' An archaeology of perpetrators. In Hamilakis, Y. and Duke, P. (eds) *Archaeology and Capitalism: From Ethics to Politics*. One World Archaeology 54. Walnut Creek, CA, Left Coast Press, pp. 217–34.

Bender, S. J. and Smith, G. S. 2000. *Teaching Archaeology in the 21st Century*. Washington, DC, Society for American Archaeology.

Berlitz, C. 1969. *The Mystery of Atlantis*. New York, W. W. Norton & Co.

Bewley, R. H. and Rączkowski, W. (eds) 2002. *Aerial Archaeology: Developing Future Practice*. NATO Series 1 Life Sciences 337. Amsterdam, IOS Press.

Binford, L. (ed.) 1977. *For Theory Building in Archaeology: Essays on Faunal Remains, Aquatic Resources, Spatial Analysis and Systematic Modelling*. Studies in Archaeology. New York, Academic Press.

Binford, L. 1981. Behavioural Archaeology and the 'Pompeii premise'. *Journal of Anthropological Research* 37, pp. 195–208.

Binford, L. 1983. *Working at Archaeology*. New York, Academic Press.

Binford, L. 1989. *Debating Archaeology*. Studies in Archaeology. San Diego, Academic Press.

Bland, R. 1996. Treasure Trove and the case for reform. *Art, Antiquity and Law* 1 (1), pp. 11–26.

Bland, R. 2004. The Treasure Act and the Portable Antiquities Scheme: a case study in developing public archaeology. In Merriman, N. (ed.) *Public Archaeology*. London, Routledge, pp. 272–91.

Boniface, P. and Fowler, P. J. 1993. *Heritage and Tourism in 'the Global Village'*. London, Routledge.

Bordes, J.-G., Vernet, R., Gonzalez-Carballo, A., Naffé, B. O. M. and Tauveron, M. 2008. Un exemple de coopération archéologie-recherche pétrolière: Ta 07–08, concession pétrolière du basin de Taoudenni, Mauretanie. In Naffé, B. O. M., Lanfranchi, R. and Schlanger, N. (eds) *L'Archéologie préventive en Afrique: enjeux et perspectives*. Saint-Maur-des-Fossés, Éditions Sepia, pp. 68–74.

Boulting, N. 1976. The law's delays: conservationist legislation in the British Isles. In Fawcett, J. (ed.) *The Future of the Past: Attitudes to Conservation 1174–1974*. London, Thames & Hudson, pp. 9–33.

Boyd. W. E. 2012. 'A frame to hang clouds on': cognitive ownership, landscape, and heritage management. In Skeates, R., McDavid, C. and Carman, J. (eds) *The Oxford Handbook of Public Archaeology*. Oxford, Oxford University Press, pp. 172–98.

Boyd, W. E., Cotter, M. M., O'Connor, W. and Sattler, D. 1996. Cognitive ownership of heritage places: social construction and cultural heritage management. *Tempus* 6, pp. 123–40.

Boyd, W. E., Cotter, M. M., Gardiner, J. and Taylor, G. 2005. 'Rigidity and a changing order … disorder, degeneracy and daemonic repetition': fluidity of cultural values and cultural heritage management. In Mathers, C., Darvill, T. and Little, B. J. (eds) *Heritage of Value, Archaeology of Renown: Reshaping*

Archaeological Assessment and Significance. Gainesville, FL, University Press of Florida, pp. 43–57.

Bradley, R. 2006. *Bridging the Two Cultures: Commercial Archaeology and the Study of British Prehistory*. Paper delivered to the Society of Antiquaries, London, 12 January 2006.

Breeze, D. 1996. Archaeological nationalism as defined by law in Britain. In Atkinson, J. A., Banks, I. and O'Sullivan, J. (eds) *Nationalism and Archaeology*. Scottish Archaeological Forum. Glagow, Cruithne Press, pp. 95–103.

Breeze, D. J. 2006. Ancient monuments legislation. In Hunter, J. and Ralston, I. (eds) *Archaeological Resource Management in the UK: An Introduction*. 2nd edition. Stroud, Sutton, pp. 57–68.

Breuil, J.-Y. 2008. Archéologie preventive et aménagement du territoire: l'exemple d'une ville du sud de la France: Nîmes. In Naffé, B. O. M., Lanfranchi, R. and Schlanger, N. (eds) *L'Archéologie préventive en Afrique: enjeux et perspectives*. Saint-Maur-des-Fossés, Éditions Sepia, pp. 196–200.

Briuer, F. L. and Mathers, W. 1996. *Trends and Patterns in Cultural Resource Significance: An Historical Perspective and Annotated Bibliography*. Alexandria, VA, US Army Corps of Engineers.

Bruning, S. B. 2010. Articulating culture in the legal sphere: heritage values, Native Americans, and the law. In Smith, G., Messenger, P. M. and Soderland, H. A. (eds) *Heritage Values in Contemporary Society*. Walnut Creek, CA, Left Coast Press, pp. 209–24.

Buchli, V. and Lucas, G. 2001. *Archaeologies of the Contemporary Past*. London, Routledge.

Burke, H. and Smith, C. (eds) 2007. *Archaeology to Delight and Instruct: Active Learning in the University Classroom*. Walnut Creek, CA, Left Coast Press.

Burke, H. and Smith, C. 2010. Vestiges of colonialism: manifestations of the culture/nature divide in Australian heritage management. In Messenger, P. M. and Smith, G. S. (eds) *Cultural Heritage Management: A Global Perspective*. Gainesville, FL, University Press of Florida, pp. 21–37.

Burnham, B. 1974. *The Protection of Cultural Property: Handbook of National Legislations*. Paris, ICOM.

Byrne, D. 2008. Heritage as social action. In Fairclough, G., Harrison, R., Jameson, J. H. Jr and Schofield, J. (eds) *The Heritage Reader*. London, Routledge, pp. 149–73.

Campana, S. and Forte, M. 2006. *From Space to Place: Second International Conference on Remote Sensing in Archaeology*. *Proceedings of the Second International Workshop, CNR, Rome, Italy, 4–7 December 2006*. Bar International Series 1568. Oxford, Archaeopress.

Canouts, V. 1992. Computerised information exchange on the local and national levels in USA. In National Museum of Denmark. *Sites and Monuments: National Archaeological Records*. Copenhagen, National Museum of Denmark, pp. 231–47.

Carman, J. 1990. Commodities, rubbish and treasure: valuing archaeological objects. *Archaeological Review from Cambridge* 9 (2), pp. 195–207.

Carman, J. 1993. The P is silent – as in archaeology. *Archaeological Review from Cambridge* 12 (1), pp. 39–53.

Carman, J. 1996. *Valuing Ancient Things: Archaeology and Law in England.* London, Leicester University Press.

Carman, J. 1997. Archaeology, politics and legislation: the British experience. In Mora, G. and Diaz-Andreu, M. (eds) *La cristalización del pasado: genesis y desarollo del marco institucional de la arqueología en España.* Malaga, University of Malaga Press, pp. 125–32.

Carman, J. 1998. Object values: landscapes and their contents. In Jones, M. and Rotherham, D. (eds) *Landscapes – Perception, Recognition and Management: Reconciling the Impossible? Landscape Archaeology and Ecology* 2. Sheffield, Landscape Conservation Forum, pp. 31–4.

Carman, J. 2000. Theorising the practice of archaeological heritage management. *Archaeologia Polona* 38, pp. 5–21.

Carman, J. 2002. *Archaeology and Heritage: An Introduction.* London and New York, Continuum.

Carman, J. 2004. Excavating excavation: a contribution to the social archaeology of archaeology. In Carver, G. (ed.) *Digging in the Dirt*, British Archaeological Reports, Oxford, Archaeopress, pp. 45–51.

Carman, J. 2005a. *Against Cultural Property: Archaeology, Heritage and Ownership.* Duckworth Debates in Archaeology. London, Duckworth.

Carman, J. 2005b. Good citizens and sound economics: the trajectory of archaeology in Britain from 'heritage' to 'resource'. In Mathers, C., Darvill, T. and Little, B. J. (eds) *Heritage of Value, Archaeology of Renown: Reshaping Archaeological Assessment and Significance.* Gainesville, FL, University Press of Florida, pp. 43–57.

Carman, J. 2011. Stories we tell: myths at the heart of 'community archaeology'. *Archaeologies: Journal of the World Archaeological Congress* 7 (3), pp. 490–501.

Carman, J. 2012. Towards an international comparative history of archaeological heritage management. In Skeates, R., McDavid, C. and Carman, J. (eds) *The Oxford Handbook of Public Archaeology.* Oxford, Oxford University Press, pp. 13–35.

Carman, J. 2013. A heritage of conflict, and conflicts of heritage. In Bergerbrant, S. and Sabatini, S. (eds) *Counterpoint: Essays in Archaeology and Heritage Studies in Honour of Professor Kristian Kristiansen.* British Archaeological Reports International Series 2508. Oxford, Archaeopress.

Carman, J. forthcoming. Heritage and economics: a view from the 'cultural' side. *International Journal of Heritage Studies.*

Carman, J. and Carman, P. 2006. *Bloody Meadows: Investigating Landscapes of Battle.* Stroud, Sutton.

Carmichael, D. L., Hubert, J., Reeves, B. and Schanche, A. (eds) 1994. *Sacred Sites, Sacred Places.* London, Routledge.

Carver, G. (ed.) 2004. *Digging in the Dirt: Excavation in a New Millennium*, BAR International Series 1256. Oxford, Archaeopress.

Carver, M. 1996. On archaeological value. *Antiquity* 70, pp. 45–56.

Chandler, S. M. 2009. Innovative approaches to mitigation. In Sebastian, L. and Lipe, W. D. (eds) *Archaeology and Cultural Resource Management: Visions for the Future*. School for Advanced Reserarch Seminar Series. Santa Fé, NM, SAR Press, pp. 115–40.

Chapman, W. 1989. The organisational context in the history of archaeology: Pitt-Rivers and other British archaeologists in the 1860s. *The Antiquaries Journal*, 69 (1), pp. 23–42.

Chippindale, C. 1983. The making of the first Ancient Monuments Act, 1882, and its administration under General Pitt-Rivers. *Journal of the British Archaeological Association* 136, pp. 23–42.

Chippindale, C., Devereux, P., Fowler, P., Jones, R. and Sebastian, T. 1990. *Who Owns Stonehenge?* London, Batsford.

Chippindale, C. and Taçon, P. 1998. *The Archaeology of Rock-Art*. Cambridge, Cambridge University Press.

Chitty, G. 1999. *Training in Professional Archaeology: A Preliminary Review*. Carnforth, Hawkshead Archaeology and Conservation.

Clark, G. 1939. *Archaeology and Society*. London, Methuen.

Clark, G. 1947. *Archaeology and Society*. 2nd edition (revised). London, Methuen.

Clark, K. 2001. *Informed Conservation: Understanding Historic Buildings and Their Landscapes for Conservation*. London, English Heritage.

Clark, K. (ed.) 2006. *Capturing the Public Value of Heritage: The Proceedings of the London Conference 25–26 January 2006*. London, English Heritage.

Clark, M. 1984. *Modern Italy 1871–1982*. London and New York, Longman.

Cleere, H. F. (ed.) 1984a. *Approaches to the Archaeological Heritage*. Cambridge, Cambridge University Press.

Cleere, H. F. 1984b. Great Britain. In Cleere, H. F. (ed.) *Approaches to the Archaeological Heritage*. Cambridge, Cambridge University Press, 54–62.

Cleere, H. F. 1984c. World cultural resource management: problems and perspectives. In Cleere, H. F. (ed.) *Approaches to the Archaeological Heritage*. Cambridge, Cambridge University Press, pp. 125–31.

Cleere, H. F. (ed.) 1989. *Archaeological Heritage Management in the Modern World*. One World Archaeology 9. London, Unwin Hyman.

Cleere, H. F. 2001. The uneasy bedfellows: universality and cultural heritage. In Layton, R., Stone, P. G. and Thomas, J. (eds) *Destruction and Conservation of Cultural Property*. London, Routledge.

Cohn, B. S. 1983. Representing authority in Victorian India. In Hobsbawm, E. and Ranger, T. (eds) *The Invention of Tradition*. Past and Present. Cambridge, Cambridge University Press, pp. 165–210.

Colley, L. 1992. *Britons: Forging the Nation, 1707–1837*. London, Yale University Press.

Cooney, G. 1996. Building the future on the past: archaeology and the construction of national identity in Ireland. In Díaz-Andreu, M. and Champion, T. (eds) *Nationalism and Archaeology in Europe*. London, UCL Press, pp. 146–63.

Cooper, M. A., Firth, A., Carman, J. and Wheatley, D. (eds) 1995. *Managing Archaeology*. Theoretical Archaeology Group. London, Routledge.

Copeland, T. 2004. Presenting archaeology to the public: constructing insights on-site. In Merriman, N. 2004. *Public Archaeology*. London, Routledge, pp. 132–44.

Corazzol, G. 1991. Electronic catalogue of historical-artistic heritage of Veneto. In Baer, N. S., Sabbioni, C. and Sors, A. I. (eds) *Science, Technology and European Cultural Heritage*. London, Butterworth-Heinemann, pp. 834–7.

Corbishley, M. 2011. *Pinning Down the Past: Archaeology, Heritage, and Education Today*. Woodbridge, Boydell Press.

Cordell, K. H. 2004. *Outdoor Recreation for the 21st Century American: A Report to the Nation: The National Survey on Recreation and the Environment*. State College, PA, Venture Publishing.

Corfield, M., Hinton, P., Nixon, T. and Pollard, M. (eds) 1998. *Preserving Archaeological Remains in situ: Proceedings of the Conference of 1st–3rd April 1996*. London, MOLAS.

Cosgrove, D. 1984. *Social Formation and Symbolic Landscape*. London, Croom Helm.

Cosgrove, D. 2000. *Apollo's Eye: A Cartographic Genealogy of the Earth in the Western Imagination*. Baltimore, MD, Johns Hopkins University Press.

Cox, M., Straker, V. and Taylor, D. (eds) 1996. *Wetlands Archaeology and Nature Conservation*. London, HMSO.

Cracknell, S. and Corbishley, M. (eds) 1986. *Presenting Archaeology to Young People*. CBA Research Report 64. London, Council for British Archaeology.

Crass, D. C. 2009. The crisis in communication: still with us? In Sebastian, L. and Lipe, W. D. (eds) *Archaeology and Cultural Resource Management: Visions for the Future*. School for Advanced Research Seminar Series. Santa Fé, NM, SAR Press, pp. 253–82.

Cross, R. 1995. *Statutory Interpretation*. 3rd edition. London, Blackwell.

Crump, T. 1987. The role of MSC funding in British archaeology. In Mytum, H. and Waugh, K. (eds) *Rescue Archaeology- What's Next? Proceedings of a Rescue Conference Held at the University of York, December 1986*. Monograph 6, York, Department of Archaeology, University of York, pp. 41–6.

Cunliffe, B. W. 1983. *Report of the Joint Working Party of the Council for British Archaeology and the Department of the Environment*. London, DoE.

Curtis, J. 2011. Relations between archaeologists and the military in the case of Iraq. In Stone, P. G. (ed.) *Cultural Heritage, Ethics and the Military*. Heritage Matters. Woodbridge, Boydell Press, pp. 193–9.

Dalglish, C. 2013. *Archaeology, the Public and the Recent Past*. Woodbridge, Boydell Press.

Daniel, G. 1978. *150 Years of Archaeology*. London, Duckworth.

Daniel, G. and Renfrew, C. 1988. *The Idea of Prehistory*. Edinburgh, Edinburgh University Press.

Darvill, T. 1987. *Ancient Monuments in the Countryside: An Archaeological Management Review*. English Heritage Archaeological Report 5. London, English Heritage.

Darvill, T. 1993. *Valuing Britain's Archaeological Resource*. Bournemouth University Inaugural Lecture. Bournemouth, Bournemouth University.

Darvill, T. 1995. Value systems in archaeology. In Cooper, M. A., Firth, A., Carman, J. and Wheatley, D. (eds) *Managing Archaeology*. London, Routledge, pp. 40–50.

Darvill, T. 2005. 'Sorted for ease and whiz'? Approaching value and importance in archaeological resource management. In Mathers, C., Darvill, T. and Little, B. J. (eds) *Heritage of Value, Archaeology of Renown: Reshaping Archaeological Assessment and Significance*. Gainesville, FL, University Press of Florida, pp. 21–42.

Darvill, T. 2010. Blowing in the wind: cultural heritage management in a risk society. In Koerner, S. and Russell, I. (eds) *Unquiet Pasts: Risk Society, Lived Cultural Heritage, Redesigning Reflexivity*. Farnham, Ashgate, pp. 389–404.

Darvill, T. and Russell, B. 2002. *Archaeology after PPG16: Archaeological Investigations in Britain 1990–1999*. Bournemouth University School of Conservation Sciences Research Report 10. Poole, Bournemouth University.

Darvill, T., Saunders, A. and Startin, B. 1987. A question of national importance: approaches to the evaluation of ancient monuments for the Monuments Protection Programme in England. *Antiquity* 61, pp. 393–408.

Davidson, I., Lovell-Jones, C. and Bancroft, R. (eds) 1995. *Archaeologists and Aborigines Working Together*. Armidale, University of New England Press.

Davis, H. A. 2009. Archaeologists looked to the future in the past. In Sebastian, L. and Lipe, W. D. (eds) 2009. *Archaeology and Cultural Resource Management: Visions for the Future*. School for Advanced Research Seminar Series. Santa Fé, NM, SAR Press, pp. 19–40.

Davis, H. A. 2010. Heritage resource management in the United States. In Messenger, P. M. and Smith, G. S. (eds) *Cultural Heritage Management: A Global Perspective*. Gainesville, FL, University Press of Florida, pp. 188–98.

Day, M. 2006. Peter Ucko and the World Archaeological Congress (WAC). In Layton, R., Shennan, S. and Stone. P. (eds) *A Future for Archaeology: The Past in the Present*. London, UCL Press, pp. 41–6.

DeBlasis, P. 2010. Twenty years of heritage resource management in Brazil: a brief evaluation 1986–2006. In Messenger, P. M. and Smith, G. S. (eds) *Cultural Heritage Management: A Global Perspective*. Gainesville, FL, University Press of Florida, pp. 38–47.

Deeben, J., Groenewoudt, B. J., Hallewas, D. P. and Willems, W. J. H. 1999. Proposals for a practical system of significance evaluation in archaeological heritage management. *European Journal of Archaeology* 2 (2), pp. 177–200.

DEMOS 2004. *Challenge and Change: Heritage Lottery Fund and Cultural Value.* London, HLF and DEMOS.

Demoule, J.-P. 2008. L'archéologie preventive en France, parcours et perspectives. In Naffé, B. O. M., Lanfranchi, R. and Schlanger, N. (eds) *L'Archéologie préventive en Afrique: enjeux et perspectives.* Saint-Maur-des-Fossés, Éditions Sepia, pp. 187–92.

Depaepe, P. 2008. Archéologie et grands travaux d'aménagement en France. In Naffé, B. O. M., Lanfranchi, R. and Schlanger, N. (eds) *L'Archéologie préventive en Afrique: enjeux et perspectives.* Saint-Maur-des-Fossés, Éditions Sepia, pp. 193–5.

Department of the Environment 1975. *Principles of Publication in Rescue Archaeology.* London, Committee for Rescue Archaeology.

Department of the Environment 1983. *Criteria for the Selection of Ancient Monuments.* London, Department of the Environment.

Department of the Environment 1990. *Archaeology and Planning: Planning Policy Guideline Note No. 16, November 1990.* London, Department of the Environment.

Derry, L. 2011. Why do people become involved with archaeology? Some answers from Alabama's Black Belt region. *Archaeologies: Journal of the World Archaeological Congress* 7 (3), pp. 538–53.

Diaz-Andreu, M. and Champion, T. (eds) 1996. *Nationalism and Archaeology in Europe.* London, Routledge.

Dickerson, R. 1975. *The Interpretation and Application of Statutes.* Boston, MA, Little Brown.

Dingli, S. M. 2006. A plea for responsibility towards the common heritage of mankind. In Scarre, C. and Scarre, G. (eds) *The Ethics of Archaeology: Philosophical Perspectives on Archaeological Practice.* Cambridge, Cambridge University Press, pp. 219–41.

Dörge, H. 1971. *Das Recht der Denkmalpflege in Baden-Württemberg.* Stuttgart, Kohlhammer.

Douglas, M. and Isherwood, B. 1979. *The World of Goods: Towards an Anthropology of Consumption.* London, Allen Lane.

Dreyfus, H. L. and Rabinow, P. 1983. *Beyond Structuralism and Hermeneutics.* Chicago, IL, University of Chicago Press.

Dromgoole, S. (ed.) 1999. *Legal Protection of the Underwater Cultural Heritage: National and International Perspectives.* The Hague, Kluwer.

Dublin, S.-A. 2008. Changing places: a cultural geography of nineteenth century Zuni, New Mexico. In Lozny, L. (ed.) *Landscapes under Pressure: Theory and Practice of Cultural Heritage Research and Preservation.* New York, Springer, pp. 97–114.

Dunnell, R. C. 1984. The ethics of archaeological significance decisions. In Green, E. L. (ed.) *Ethics and Values in Archaeology.* New York, Free Press, pp. 62–74.

Dunnell, R. C. 1992. The notion site. In Rossignol, J. and Wandsnider, L. (eds) *Space, Time and Archaeological Landscapes*. New York, Plenum Press, pp. 21–41.

Dunnell, R. C. and Dancey, W. S. 1983. The siteless survey: a regional scale data collection strategy. In Schiffer, M. B. (ed.) *Advances in Archaeological Method and Theory* 6. San Diego, CA, Academic Press, pp. 267–87.

Eberl, W., Schiedermair, W. and Petzet, M. 1975. *Bayerisches Denkmalschutzgesetz*. Munich, Deutscher Gemeindeverlag.

Edgeworth, M. 2003. *Acts of Discovery: An Ethnography of Archaeological Practice*. BAR International Series 1311. Oxford, Archaeopress.

Edgeworth, M. (ed.) 2006. *Ethnographies of Archaeological Practice: Cultural Encounters, Material Transformations*. Worlds of Archaeology. Walnut Creek, CA, Left Coast Press.

Embree, L. 1990. The structure of American theoretical archaeology: a preliminary report. In Pinsky, V. and Wylie, A. (eds) *Critical Traditions in Contemporary Archaeology*. New Directions in Archaeology. Cambridge, Cambridge University Press, pp. 28–37.

Endere, M. L. 2010. The challenge of protecting archaeological heritage in Argentina. In Messenger, P. M. and Smith, G. S. (eds) *Cultural Heritage Management: A Global Perspective*. Gainesville, FL, University Press of Florida, pp. 8–20.

English Heritage 1991. *Managing Archaeological Projects (MAP2)*. London, English Heritage.

English Heritage 1992. *An Evaluation of the Impact of PPG 16 on Archaeology and Planning*. London, English Heritage.

English Heritage 1997. *The Monuments Protection Programme 1986–96 in Retrospect*. London, English Heritage.

English Heritage 2000. *MPP 2000: A Review of the Monuments Protection Programme, 1986–2000*. London, English Heritage.

Evans, C. 1994. Natural wonders and national monuments: a meditation upon the fate of the tolmen. *Antiquity* 68, pp. 200–8.

Everill, P. 2007. British commercial archaeology: antiquarian and labourers; developers and diggers. In Hamilakis, Y. and Duke, P. (eds) *Archaeology and Capitalism: From Ethics to Politics*. One World Archaeology 54. Walnut Creek, CA, Left Coast Press, pp. 119–36.

Everill, P. 2009. *The Invisible Diggers: A Study of British Commercial Archaeology*. Oxford, Oxbow Books.

Fairclough, G. 2006. From assessment to characterisation: current approaches to understanding the historic environment. In Hunter, J. and Ralston, I. (eds) *Archaeological Resource Management in the UK: An Introduction*. 2nd edition. Stroud, Sutton, pp. 253–75.

Fairclough, G. 2008. A new landscape for cultural heritage management: characterisation as a management tool. In Lozny, L. R. (ed.) *Landscapes under Pressure: Theory and Practice of Cultural Heritage Research and Preservation*. New York, Springer, pp. 55–74.

Fairclough, G. 2009. Conservation and the British. In Schofield, J. (ed.) *Defining Moments: Dramatic Archaeologies of the Twentieth Century*. BAR International Series 2005. Oxford, Archeopress, pp. 157–64.

Fasham, P. J. 1980. *Fieldwalking for Archaeologists*. Aldershot, Hampshire Field Club and Archaeological Society.

Faulkner, N. 2000. Archaeology from below. *Public Archaeology* 1, pp. 21–33.

Fawcett, J. (ed.) 1976. *The Future of the Past: Attitudes to Conservation 1174–1974*. London, Thames & Hudson.

Ferguson, L. 1992. *Uncommon Ground: Archaeology and Early African America, 1650–1800*. Washington, DC, Smithsonian Institution Press.

Ferguson, T. J. 2009. Improving the quality of archaeology in the United States through consultation and collaboration with Native Americans and Descendant Communities. In Sebastian, L. and Lipe, W. D. (eds) 2009. *Archaeology and Cultural Resource Management: Visions for the Future*. School for Advanced Research Seminar Series. Santa Fé, NM, SAR Press, pp. 169–94.

Fforde, C., Hubert, J. and Turnbull, P. (eds) 2002. *The Dead and Their Possessions: Repatriation in Principle, Policy and Practice*. London and New York, Routledge.

Field, J., Barker, J., Barker, R., Coffey, E., Coffey, L., Crawford, E., Darcy, L., Fields, T., Lord, G. Steadman, B. and Colley, S. 2000. 'Coming back': aborigines and archaeologists at Cuddie Springs. *Public Archaeology* 1 (1), pp. 35–48.

Firth, A. 1995. Ghosts in the machine. In Cooper, M. A., Firth, A., Carman, J. and Wheatley, D. (eds) *Managing Archaeology*. London, Routledge, pp. 51–67.

Firth, A. 1999. Making archaeology: the history of the Protection of Wrecks Act 1973 and the constitution of an archaeological resource. *International Journal of Nautical Archaeology* 28, pp. 10–24.

Fitz, S. 1991. Monufakt: the Federal Environmental Agency's database for the protection of historic monuments and cultural heritage. In Baer, N. S., Sabbioni, C. and Sors, A. I. (eds) *Science, Technology and European Cultural Heritage*. London, Butterworth-Heinemann, pp. 830–33.

Fleming, A. K. and Campbell, I. L. 2010. Cultural heritage and the development process: policies and performance standards of the World Bank Group. In Messenger, P. M. and Smith, G. S. (eds) *Cultural Heritage Management: A Global Perspective*. Gainesville, FL, University Press of Florida, pp. 243–50.

Foard, G. and Morris, R. 2012. *The Archaeology of English Battlefields: Conflict in the Pre-Industrial Landscape*. CBA Research Report 168. York, Council for British Archaeology.

Foley, R. 1981. *Off-Site Archaeology and Human Adaptation in East Africa*. BAR International Series 97. Cambridge Monographs in African Archaeology 3. Oxford, BAR.

Foucault, M. 1970. *The Order of Things: An Archaeology of the Human Sciences*. London, Tavistock.

Foucault, M. 1972. *The Archaeology of Knowledge and the Discourse on Language*. London, Tavistock.

Foucault, M. 1977. *Discipline and Punish: The Birth of the Prison*. French edition 1975, entitled *Surveiller et punir: naissance de la prison*. Trans. A. Sheridan. London, Allen Lane.

Fourmile, H. 1996. The law of the land: whose law? Whose land? In Clark, A. and Smith, L. (eds) *Issues in Management Archaeology*. St Lucia, Tempus Publications, University of Queensland, pp. 45–50.

Fowler, D. D. 1984. Ethics in contract archaeology. In Green, E. L. (ed.) *Ethics and Values in Archaeology*. New York, Free Press, pp. 108–16.

Fowler, D. D. 1986. Conserving American archaeological resources. In Meltzer, D. J., Fowler, D. D. and Sabloff, J. A. (eds) *American Archaeology Past and Future: A Celebration of the Society for American Archaeology 1935–1985*. Washington, DC, Smithsonian Institution, pp. 135–62.

Fox, R. 1993. Review of the *One World Archaeology* series: an appraisal. *Anthropology Today* 9 (5), pp. 6–10.

Fraser, D. and Newman, M. 2006. The British archaeological database. In Hunter, J. and Ralston, I. (eds) *Archaeological Resource Management in the UK: An Introduction*. 2nd edition. Stroud, Sutton, pp. 23–36.

Franklin, M. E. and Moe, J. M. 2012. A vision for archaeological literacy. In Skeates, R., McDavid, C. and Carman, J. (eds) *The Oxford Handbook of Public Archaeology*. Oxford, Oxford University Press, pp. 566–80.

Freestone, R., Marsden, S. and Garnaut, C. 2008. A methodology for assessing the heritage of planned urban environments: an Australian study of national heritage values. *International Journal of Heritage Studies* 14 (1), pp. 165–75.

Frost, K. E. S. 2004. Archaeology and public education in North America: view from the beginning of the millennium. In Merriman, N. (ed.) *Public Archaeology*. London, Routledge, pp. 59–84.

Funari, P. P. A. 2004. Public archaeology in Brazil. In Merriman, N. (ed.) *Public Archaeology*. London, Routledge, pp. 202–10.

Funari, P. P. A. 2005. Reassessing archaeological significance: heritage of value and archaeology of renown in Brazil. In Mathers, C., Darvill, T. and Little, B. (eds) *Heritage of Value, Archaeology of Renown: Reshaping Archaeological Assessment and Significance*. Gainesville, FL, University Press of Florida, pp. 125–36.

Funari, P. P. A., Hall, M. and Jones, S. (eds) 1999. *Historical Archaeology: Back from the Edge*. One World Archaeology 31. London, Routledge.

Gaffney, C. F., Gater, J. A. and Ovenden, S. M. 2002. *The Use of Geophysical Techniques in Archaeological Evaluations*. Institute of Field Archaeology Technical Paper 6. Reading, Institute of Field Archaeology.

Gallant, T. W. 2001. *Modern Greece*. London, Arnold.

Garden, M.-C. E. 2006. The heritagescape: looking at landscapes of the past. *International Journal of Heritage Studies* 12 (5), pp. 394–411.

Gatsov, I. 2001. From isolation to integration: some remarks about Bulgarian archaeology 1944–1989. In Kobyliński, Z. (ed.) 2001. *Quo Vadis Archaeologia? Whither European Archaeology in the 21st Century? Proceedings of the European*

Science Foundation Exploratory Workshop, Madralin near Warsaw, 12–13 October 2001. Warsaw, Institute of Archaeology and Ethnography Polish Academy of Sciences and Foundation 'Res Publica Multiethnica', pp. 66–8.

Gellner, E. 1983. *Nations and Nationalism*. Oxford, Oxford University Press.

Gianighian, G. 2001. Italy, in Pickard, R. (ed.) *Policy and Law in Heritage Conservation*. London and New York, Spon, pp. 184–206.

Gibbs, J. G. 2008. The archaeologist as playwright. In Fairclough, G., Harrison, R., Jameson, J. H. Jr and Schofield, J. (eds) *The Heritage Reader*. London, Routledge, pp. 545–55.

Giddens, A. 1998. *Conversations with Anthony Giddens: Making Sense of Modernity*. Stanford, CA, Stanford University Press.

Gill, E., Abdi, M. O. and Fonseca, S. 2008. Le projet Walata: la protection du patrimoine dans le cadre d'un programme de coopération pour le développement en Mauritanie. In Naffé, B. O. M., Lanfranchi, R. and Schlanger, N. (eds) *L'Archéologie préventive en Afrique: enjeux et perspectives*. Saint-Maur-des-Fossés, Éditions Sepia, pp. 64–7.

Gomes, S. 2010. Nation, identity and ideology: *Romanità* and *Portugalidade* under Fascist dictatorships. In Koerner, S. and Russell, I. (eds) *Unquiet Pasts: Risk Society, Lived Cultural Heritage, Redesigning Reflexivity*. Heritage, Culture and Identity. Farnham, Ashgate, pp. 63–80.

Gould, S. 1999. Planning, development and social archaeology. In Tarlow, S. and West, S. (eds) *The Familiar Past? Archaeologies of Later Historical Britain*. London, Routledge, pp. 140–54.

Graham, R. E. 2010. The protection of heritage values while utilizing World Heritage sites for the benefit of the community. In Smith, G., Messenger, P. M. and Soderland, H. A. (eds) *Heritage Values in Contemporary Society*. Walnut Creek, CA, Left Coast Press, pp. 267–78.

Graves-Brown, P. 2000. *Matter, Materiality and Modern Culture*. London, Routledge.

Graves-Brown, P., Jones, S. and Gamble, C. (eds) 1996. *Cultural Identity and Archaeology: The Construction of European Identities*. London, Routledge.

Green, E. L. (ed.) 1984. *Ethics and Values in Archaeology*. New York, Free Press.

Green, L. 1990. *The Authority of the State*. Oxford, Clarendon Press.

Grenville, J. 2006. The curator's egg: a new overview. In Hunter, J. and Ralston, I. (eds) *Archaeological Resource Management in the UK: An Introduction*. 2nd edition (revised). Stroud, Sutton, pp. 158–76.

Groarke, L. and Warrick, G. 2006. Stewardship gone astray? Ethics and the SAA. In Scarre, C. and Scarre, G. (eds) *The Ethics of Archaeology: Philosophical Perspectives on Archaeological Practice*. Cambridge, Cambridge University Press, pp. 163–77.

Groenewoudt, B. J. and Bloemers, J. H. F. 1997. Dealing with significance: concepts, strategies and priorities for archaeological heritage management and occupation history. In Willems, W. J. H., Kars, H. and Hallewas, D. P. (eds) *Archaeological Heritage Management in the Netherlands: Fifty Years State Service for Archaeological Investigations.* Amersfoort, Rijkdienst voor het Oudheidkundig Bodemonderzoek, pp. 119–72.

Guidi, A. 1996. Nationalism without a nation: the Italian case. In Diaz-Andreu, M. and Champion, T. (eds) *Nationalism and Archaeology in Europe.* London, Routledge, pp. 108–18.

Gustafsson, A. and Karlsson, H. 2006. Among totem poles and clan power in Tanum, Sweden: an ethnographic perspective on communicative artefacts of heritage management. In Edgeworth, M. 2006. *Ethnographies of Archaeological Practice: Cultural Encounters, Material Transformations.* Worlds of Archaeology. Walnut Creek, CA, Left Coast Press, pp. 137–47.

Gustafsson, A. and Karlsson, H. 2012. 'Changing of the guards': the ethics of public interpretation at heritage sites. In Skeates, R., McDavid, C. and Carman, J. (eds) *The Oxford Handbook of Public Archaeology.* Oxford, Oxford University Press, pp. 478–95.

Hamilakis, Y. and Duke, P. (eds) 2007. *Archaeology and Capitalism: From Ethics to Politics.* One World Archaeology 54. Walnut Creek, CA, Left Coast Press.

Hancock, G. 2002. *Underworld: Flooded Kingdoms of the Ice Age.* London, Michael Joseph.

Hangartner, Y. 1981. *Rechtsfragen der Denkmalpflege.* St Gallen, Schweizerischer Institut für Verwaltungskurse an der Hochschule St Gallen.

Hardesty, D. L. and Little, B. J. 2009. *Assessing Site Significance.* Plymouth, AltaMira Press.

Harris, E. C. 1979. *Principles of Archaeological Stratigraphy.* London, Academic Press.

Harrison, R. 2010. What is heritage? In Harrison, R. (ed.) *Understanding the Politics of Heritage.* Manchester and Milton Keynes, Manchester University Press and the Open University, pp. 5–42.

Harrison, R. and Schofield, J. 2010. *After Modernity: Archaeological Approaches to the Contemporary Past.* Oxford, Oxford University Press.

Harrowfield, D. L. 2005. Archaeology on ice: a review of historical archaeology in Antarctica. *New Zealand Journal of Archaeology* 26, pp. 5–28.

Hausmann, A. 2007. Cultural tourism: marketing challenges and opportunities for German cultural heritage. *International Journal of Cultural Heritage* 13 (2), pp. 170–84.

Hearder, H. 1990. *Italy: A Short History.* Cambridge, Cambridge University Press.

von Henneborg, K. and Ascoli, A. R. 2001. Introduction: nationalism and the uses of Risorgimento culture. In Ascoli, A. R. and von Henneberg, K. (eds) *Making and Remaking Italy: The Cultivation of National Identity around the Risorgimento.* Oxford and New York, Berg, pp. 1–26.

Henson, F. G. 1989. Historical development and attendant problems of cultural resource management in the Philippines. In Cleere, H. F. (ed.) *Archaeological Heritage Management in the Modern World.* One World Archaeology 9. London, Unwin Hyman, pp. 109–17.

Hewison, R. and Holden, J. 2006. Public value as a framework for analysing the value of heritage: the ideas. In Clark, K. (ed.) *Capturing the Public Value of Heritage: The Proceedings of the London Conference* 25–26 January 2006. London, English Heritage, pp. 14–18.

Hey, G. and Lacey, M. 2001. *Evaluation of Archaeological Decision-Making Processes and Sampling Strategies*. Canterbury, Kent County Council.

Heyerdahl, T. 1950. *Kon-Tiki*. Chicago, IL, Rand McNally.

Heyerdahl, T. 1958. *Aku Aku: The Secret of Easter Island*. London, George Allen & Unwin.

Heyerdahl, T. 1970. *The Ra Expedition*. London, George Allen & Unwin.

Hicks, D. and Beaudry, M. C. (eds) 2006. *The Cambridge Companion to Historical Archaeology*. Cambridge, Cambridge University Press.

Higginbottom, G. and Tonner, P. 2010. Archaeologies and geographies of value. In Koerner, S. and Russell, I. (eds) *Unquiet Pasts: Risk Society, Lived Cultural Heritage, Redesigning Reflexivity,*. Ashgate, Farnham, pp. 291–304.

Hill, G. F. 1936. *Treasure Trove in Law and Practice*. Oxford, Clarendon Press.

Hills, C. and Richards, J. D. 2006. The dissemination of information. In Hunter, J. and Ralston, I. (eds) *Archaeological Resource Management in the UK: An Introduction*. 2nd edition (revised). Stroud, Sutton, pp. 304–15.

Hobsbawm, E. 1990. *Nations and Nationalism since 1780: Programme, Myth, Reality*. Cambridge, Cambridge University Press.

Hocke, M. 1975. *Denkmalschutz in Österreich*. Vienna, Jupiter-Verlag.

Hodder, I. 1986. *Reading the Past: Current Approaches to Interpretation in Archaeology*. Cambridge, Cambridge University Press.

Hodder, I. (ed.) 1991. *Archaeological Theory in Europe: The Last Three Decades*. London, Routledge.

Hodder, I. 1999. *The Archaeological Process*. Oxford, Blackwell.

Hodder, I., Shanks, M., Alexandri, A., Buchli, V., Carman, J., Last, J. and Lucas, G. (eds) 1995. *Interpreting Archaeology: Finding Meaning in the Past*. London, Routledge.

Holtorf, C, 2001. Is the past a non-renewable resource? In Layton, R., Stone, P. G. and Thomas, J. (eds) *The Destruction and Conservation of Cultural Property*. London, Routledge pp. 286–97.

Holtorf, C. 2005. Iconoclasm: the destruction and loss of heritage reconsidered. In Coulter-Smith, G. and Owen, M. (eds) Art *in the Age of Terrorism*. London, Paul Holberton, pp. 229–39.

Holtorf, C. 2010. Heritage values in contemporary popular culture. In Smith, G., Messenger, P. M. and Soderland, H. A. (eds) *Heritage Values in Contemporary Society*. Walnut Creek CA, Left Coast Press, pp. 43–54.

Holtorf, C. 2012. The heritage of heritage. *Heritage & Society* 5 (2), pp. 153–74.

Holtorf, C. 2013. On pastness: a reconsideration of materiality in archaeological object authenticity. *Anthropological Quarterly* 86, pp. 427–44.

Holtorf, C. and Schadla-Hall, T. 2000. Age as artefact. *European Journal of Archaeology* 2 (2), pp. 229–48.

Howard, P. 2001. *Heritage: Management, Interpretation, Identity*. London, Continuum.

Howard, S. 2013. Understanding the concept of sustainability as applied to archaeological heritage. *Rosetta* 14, pp. 1–19.

Hudson, K. 1987. *Museums of Influence*. Cambridge, Cambridge University Press.

Hunter, M. (ed.) 1996. *Preserving the Past: The Rise of Heritage in Modern Britain*. Stroud, Sutton.

Hunter, J. and Ralston, I. (eds) 1993. *Archaeological Resource Management in the UK: An Introduction*. Stroud, Sutton.

Hunter, J. and Ralston, I. (eds) 2006. *Archaeological Resource Management in the UK: An Introduction*. 2nd edition (revised). Stroud, Sutton.

Hutchinson, J. and Smith, A. D. (eds) 1994. *Nationalism*. Oxford, Oxford University Press.

Ickerodt, U. 2010. The social and political significance of prehistoric archaeology in modern and post-modern societies. In Koerner, S. and Russell, I. (eds) *Unquiet Pasts: Risk Society, Lived Cultural Heritage, Redesigning Reflexivity*. Heritage, culture and identity. Farnham, Ashgate, pp. 81–98.

ICOMOS 2006. *ICOMOS Ename Charter for the Interpretation of Cultural Heritage Sites*. Paris, ICOMOS.

Ide, O. A. 2008. Archéologie preventive et preservation du patrimoine au Niger. In Naffé, B. O. M., Lanfranchi, R. and Schlanger, N. (eds) *L'Archéologie préventive en Afrique: enjeux et perspectives*. Saint-Maur-des-Fossés, Éditions Sepia, pp. 103–9.

Institute for Archaeologists 1994 (revised to 2012). *Standard and Guidance for Historic Environment Desk-Based Assessment*. Reading, IfA.

Isakhan, B. 2015. Creating the Iraqi Cultural Heritage Destruction Database: calculating a heritage destruction index. *International Journal of Heritage Studies* 21 (1), pp. 1–21.

Jameson, J. H. Jr. 2004. Public archaeology in the United States. In Merriman, N. (ed.) *Public Archaeology*. London, Routledge, pp. 21–58.

Jameson, J. H. Jr. 2008. Presenting archaeology to the public, then and now: an introduction. In Fairclough, G., Harrison, R., Jameson, J. H. Jr and Schofield, J. (eds) *The Heritage Reader*. London, Routledge, pp. 427–56.

Jansen, W. H. II. 2010. Cultural heritage in the global policy arena: issues, institutions, and resources in the policy mix. In Messenger, P. M. and Smith, G. S. (eds) *Cultural Heritage Management: A Global Perspective*. Gainesville, FL, University Press of Florida, pp. 230–42.

Jeppson, P. J. 2012. Public archaeology and the US culture wars. In Skeates, R., McDavid, C. and Carman, J. (eds) *The Oxford Handbook of Public Archaeology*. Oxford, Oxford University Press, pp. 581–602.

Johnson, M. 1999. *Archaeological Theory: An Introduction*. Oxford, Blackwell.

Johnson, M. 2007. *Ideas of Landscape*. Oxford, Blackwell.

Johnston, C. 1994. *What is Social Value? A Discussion Paper*. Australian Heritage Commission Technical Publication 3. Canberra, Australian Government Publishing Services.

Jones, S. 2004. *Early Medieval Sculpture and the Production of Meaning, Value and Place: The Case of Hilton of Cadboll*. Edinburgh, Historic Scotland.

Jones, S. 2013. Dialogues between past, present and future: reflections on engaging the recent past. In Dalglish, C. (ed.) *Archaeology, the Public and the Recent Past*. Woodbridge, Boydell Press, pp. 163–75.

Jowell, T. 2004. *Government and the Value of Culture*. London, DCMS.

Jowell, T. 2005. *Better Places to Live: Government, Identity and the Value of the Historic and Built Environment*. London, DCMS.

Jowell, T. 2006. From consultation to conversation: the challenge of *Better Places to Live*. In Clark, K. (ed.) *Capturing the Public Value of Heritage: The Proceedings of the London Conference 25–26 January 2006*. London, English Heritage, pp. 7–13.

Kaitavuori, K. 2010. Open to the public: the use and accessibility of the object for the benefit of the public. In Pettersson, S., Hagedorn-Saupe, M., Jyrkkiö, T. and Weij, A. (eds) *Encouraging Collections Mobility: A Way Forward for Museums in Europe*. Helsinki, Finnish National Gallery, pp. 276–98.

Karskens, G. 2001. Small things, big pictures: new perspectives from the archaeology of Sydney's Rocks neighbourhood. In Mayne, A. and Murray, T. (eds) *The Archaeology of Urban Landscapes: Explorations in Slumland*. Cambridge, Cambridge University Press, pp. 69–85.

Kehoe, A. B. 2007. Archaeology within marketing capitalism. In Hamilakis, Y. and Duke, P. (eds) 2007. *Archaeology and Capitalism: From Ethics to Politics*. One World Archaeology 54. Walnut Creek, CA, Left Coast Press, pp. 169–78.

Kehoe, A. B. 2012. Public education in archaeology in North America: the long view. In Skeates, R., McDavid, C. and Carman, J. (eds) *The Oxford Handbook of Public Archaeology*. Oxford, Oxford University Press, pp. 537–51.

Keitumetse, S. 2009. Methods for investigating locals' perceptions of a cultural heritage product for tourism: lessons from Botswana. In Sørensen, M. L. S. and Carman, J. (eds) *Heritage Studies: Methods and Approaches*. London, Routledge, pp. 201–16.

Kennedy, D. and Bewley, R. 2004. *Ancient Jordan from the Air*. London, Council for British Research in the Levant.

Kerrell, E, Briggs, D. J., Reeve, D. and Wright, A. 1991. The Corine environmental evaluation system: applications to the protection of Europe's cultural heritage. In Baer, N. S., Sabbioni, C. and Sors, A. I. (eds) *Science, Technology and European Cultural Heritage*. London, Butterworth-Heinemann, pp. 825–9.

King, J. L., Gonzalez, R. L. and Gonzalez M. del R. 1980. *Archaeología y derecho en México*. Mexico City, Universidad Nacional Autónoma de México.

King, T. F. 2003. *Places That Count: Traditional Cultural Properties in Cultural Resource Management*. Walnut Creek, CA, AltaMira Press.

King, T. F. 2007. *Saving Places That Matter: A Citizen's Guide to the National Historic Preservation Act*. Walnut Creek, CA, Left Coast Press.

King, T. F., Hickman, P. P. and Berg, G. 1977. *Anthropology in Historic Conservation: Caring for Culture's Clutter*. New York, Academic Press.

Knudson, R. 1986. Contemporary cultural resource management. In Meltzer, D. J., Fowler, D. D. and Sabloff, J. A. (eds) *American Archaeology Past and Future: A Celebration of the Society for American Archaeology 1935–1985*. Washington, DC, Smithsonian Institution, pp. 395–414.

Kobyliński, Z. (ed.) 2001. *Quo Vadis Archaeologia? Whither European Archaeology in the 21st Century? Proceedings of the European Science Foundation Exploratory Workshop, Madralin near Warsaw, 12–13 October 2001*. Warsaw, Institute of Archaeology and Ethnography Polish Academy of Sciences and Foundation 'Res Publica Multiethnica'.

Kobyliński, Z. 2003. Wet archaeological sites: problems of research and conservation. In Bauerochse, A. and Hassmann, H. (eds) *Peatlands: Archaeological Sites – Archives of Nature – Nature Conservation – Wise Use*. Rahden, Westfalia, Verlag Marie Leidorf, pp. 132–42.

Kobyliński, Z. 2010. Management of archaeological resources in Poland at the beginning of the twenty-first century. In Messenger, P. M. and Smith, G. S. (eds) *Cultural Heritage Management: A Global Perspective*. Gainesville, FL, University Press of Florida, pp. 136–52.

Kohl, P. L. and Fawcett, C. (eds) 1995. *Nationalism, Politics and the Practice of Archaeology*. Cambridge, Cambridge University Press.

Kristiansen, K. 1984. Denmark. In Cleere, H. F. (ed.) *Approaches to the Archaeological Heritage*. Cambridge, Cambridge University Press, pp. 21–36.

Kristiansen, K. 1989. Perspectives on the archaeological heritage: history and future. In Cleere, H. F. (ed.) *Archaeological Heritage Management in the Modern World*. London, Unwin Hyman, pp. 23–9.

Kristiansen, K. 1993. 'The strength of the past and its great might': an essay on the use of the past. *Journal of European Archaeology* 1, pp. 3–32.

Kristiansen, K. 1996. The destruction of the archaeological heritage and the formation of museum collections: the case of Denmark. In Kingery, W. D. (ed.) *Learning from Things: Method and Theory of Material Culture Studies*. Washington, DC, Smithsonian Institution Press, pp. 82–101.

Kristiansen, K. 2012. Archaeological communities and languages. In Skeates, R., McDavid, C. and Carman, J. (eds) *The Oxford Handbook of Public Archaeology*. Oxford, Oxford University Press, pp. 461–77.

Lagerqvist, B and Rosvall, J. 1991. Documentation and data processing in integrated conservation. In Baer, N. S., Sabbioni, C. and Sors, A. I. (eds) *Science, Technology and European Cultural Heritage*. London, Butterworth-Heinemann, pp. 821–4.

Lammy, D. 2006. Community, identity and heritage. In Clark, K. (ed.) *Capturing the Public Value of Heritage: The Proceedings of the London Conference 25–26 January 2006*. London, English Heritage, pp. 65–9.

Lape, P. V. 2002.. Historic maps and archaeology as a means of understanding late precolonial settlement in the Banda Island, Indonesia. *Asian Perspectives* 4 (1), pp. 43–70.

LaRoche, C. J. 2011. Archaeology, the activist community, and the redistribution of power in New York City. *Archaeologies: Journal of the World Archaeological Congress* 7 (3), pp. 619–34.

Layton, R. (ed.) 1989. *Conflict in the Archaeology of Living Traditions*. London, Routledge.

Layton, R., Stone, P. and Thomas, J. (eds) 2000. *Destruction and Conservation of Cultural Property*. One World Archaeology 41. London, Routledge.

Leaman, O. 2006. Who guards the guardians? In Scarre, C. and Scarre, G. (eds) *The Ethics of Archaeology: Philosophical Perspectives on Archaeological Practice*. Cambridge, Cambridge University Press, pp. 32–45.

Lee Long, D. 2000. Cultural heritage management in post-colonial polities: not the heritage of the other. *International Journal of Heritage Studies* 6 (4), pp. 317–22.

Leone, M. and Potter, P. B. 1992. Legitimation and the classification of archaeological sites. *American Antiquity* 57 (1), pp. 137–45.

Leone. M., Potter, P. B. and Shackel, P. A. 1987. Toward a critical archaeology. *Current Anthropology* 57 (1), pp. 137–45.

Levin, J. 2011. Activism leads to excavation: the power of place and the power of the people at the President's House in Philadelphia. *Archaeologies: Journal of the World Archaeological Congress* 7 (3), pp. 596–618.

Lilley, I. and Williams, M. 2005. Archaeology and indigenous significance: a view from Australia. In Mathers, C., Darvill, T. and Little, B. (eds) *Heritage of Value, Archaeology of Renown: Reshaping Archaeological Assessment and Significance*. Gainesville, FL, University Press of Florida, pp. 227–47.

Lipe, W. D. 1974. A conservation model for American archaeology. *The Kiva* 39 (3–4), pp. 213–45.

Lipe, W. D. 1977. A conservation model for American archaeology. In Schiffer, M. B. and Gumerman, G. J. (eds) 1977. *Conservation Archaeology: A Handbook for Cultural Resource Management Studies*. Studies in Archaeology. New York, Academic Press, pp. 19–42.

Lipe, W. D. 1984. Value and meaning in cultural resources. In Cleere, H. F. (ed.) *Approaches to the Archaeological Heritage*. Cambridge, Cambridge University Press, pp. 1–11.

Lipe, W. D. 2009. Archaeological values and resource management. In Sebastian, L. and Lipe, W. D. (eds) *Archaeology and Cultural Resource Management: Visions for the Future*. School for Advanced Research Seminar Series. Santa Fé, NM, SAR Press, pp. 41–64.

Little, B. J. 1992. *Text-Aided Archaeology*. Boca Raton, FL, CRC Press.

Little, B. J. 2007. *Historical Archaeology: Why the Past Matters*. Walnut Creek, CA, Left Coast Press.

Loechl, S. K., Enscore, S. I., Tooker, M. W. and Batzli, S. A. 2009. *Guidelines for Identifying and Evaluating Historic Military Landscapes*. Legacy Resource Management Program 05–197. ERCD/CERL TR-09-06. Arlington, VA, US Army Corps of Engineers Engineer Research and Development Center.

Lozny, L. 2008. Place, historical ecology and cultural landscape: new approaches for applied archaeology. In Lozny, L. (ed.) *Landscapes under Pressure: Theory and Practice of Cultural Heritage Research and Preservation*. New York, Springer, pp. 15–26.

Lucas, G. 2001a. *Critical Approaches to Fieldwork: Contemporary and Historical Archaeological Practice*. London, Routledge.

Lucas, G. 2001b. Destruction and the rhetoric of excavation. *Norwegian Archaeological Review* 34 (1), pp. 35–46.

Lucas, G. 2006. Changing configurations: the relationship between theory and practice. In Hunter, J. and Ralston, I. (eds) *Archaeological Resource Management in the UK: An Introduction*. 2nd edition (revised). Stroud, Sutton, pp. 15–22.

Luke, C. and Kersel, M. M. 2013. *U.S. Cultural Diplomacy and Archaeology: Soft Power, Hard Heritage*. London, Routledge.

Lynott, M. J. 1980. The dynamics of significance: an example from central Texas. *American Antiquity* 45 (1), pp. 117–20.

MacCormick, D. N. and Summers, R. S. (eds) 1991. *Interpreting Statutes: A Comparative Study*. Aldershot, Dartmouth Publishing.

MacRory, R. and Kirwan, S. 2001. Ireland. In Pickard, R. (ed.) *Policy and Law in Heritage Conservation*. London and New York, Spon, pp. 158–83.

Manders, M. R., Van Tilburg, H. K. and Staniforth, M. 2012. Unit 6: significance assessment. In Manders, M. R. and Underwood, C. J. (eds) *Training Manual for the UNESCO Foundation Course on the Protection and Management of Underwater Cultural Heritage in Asia and the Pacific* (electronic resource). Bangkok, UNESCO.

Mapunda, B. and Lane, P. 2004. Archaeology for whose interest: archaeologists or the locals? In Merriman, N. (ed.) *Public Archaeology*. London, Routledge, pp. 211–23.

de Maret, P., Lavachery, P. and Gouem, B. G. 2008. Large-scale public works: major archaeological opportunities? Evaluating a century of experience in Africa. In Naffé, B. O. M., Lanfranchi, R. and Schlanger, N. (eds) *L'Archéologie préventive en Afrique: enjeux et perspectives*. Saint-Maur-des-Fossés, Éditions Sepia, pp. 142–52.

Martin, P. L. [n.d.] Rethinking significance: an archaeological approach to architectural and historical significance. *Heritage Spring Supplement*. Kentucky Heritage Council, pp. 7–13.

Masson, V. M. 1989. Archaeological heritage management in the USSR. In Cleere, H. F. (ed.) *Archaeological Heritage Management in the Modern World*. One World Archaeology 9. London, Unwin Hyman, pp. 195–206.

Mathers, C., Darvill, T. and Little, B. (eds) 2005a. *Heritage of Value, Archaeology of Renown: Reshaping Archaeological Assessment and Significance*. Gainesville, FL, University Press of Florida.

Mathers, C., Schelberg, J. and Kneebone, R. 2005b. Drawing distinctions: towards a scalar model of value and significance. In Mathers, C., Darvill, T. and Little, B. (eds) *Heritage of Value, Archaeology of Renown: Reshaping Archaeological Assessment and Significance*. Gainesville, FL, University Press of Florida, pp. 159–91.

Matthews, C. 2008. The idea of the site: history, heritage, and locality in community archaeology. In Lozny, L. (ed.) *Landscapes under Pressure: Theory and Practice of Cultural Heritage Research and Preservation*. New York, Springer, pp. 75–94.

McCarthy, J. P. 2008. More than just 'telling the story': interpretive narrative archaeology. In Fairclough, G., Harrison, R., Jameson, J. H. Jr and Schofield, J. (eds) *The Heritage Reader*. London, Routledge, pp. 536–44.

McClanahan, A. 2007. Constructing world heritage: strategies for exploring perceptions and practices. In White, R. and Carman, J. (eds) *World Heritage: Global Challenges, Local Solutions: Proceedings of a Conference Held at Coalbrookdale, 4–7 May 2006 hosted by the Ironbridge Institute*. BAR International Series 1698. Oxford, Archaeopress, pp. 33–8.

McDavid, C. 2000. Archaeology as cultural critique: pragmatism and the archaeology of a southern states plantation. In Holtorf, C. and Karlsson, H. (eds) *Philosophy and Archaeological Practice: Perspectives for the 21st Century*. Gothenburg, Göteborg Institutionen för Arkeologi.

McDavid, C. 2002. Archaeology that hurts; descendants that matter: a pragmatic approach to collaboration in the public interpretation of African-American archaeology. *World Archaeology* 34 (2), pp. 303–14.

McDavid, C. 2004. Towards a more democratic archaeology? The internet and public archaeological practice. In Merriman, N. (ed.) *Public Archaeology*. London, Routledge, pp. 159–87.

McDavid, C. 2009. The public archaeology of African America: reflections on pragmatic methods and their results. In Sørensen, M. L. S. S. and Carman, J. (eds) *Heritage Studies: Methods and Approaches*. London, Routledge, pp. 217–34.

McDavid, C. and Jeppson, P. 2007. *Call for Papers: Pathways to Justice: Exploring the Intersections between the Global Justice Movement, Archaeology and Anthropology*. Session submitted for the 2007 Annual Meetings of the American Anthropological Association, Washington, DC.

McDonald, J. D., Zimmerman, L. J., McDonald, A. L., Tall Bull, W. and Rising Sun, T. 1991. The northern Cheyenne outbreak of 1879: using oral history and archaeology as tools of resistance. In Paynter, R. and McGuire, R. (eds) *The Archaeology of Inequality*. Oxford, Blackwell, pp. 64–78.

McEwan, J. M. 2003. *Archaeology and Ideology in Nineteenth Century Ireland: Nationalism or Neutrality?* British Archaeological Reports British Series 354. Oxford, John and Erica Hedges Ltd.

McGimsey, C. R. 1972. *Public Archaeology*. New York, Seminar Books.

McGimsey, C. R. 1984. The value of archaeology. In Green, E. L. (ed.) *Ethics and Values in Archaeology*. New York, Free Press, pp. 171–4.

McGimsey, C. R. and Davis, H. R. (eds) 1977. *The Management of Archaeological Resources: The Airlie House Report*. Washington, DC, Society for American Archaeology.

McKinley, J. R. and Jones, R. (eds) 1979. *Archaeological Resource Management in Australia and Oceania*. Wellington, NZ, New Zealand Historic Places Trust.

McManamon, F. P. 1991. The many publics for archaeology. *American Antiquity* 56, pp. 121–30.

McManamon, F. P. 2000. Archaeological messages and messengers. *Public Archaeology* 1, pp. 5–20.

McManamon, F. P. and Hatton, A. (eds) 2000. *Cultural Resource Management in Contemporary Society: Perspectives on Managing and Presenting the Past*. One World Archaeology 33. London, Routledge.

Merriman, N. 1991. *Beyond the Glass Case: The Past, the Heritage and the Public in Britain*. Leicester, Leicester University Press.

Merriman, N. 2004a. Introduction: diversity and dissonance in public archaeology. In Merriman, N. (ed.) *Public Archaeology*. London, Routledge, pp. 1–17.

Merriman, N. (ed.) 2004b. *Public Archaeology*. London, Routledge.

Meskell, L. 1998. *Archaeology under Fire: Nationalism, Politics, and Heritage in the Eastern Mediterranean and Middle East*. London, Routledge.

Messenger, P. M. and Smith, G. S. (eds) 2010. *Cultural Heritage Management: A Global Perspective*. Gainesville, FL, University Press of Florida.

Min, Z. 1989. The administration of China's archaeological heritage. In Cleere, H. F. (ed.) *Archaeological Heritage Management in the Modern World*. One World Archaeology 9. London, Unwin Hyman, pp. 102–8.

Morgan, D. W. 2010. Descendant communities, heritage resource law, and heritage areas: strategies for managing and interpreting Native American traditional and cultural places. In Messenger, P. M. and Smith, G. S. (eds) *Cultural Heritage Management: A Global Perspective*. Gainesville, FL, University Press of Florida, pp. 199–211.

Moscardo, G. 1996. Mindful visitors: heritage and tourism. *Annals of Tourism Research* 231, pp. 376–97.

Moser, S., Glazier, D., Phillips, J. E., Nasr el Namr. L., Mouier, M. S., Aiesh, R. N., Richardson, S., Conner, A. and Seymour, M. 2002. Transforming archaeology through practice: strategies for collaborative archaeology and the community archaeology project at Quesir, Egypt. *World Archaeology* 34 (2), pp. 220–48.

Moshenska, G. and Dhanjal, S. (eds) 2011. *Community Archaeology: Themes, Methods and Practices*. Oxford, Oxbow Books.

Mouliou, M. 1996. Ancient Greece, its classical heritage and the modern Greeks: aspects of nationalism in museum exhibitions. In Atkinson, J. A., Banks, I. and O'Sullivan, B. (eds) *Nationalism and Archaeology: Scottish Archaeological Forum*. Glasgow, Cruithne Press, pp. 174–99.

Mourad, T. O. 2007. An ethical archaeology in the Near East: confronting empire, war and colonization. In Hamilakis, Y. and Duke, P. (eds) *Archaeology and Capitalism: From Ethics to Politics*. One World Archaeology 54. Walnut Creek, CA, Left Coast Press, pp. 151–67.

Murray, T. 1990. The history, philosophy and sociology of archaeology: the case of the Ancient Monuments Protection Act 1882. In Pinsky, V. and Wylie, A. (eds) *Critical Traditions in Contemporary Archaeology*. Cambridge, Cambridge University Press, pp. 55–67.

Mydland, L. and Grahn, W. 2012. Identifying heritage values in local communities. *International Journal of Heritage Studies* 18 (6), pp. 564–87.

Myles, K. 1989. Cultural resource management in sub-Saharan Africa: Nigeria, Togo and Ghana. In Cleere, H. F. (ed.) *Archaeological Heritage Management in the Modern World*. One World Archaeology 9. London, Unwin Hyman, pp. 118–27.

Naffé, B. O. M., Lanfranchi, R. and Schlanger, N. (eds) 2008. *L'Archéologie préventive en Afrique: enjeux et perspectives*. Saint-Maur-des-Fossés, Éditions Sepia.

Nao, O. 2008. Preventive archaeology and the preservation of the cultural heritage in Burkino Faso. In Naffé, B. O. M., Lanfranchi, R. and Schlanger, N. (eds) *L'Archéologie préventive en Afrique: enjeux et perspectives*. Saint-Maur-des-Fossés, Éditions Sepia, pp. 100–2.

National Museum of Denmark 1992. *Sites and Monuments: National Archaeological Records*. Copenhagen, National Museum of Denmark.

Nietzche, F. 1899. *On the Genealogy of Morality*; translated from the German by William A. Haussmann and J. Gray. London, T. Fisher Unwin.

Nixon, T. (ed.) 2004. *Preserving Archaeological Remains in situ? Proceedings of the 2nd Conference 12–14 September 2001*. London, Museum of London Archaeological Service.

Noble, V. E. 1987. A problem of preservation: assessing significance of historic cultural resources in Illinois. In Emerson, T. E. and Rohrbaugh, C. L. (eds) *Nineteenth Century Archaeology in Illinois*. Springfield, IL, Illinois Historic Preservation Agency, pp. 33–43.

Nuttall, M. 1997. Packaging the wild: tourism development in Alaska. In Abram, S., Waldren, J. and Macleod, D. (eds) *Tourists and Tourism: Identifying People with Places*. Oxford, Berg, pp. 223–38.

Nye, E. 1987. *Ley Lines Worldwide: Explained with History, Map and Examples*. London, DLM Publications.

Nzewunwa, N. 1984. Nigeria. In Cleere, H. F. (ed.) *Approaches to the Archaeological Heritage*. Cambridge, Cambridge University Press, pp. 101–8.

Okamura, K. 2010. A consideration of heritage values in contemporary society. In Smith, G., Messenger, P. M. and Soderland, H. A. (eds) *Heritage Values in Contemporary Society*. Walnut Creek, CA, Left Coast Press, pp. 55–62.

Okamura, K. and Matsuda, A. 2010. Archaeological heritage management in Japan. In Messenger, P. M. and Smith, G. S. (eds) *Cultural Heritage Management: A Global Perspective*. Gainesville, FL, University Press of Florida, pp. 99–110.

O'Keefe, P. J. and Prott. L. V. 1984. *Law and the Cultural Heritage, Volume 1: Discovery and Excavation*. Abingdon, Professional Books.

Olivier, A. and Clark, K. 2001. Changing approaches to the historic environment. In Kobyliński, Z. (ed.) 2001. *Quo Vadis Archaeologia? Whither European Archaeology in the 21st Century? Proceedings of the European Science Foundation Exploratory Workshop, Madralin near Warsaw, 12–13 October 2001*. Warsaw, Institute of Archaeology and Ethnography Polish Academy of Sciences and Foundation 'Res Publica Multiethnica', pp. 92–102.

Omland, A. 2006. The ethics of the world heritage concept. In Scarre, C. and Scarre, G. (eds) *The Ethics of Archaeology: Philosophical Perspectives on Archaeological Practice*. Cambridge, Cambridge University Press, pp. 242–59.

Ota, S. B. 2010. Archaeological heritage management in India. In Messenger, P. M. and Smith, G. S. (eds) *Cultural Heritage Management: A Global Perspective*. Gainesville, FL, University Press of Florida, pp. 82–98.

Palmer, C. 2009. Reflections on the practice of ethnography within tourism. In Sørensen, M. L. S. and Carman, J. (eds) *Heritage Studies: Methods and Approaches*. London, Routledge, pp. 123–39.

Palmer, N. 1993. Treasure Trove and title to discovered antiquities. *International Journal of Cultural Property* 2 (2), pp. 275–318.

Parker Pearson, M. and Pryor, F. 2006. Visitors and viewers welcome? In Hunter, J. and Ralston, I. (eds) *Archaeological Resource Management in the UK: An Introduction*. 2nd edition (revised). Stroud, Sutton, pp. 316–27.

Patrik, L. E. 1985. Is there an archaeological record? In Schiffer, M. B. (ed.) *Advances in Archaeological Method and Theory* 8. New York, Academic Press, pp. 27–62.

Pearce, S. 2006. Museum archaeology. In Hunter, J. and Ralston, I. (eds) *Archaeological Resource Management in the UK: An Introduction*. 2nd edition. Stroud, Sutton Publishing, pp. 328–38.

Pellati, F. 1932. La Législation des monuments historiques en Italie. *Museion*, 17–18, pp. 26–9.

Perkin, H. 1989. *The Rise of Professional Society: England since 1880*. London, Routledge.

Petrov, N. 2010. Cultural heritage management in Russia. In Messenger, P. M. and Smith, G. S. (eds) *Cultural Heritage Management: A Global Perspective*. Gainesville, FL, University Press of Florida, pp. 153–61.

Pickard, R. (ed.) 2001a. Introduction. In Pickard, R. (ed.) *Policy and Law in Heritage Conservation*. London and New York, Spon, pp. 1–11.

Pickard, R. (ed.) 2001b. *Policy and Law in Heritage Conservation*. London and New York, Spon.

Pickard, R. (ed.) 2001c. Review. In Pickard, R. (ed.) *Policy and Law in Heritage Conservation*. London and New York, Spon, pp. 315–41.

Pokotylo, D. and Mason, A. R. 2010. Archaeological heritage resource protection on Canada: the legislative basis. In Messenger, P. M. and Smith, G. S. (eds) *Cultural*

Heritage Management: A Global Perspective. Gainesville, FL, University Press of Florida, pp. 48–69.

Politis, G. 1995. The socio-politics of the development of archaeology in Hispanic South America. In Ucko, P. J. (ed.) *Theory in Archaeology: A World Perspective*. London, Routledge, pp. 197–228.

Potter, P. B. 1994. *Public Archaeology in Annapolis: A Critical Approach to History in Maryland's Ancient City*. Washington, DC, Smithsonian Institution Press.

Potter, P. B. 1997. The archaeological site as an interpretive environment. In Jameson, J. H. (ed.) *Presenting Archaeology to the Public: Digging for Truths*. Walnut Creek, CA, AltaMira Press, pp. 35–44.

Potter, P. B. and Leone, M. P. 1986. Liberation not replication: 'Archaeology in Annapolis' analyzed. *Journal of the Washington Academy of Sciences* 76 (2), pp. 97–105.

Potter, P. B. and Leone, M. P. 1987. Archaeology in public in Annapolis: four seasons, six sites, seven tours, and 32,000 visitors. *American Archaeology* 6 (1), pp. 51–61.

Potter, P. B. and Leone, M. P. 1992. Establishing the roots of historical consciousness in modern Annapolis, Maryland. In Karp, I., Kramer, C. M. and Lavine, S. D. (eds) *Museums and Communities*. Washington, DC, Smithsonian Institution Press.

Prangnell, J., Ross, A. and Coghill, B. 2011. Power relations and community involvement in landscape-based cultural heritage management practice: an Australian case study. In Waterton, E. and Watson, S. (eds) *Heritage and Community Engagement: Collaboration or Contestation?* London, Routledge, pp. 148–64 [= *International Journal of Heritage Studies* 16 [1–2], pp. 140–45].

Priede, C. 2009. *Understanding Landscape Values: A Scottish Highland Case Study*. British Archaeological Reports British Series 502. Oxford, Archaeopress.

Pryor, F. 1989. Look what we've found: a case study in public archaeology. *Antiquity* 63, pp. 51–61.

Pugh-Smith, J. and Samuels, J. 1996. *Archaeology in Law*. London, Sweet and Maxwell.

Rahtz, P. 1976. *Rescue Archaeology*. Harmondsworth, Penguin.

RCHME 1998. *Thesaurus of Archaeological Terms*. London, Royal Commission on Historic Monuments for England.

Reed, A. D. 1987. A technique for ranking prehistoric sites in terms of scientific significance. *American Archaeology* 6 (2), pp. 127–30.

Reichstein, C. 1984. Federal Republic of Germany. In Cleere, H. F. (ed.) *Approaches to the Archaeological Heritage*. Cambridge, Cambridge University Press, pp. 37–47.

Reidlmayer, A. J. 2002. *Destruction of Cultural Heritage in Bosnia-Herzegovina, 1992–1996: A Post-War Survey of Selected Municipalities*. No. P486. The Hague, International Criminal Tribunal for the Former Yugoslavia.

Renfrew, C. 1983. 'Divided we stand': aspects of archaeology and information. *American Antiquity* 48 (1), pp. 3–16.

Renfrew, C. 1986. Introduction: peer polity interaction and socio-political change. In Renfrew, C. and Cherry, J. (eds) *Peer Polity Interaction and Socio-Political Change*. Cambridge, Cambridge University Press, pp. 1–18.

Riall, L. 2000. 'Garibaldi and the south', in Davis, J. A. (ed.), *Italy in the Nineteenth Century 1796–1900*. Oxford, Oxford University Press, pp. 132–53.

Rigambert, C. 1996. *Le Droit de l'archéologie française*. Paris, Picard.

Ronayne, M. 2007. The culture of caring and its destruction in the Middle East: women's work, water, war and archaeology. In Hamilakis, Y. and Duke, P. (eds) *Archaeology and Capitalism: From Ethics to Politics*. One World Archaeology 54. Walnut Creek, CA, Left Coast Press, pp. 247–66.

Roskams, S. 2001. *Excavation*. Cambridge Manuals in Archaeology. Cambridge, Cambridge University Press.

Rubertone, P. E. (ed.) 2008a. *Archaeologies of Placemaking: Monuments, Memories, and Engagement in Native North America*. One World Archaeology 59. Walnut Creek, CA, Left Coast Press.

Rubertone, P. E. 2008b. Engaging monuments, memories, and archaeology. In Rubertone, P. E. (ed.) *Archaeologies of Placemaking: Monuments, Memories, and Engagement in Native North America*. One World Archaeology 59. Walnut Creek, CA, Left Coast Press, pp. 13–33.

Russell, I. 2010. Heritages, identities, and roots: a critique of arborescent models of heritage and identity. In Smith, G. S., Messenger, P. M. and Soderland, H. (eds) *Heritage Values in Contemporary Society*. Walnut Creek, CA, Left Coast Press, pp. 29–42.

Saitta, D. 2007. Ethics, objectivity and emancipatory archaeology. In Hamilakis, Y. and Duke, P. (eds) *Archaeology and Capitalism: From Ethics to Politics*. One World Archaeology 54. Walnut Creek CA, Left Coast Press, pp. 267–80.

Salmon, M. H. 1982. *Philosophy and Archaeology*. New York, Academic Press.

Sanogo, K. 2008. Fondements et prémices d'une archéologie preventive au Mali. In Naffé, B. O. M., Lanfranchi, R. and Schlanger, N. (eds) *L'Archéologie préventive en Afrique: enjeux et perspectives*. Saint-Maur-des-Fossés, Éditions Sepia, pp. 97–9.

Saunders, A. 1983. A century of ancient monuments legislation, 1882–1982. *The Antiquaries Journal* 63, pp. 11–29.

Savile, A. 2006. Portable antiquities. In Hunter, J. and Ralston, I. (eds) *Archaeological Resource Management in the UK: An Introduction*. 2nd edition. Stroud, Sutton Publishing, pp. 69–84.

Scarre, C. and Scarre, G. (eds) 2006. *The Ethics of Archaeology: Philosophical Perspectives on Archaeological Practice*. Cambridge, Cambridge University Press.

Schaafsma, C. F. 1989. Significant until proven otherwise: problems versus representative samples. In Cleere, H. F. (ed.) *Archaeological Heritage Management in the Modern World*. One World Archaeology 9. London, Unwin Hyman, pp. 38–51.

Schadla-Hall, T. 2004. The comforts of unreason: the importance and relevance of alternative archaeology. In Merriman, N. (ed.) *Public Archaeology*. London, Routledge, pp. 255–71.

Schiffer, M. B. 1972. Systemic context and archaeological context. *American Antiquity* 37, pp. 156–65.

Schiffer, M. B. 1987. *Formation Process of the Archaeological Record*. Albuquerque, NM, University of New Mexico Press.

Schiffer, M. B. 1988. The structure of archaeological theory. *American Antiquity* 53 (3), pp. 461–85.

Schiffer, M. B. and Gumerman, G. J. (eds) 1977. *Conservation Archaeology: A Handbook for Cultural Resource Management Studies*. Studies in Archaeology. New York, Academic Press.

Schlanger, N. and Aitchison, K. (eds) 2010. *Archaeology and the Global Economic Crisis: Multiple Impacts, Possible Solutions*. Tervuren, Culture Lab Éditions.

Schnapp, A. 1984. France. In Cleere, H. F. (ed.) *Approaches to the Archaeological Heritage*. Cambridge, Cambridge University Press, pp. 48–53.

Schnapp, A. 1996. *The Discovery of the Past: The Origins of Archaeology*. London, British Museum Press.

Schnapp, A. and Kristiansen, K. 1999. Discovering the past. In Barker, G. (ed.) *Companion Encyclopedia of Archaeology*. London, Routledge, pp. 3–47.

Schofield, J., Carman, J. and Belford, P. 2011. *Archaeological Practice in Great Britain: A Heritage Handbook*. World Archaeological Congress Cultural Heritage Manuals. New York, Springer.

Schofield, J., Kiddey, R. and Lashua, B. D. 2012. People and landscape. In Skeates, R., McDavid, C. and Carman, J. 2012. *The Oxford Handbook of Public Archaeology*. Oxford, Oxford University Press, pp. 296–318.

Schwarz, M. and Thompson, M. 1990. *Divided We Stand: Redefining Politics, Technology and Social Choice*. Hemel Hempstead, Harvester Wheatsheaf.

Scollar, I, Tabbaugh, A., Hesse, A. and Herzog, I. 1990. *Archaeological Prospecting and Remote Sensing: Topics in Remote Sensing*. Cambridge, Cambridge University Press.

Scott, D., Babits, L. and Haecker, C. (eds) 2007. *Fields of Conflict: Battlefield Archaeology from the Roman Empire to the Korean War*, 2 vols. Westport, CT, Praeger.

Sebastian, L. and Lipe, W. D. (eds) 2009. *Archaeology and Cultural Resource Management: Visions for the Future*. School for Advanced Research Seminar Series. Santa Fé, NM, SAR Press.

Segobye, A. K. 2008. Layered histories and identities in the development of public archaeology in southern Africa. In Naffé, B. O. M., Lanfranchi, R. and Schlanger, N. (eds) *L'Archéologie préventive en Afrique: enjeux et perspectives*. Saint-Maur-des-Fossés, Éditions Sepia, pp. 164–86.

Shackel, P. A., Smith, L. and Campbell, G. 2011. Editorial: Labour's heritage. *International Journal of Heritage Studies* 17 (4), pp. 291–300.

Shanks, M. and McGuire, R. H. 1996. The craft of archaeology. *American Antiquity* 61 (1), pp. 75–88.

Shanks, M. and Tilley, C. 1987. *Reconstructing Archaeology: Theory and Practice.* Cambridge, Cambridge University Press.

Shannon, R. 1976. *The Crisis of Imperialism, 1865–1915.* London, Paladin.

Shaw, David, J. (ed). 2005. *Books and Their Owners: Provenance Information and the European Cultural Heritage.* London, Consortium of European Research Libraries.

Shen, C. 2010. Evaluating values of World Heritage sites and cultural tourism in China. In Smith, G., Messenger, P. M. and Soderland, H. A. (eds) *Heritage Values in Contemporary Society.* Walnut Creek, CA, Left Coast Press, pp. 255–66.

Shen, C. and Chen, H. 2010. Cultural heritage management in China: current practices and problems. In Messenger, P. M. and Smith, G. S. (eds) *Cultural Heritage Management: A Global Perspective.* Gainesville, FL, University Press of Florida, pp. 70–81.

Sherfy, M. and Luce, W. R. 1979. *How to Evaluate and Nominate Potential National Register Properties That Have Achieved Significance within the Last Fifty Years.* Washington, DC, US Department of the Interior Heritage Conservation and Recreation Service.

Silberman, N. A. 2010. Technology, heritage values and interpretation. In Smith, G., Messenger, P. M. and Soderland, H. A. (eds) *Heritage Values in Contemporary Society.* Walnut Creek, CA, Left Coast Press, pp. 63–74.

Sillevis, J. 1981. The Hague, Panorama Mesdag, 1881–1981. *The Burlington Magazine* 123 (945), pp. 766–7, 769.

Silverman, H. 2011. Border wars: the ongoing temple dispute between Thailand and Cambodia and UNESCO's World Heritage list. *International Journal of Heritage Studies* 17 (1), pp. 1–21.

Singh, M. 1994. Intellectuals in South Africa and the reconstructive agenda. In Bond, G. C. and Gilliam, S. (eds) *Social Construction of the Past: Representation as Power.* One World Archaeology 24. London, Routledge, pp. 203–23.

Skeates, R. 2000a. *Debating the Archaeological Heritage.* London, Duckworth.

Skeates, R. 2000b. *The Collecting of Origins: Collectors and Collections of Italian Prehistory and the Cultural Transformation of Value 1550–1999.* BAR International Series 868. Oxford, Archaeopress.

Skeates, R., McDavid, C. and Carman, J. 2012. *The Oxford Handbook of Public Archaeology.* Oxford, Oxford University Press.

Smardz, K. and Smith, S. J. (eds) 2000. *Archaeology Education Handbook: Sharing the Past with Kids.* Walnut Creek, CA, AltaMira Press.

Smith, C. (ed.) 2013. *Encyclopaedia of Global Archaeology.* New York, Springer.

Smith, C. and Burke, H. 2007. *Digging It Up Down Under: A Practical Guide to Doing Archaeology in Australia.* World Archaeological Congress Cultural Heritage Manual Series. New York, Springer.

Smith, G., Messenger, P. M. and Soderland, H. A. (eds) 2010. *Heritage Values in Contemporary Society.* Walnut Creek, CA, Left Coast Press.

Smith, L. 1993. Towards a theoretical framework for archaeological heritage management. *Archaeological Review from Cambridge* 12 (1), pp. 55–75.

Smith, L. 1996. Significance concepts in Australian management archaeology. In Clark, A. and Smith, L. (eds) *Issues in Management Archaeology*. St Lucia, Tempus Publications, University of Queensland, pp. 67–77.

Smith, L. 2004. *Archaeological Theory and the Politics of Cultural Heritage*. London, Routledge.

Smith, L. 2006. *Uses of Heritage*. London, Routledge.

Smith, L. and Akagawa, N. (eds) 2009. *Intangible Heritage*. Key Issues in Cultural Heritage. London, Routledge.

Smith, L. and Campbell, G. 1998. Governing material culture. In Dean, M. and Hindess, B. (eds) *Governing Australia: Studies in Contemporary Rationalities of Government*. Cambridge, Cambridge University Press, pp. 173–93.

Smith, L., Morgan, A. and van der Meer, A. 1993. Community-driven research in cultural heritage management: the Waanyi Women's History Project. *International Journal of Heritage Studies* 9 (1), pp. 65–80.

Smith, L. and Waterton, E. 2009. *Heritage, Communities and Archaeology*. Duckworth Debates in Archaeology. London, Duckworth.

Society for American Archaeology (SAA) 2000. Principles of archaeological ethics. In Lynott, M. J. and Wylie, A. (eds) *Ethics in American Archaeology*. 2nd edition. Washington, DC, Society for American Archaeology, pp. 11–12.

Soderland, H. A. 2009. The history of heritage: a method in analysing legislative historiography. In Sørensen, M. L. S. and Carman, J. (eds) *Heritage Studies: Methods and Approaches*. London, Routledge, pp. 55–84.

Soderland, H. A. 2012. America's cherished reserves: the enduring significance of the 1916 National Park Organic Act. In Skeates, R., McDavid, C. and Carman, J. (eds) *The Oxford Handbook of Public Archaeology*. Oxford, Oxford University Press, pp. 36–59.

Spector, J. 1993. *What This Awl Means: Feminist Archaeology at Dakota Village*. St Paul, MN, Minnesota Historical Society Press.

Spennemann, D. 2006. Out of this world: issues in managing tourism and humanity's heritage on the moon. *International Journal of Heritage Studies* 12 (4), pp. 356–71.

Schrire, C. 1995. *Digging through Darkness: Chronicles of an Archaeologist*. Charlottesville, FL, University Press of Florida.

Stancic, Z. and Veljankovski, T. (eds) 2001. *Computing Archaeology for Understanding the Past, CAA 98: Computer Applications and Qualitative Methods in Archaeology: Proceedings of the 28th Conference, Ljubljana, April 2000*. Oxford, Archeopress.

Startin, B. 1993. Assessment of field remains. In Hunter, J. and Ralston, I. (eds) *Archaeological Resource Management in the UK: An Introduction*. 1st edition. Stroud, Allan Sutton/IFA, pp. 184–96.

Stone, P. G. 2005. The identification and protection of cultural heritage during the Iraq conflict: a peculiarly English tale. *Antiquity* 79, pp. 933–43.

Stone, P. 2006. 'All smoke and mirrors . . . ': The World Archaeological Congress, 1986–2004. In Layton, R., Shennan. S. and Stone. P. (eds) *A Future for Archaeology: The Past in the Present*. London, UCL Press, pp. 53–64.

Stone, P. G. 2011. Introduction: the ethical challenges for cultural heritage experts working with the military. In Stone, P. G. (ed.) *Cultural Heritage, Ethics and the Military*. Heritage Matters. Woodbridge, Boydell Press, pp. 1–28.

Stone, P. and MacKenzie, R. (eds) 1990a. Introduction: the concept of the excluded past. In Stone, P. and MacKenzie, R. (eds) *The Excluded Past: Archaeology in Education*. London, Routledge, pp. 1–14.

Stone, P. and MacKenzie, R. (eds) 1990b. *The Excluded Past: Archaeology in Education*. London, Routledge.

Stone, P. G. and Planel, P. 1999. *The Constructed Past: Experimental Archaeology, Education and the Public*. One World Archaeology 36. London, Routledge.

Sullivan, D. 2000. *Ley Lines: A Comprehensive Guide to Alignments*. London, Piatkus Books.

Summers, R. S. 1991. Statutory interpretation in the United States. In MacCormick, D. N. and Summers, R. S. (eds) *Interpreting Statutes: A Comparative Study*. Aldershot, Dartmouth Publishing, pp. 407–60.

Summers, R. S. and Taruffo, M. 1991. Interpretation and comparative analysis. In MacCormick, D. N. and Summers, R. S. (eds) *Interpreting Statutes: A Comparative Study*. Aldershot, Dartmouth Publishing, pp. 461–510.

Sweeney, S. and Hodder, I. (eds) 2002. *The Body*. Cambridge, Cambridge University Press.

Swidler, N, Dongoske, K. E., Anyon, R. and Downer, A. S. (eds) 1997. *Native Americans and Archaeologists: Stepping Stones to Common Ground*. Walnut Creek, CA, AltaMira Press.

Swidler, N. and Yeatts, M. 2005. Traditional cultural properties and the national preservation program in the United States. In Mathers, C., Darvill, T. and Little, B. (eds) *Heritage of Value, Archaeology of Renown: Reshaping Archaeological Assessment and Significance*. Gainesville, FL, University Press of Florida, pp. 276–86.

Tainter, J. A. and Bagley, B. 2005. Shaping and suppressing the archaeological record: significance in American cultural resource management. In Mathers, C., Darvill, T. and Little, B. J. (eds) *Heritage of Value, Archaeology of Renown: Reshaping Archaeological Assessment and Significance*. Gainesville, FL, University Press of Florida, pp. 58–73.

Tainter, J. A. and Lucas, J. G. 1983. Epistemology of the significance concept. *American Antiquity* 48, pp. 707–19.

Tanaka, M. 1984. Japan. In Cleere, H. F. (ed.) *Approaches to the Archaeological Heritage*. Cambridge, Cambridge University Press, pp. 82–8.

Tarello, G. 1980. *L'interpretazione della legge*. Milan, Giuffry.

Tarlow, S. 2001. Decoding ethics. *Public Archaeology* 1, pp. 245–51.

Taylor, K. and Lennon, J. L. (eds) 2012. *Managing Cultural Landscapes*. Key Issues in Cultural Heritage. London, Routledge.

Thapar, B. K. 1984. India. In Cleere, H. F. (ed.) *Approaches to the Archaeological Heritage*. Cambridge, Cambridge University Press, pp. 63–72.

Thomas, J. 2004. *Archaeology and Modernity*. London, Routledge.

Thomas, S. 2012. Archaeologists and metal-detector users in England and Wales: past, present, and future. In Skeates, R., McDavid, C. and Carman, J. (eds) *The Oxford Handbook of Public Archaeology*. Oxford, Oxford University Press, pp. 60–81.

Thomason, A. K. 2005. *Luxury and Legitimation: Royal Collecting in Ancient Mesopotamia*. Perspectives on Collecting. Aldershot, Ashgate.

Thompson, M. 1979. *Rubbish Theory: The Creation and Destruction of Value*. Oxford, Clarendon Press.

Thornes, R. and Bold, J. (eds) 1998. *Documenting the Cultural Heritage*. Los Angeles, CA, J. Paul Getty Trust.

Tilley, C. 1989. Excavation as theatre. *Antiquity* 63, pp. 275–80.

Tilley, C. 1994. *A Phenomenology of Landscape*. Oxford, Berg.

Trigger, B. G. 1984. Alternative archaeologies: nationalist, colonialist, imperialist. *Man* 19, pp. 355–70.

Trigger, B. G. 1989. *A History of Archaeological Thought*. 2nd edition 2006. Cambridge, Cambridge University Press.

Troper, M., Grzegorczyk, C. and Gardies, J.-L. 1991. Statutory interpretation in France. In MacCormick, D. N. and Summers, R. S. (eds) *Interpreting Statutes: A Comparative Study*. Aldershot, Dartmouth Publishing, pp. 171–212.

Trow, S. and Grenville, J. 2012. Agriculture, environment, and archaeological curation in historic landscapes. In Skeates, R., McDavid, C. and Carman, J. (eds) *The Oxford Handbook of Public Archaeology*. Oxford, Oxford University Press, pp. 332–50.

Turner, S. and Fairclough, G. 2007. Common culture: the archaeology of landscape character in Europe. In Hicks, D., McAtackney, L. and Fairclough, G. (eds) *Envisioning Landscape: Situations and Standpoints in Archaeology and Heritage*. One World Archaeology 52. Walnut Creek, CA, Left Coast Press, pp. 120–45.

Twohig, E. 1987. Pitt Rivers in Munster 1862–65/6. *Journal of the Cork Historical and Archaeological Society* XCII (251), January–December 1987, pp. 34–46.

Ucko, P. J. 1986. *Academic Freedom and Apartheid*. London, Duckworth.

Ucko, P. J. (ed.) 1995. *Theory in Archaeology: A World Perspective*. London, Routledge.

Urry, J. 1990. *The Tourist Gaze*. London, Sage.

U.S. Advisory Council on Historic Preservation 2007. Section 106 Archaeology Guidance. Washington, DC, ACHP.

U.S. Department of the Interior 1989–90. *Federal Historic Preservation Laws*. Edited by Blumenthal, S. K. Washington, DC, US Department of the Interior.

Uzzell, D. and Ballantyne, R. 2008. Heritage that hurts: interpretation in a postmodern world. In Fairclough, G., Harrison, R., Jameson, J. H. Jr and Schofield, J. (eds) *The Heritage Reader*. London, Routledge, pp. 502–13.

Vitelli, K. D. (ed.) 1996. *Archaeological Ethics*. Walnut Creek, CA, AltaMira Press.

Wainright, G. J. 1989. The management of the English landscape. In Cleere, H. F. (ed.) *Archaeological Heritage Management in the Modern World*. One World Archaeology 9. London, Unwin Hyman, pp. 164–70.

Waterton, E. and Smith, L. (eds) 2010. *Taking Archaeology Out of Heritage*. Cambridge, Cambridge Scholars Press.

Waterton, E. and Watson, S. (eds) 2011. *Heritage and Community Engagement: Collaboration or Contestation?* London, Routledge [= *International Journal of Heritage Studies* 16 (1–2)].

Watkins, A. 1925. *The Old Straight Track: Its Mounds, Beacons, Moats, Sites and Mark Stones*. London, Methuen & Co.

Watkins, J. 2012. Public archaeology and indigenous archaeology: intersections and divergencies from a Native American perspective. In Skeates, R., McDavid, C. and Carman, J. (eds) *The Oxford Handbook of Public Archaeology*. Oxford, Oxford University Press, pp. 659–72.

Watson, P. J., Leblanc, S. A. and Redman, C. L. 1971. *Explanation in Archaeology: An Explicitly Scientific Archaeology*. New York, Columbia University Press.

Watson, R. A. 1991. What the new archaeology has accomplished. *Current Anthropology* 32 (3), pp. 275–91.

Wedgwood, C. 1957. *The Thirty Years' War*. London, Pelican.

Weissner, S. 1999. Rights and status of indigenous peoples: a global comparative and international legal analysis. *Harvard Human Rights Journal* 12, pp. 57–128.

Wheeler, R. E. M., 1954. *Archaeology from the Earth*. Oxford, Clarendon Press.

Welch, E. 2005. *Shopping in the Renaissance: Consumer Cultures in Italy, 1400–1600*. London, Yale University Press.

Wester, K. W. 1990. The current state of cultural resource management in the United States. In Andah, B. W. (ed.) Cultural Resource Management: An African Dimension. Forum on Cultural Resource Management at the Conference in Honour of Prof. Thurstan Shaw. *West African Archaeology* 20, pp. 80–88.

White, R. and Carman, J. (eds) 2007. *World Heritage: Global Challenges, Local Solutions: Proceedings of a Conference at Coalbrookdale, 4–7 May 2006 Hosted by the Ironbridge Institute*. BAR International Series 1698. Oxford, Archaeopress.

Whitelaw, G. 2005. Plastic value: archaeological significance in South Africa. In Mathers, C., Darvill, T. and Little, B. (eds) *Heritage of Value, Archaeology of Renown: Reshaping Archaeological Assessment and Significance*. Gainesville, FL, University Press of Florida, pp. 137–56.

Wilkie, L. A. 2006. Documentary archaeology. In Hicks, D. and Beaudry, M. C. (eds) *The Cambridge Companion to Historical Archaeology*. Cambridge, Cambridge University Press, pp. 13–33.

Willems, W. J. H. 1997. Archaeological heritage management in the Netherlands: past, present and future. In Willems, W. J. H., Kars, H. and Hallewas, D. P. (eds) *Archaeological Heritage Management in the Netherlands: Fifty Years State Service for Archaeological Investigations*. Amersfoort, Rijkdienst voor het Oudheidkundig Bodemonderzoek, pp. 3–34.

Willems, W. J. H. 2010. Laws, language and learning: managing archaeological heritage resources in Europe. In Messenger, P. M. and Smith, G. S. (eds) *Cultural Heritage Management: A Global Perspective*. Gainesville, FL, University Press of Florida, pp. 212–29.

Willems, W. J. H. and Brandt, R. W. 2004. *Dutch Archaeology Quality Standard*. The Hague, Dutch State Inspectorate for Archaeology.

Willems, W. J. H., Kars, H. and Hallewas, D. P. (eds) 1997. *Archaeological Heritage Management in the Netherlands: Fifty Years State Service for Archaeological Investigations*. Amersfoort, Rijkdienst voor het Oudheidkundig Bodemonderzoek.

Wood, J. 2006. Historic buildings. In Hunter, J. and Ralston, I. (eds) *Archaeological Resource Management in the UK: An Introduction*. 2nd edition. Stroud, Sutton, pp. 97–109.

Woolley, L. 1950. *Ur of the Chaldees*. Harmondsworth, Penguin.

Woolley, L. 1982. *Ur 'of the Chaldees': The Final Account, Excavations at Ur, revised and updated by P. R. S. Mooney*. London, Herbert Press.

World Archaeology 34 (2). 2002. *Community Archaeology*.

Yentsch, A. E. 1994. *A Chesapeake Family and their Slaves: A Study in Historical Archaeology*. Cambridge, Cambridge University Press.

Young, J. O. 2006. Cultures and the ownership of archaeological finds. In Scarre, C. and Scarre, G. (eds) *The Ethics of Archaeology: Philosophical Perspectives on Archaeological Practice*. Cambridge, Cambridge University Press, pp. 15–31.

Yu, P.-L. 2010. Experiencing heritage values among the Doro Ana Pumé of Venezuela. In Smith, G., Messenger, P. M. and Soderland, H. A. (eds) *Heritage Values in Contemporary Society*. Walnut Creek, CA, Left Coast Press, pp. 199–208.

Zimmerman, L. J. 1998. When data becomes people: archaeological ethics, reburial and the past as public heritage. *International Journal of Cultural Property* 7 (1), pp. 69–88.

Zimmerman, L. J. 2000. Regaining our nerve: ethics, values and the transformation of archaeology. In Lynott, M. J. and Wylie, A. (eds) *Ethics in American Archaeology*. 2nd edition. Washington, DC, Society for American Archaeology, pp. 71–4.

INDEX

access 5, 7, 22, 49–50, 56, 82, 91, 103, 143, 150,
    152, 154, 158–159, 168, 197
activism 49–50, 157, 197
activities (see also practices) 85–86, 96,
    119–120, 160, 179
administration 13–14, 54, 59, 67, 71–74,
    94–95, 111, 132–136, 141, 144, 154
Africa (and see individual countries) 41, 69,
    102, 118, 134, 137, 146, 149, 192, 198
alienation, from archaeology 40–41
American Anthropological Association
    (AAA) 75
Annapolis 164
antiquarian/ism 4, 91, 157
archaeological record 79–83, 102–103, 143,
    171–173, 191, 193–194
archaeological resource 7, 11, 31, 42, 79–83,
    103–106, 129–130, 135, 167, 171, 191
Archaeological Survey of India 16, 22–23
archaeology: alternative 179–180;
    general 57–58, 180; history 3–5, 37, 39–40,
    168–169, 187, 57; role 37, 156, 164, 167,
    169, 181, 196–197
Argentina 99, 132–133, 135–137, 140, 144, 146
Arthur, king 6, 19
Asia (and see individual countries) 69, 89,
    102, 134, 137
Athens 6, 13
Australia 6, 24–26, 34–37, 42, 46, 47, 55–56,
    69, 71, 80, 91, 94, 99, 110–111, 113, 118,
    121–127, 132–133, 135–137, 140, 146, 148,
    174, 198
Austria 13, 15, 53, 102
authority 5, 25, 68, 73–74, 98–103, 143, 154,
    178–180, 188–189

Babylon 4
Balkans 101–102
battlefields 165–166
Belgium 175
Benin 135
Bolivia 136, 138
Brazil 41, 99, 113, 132–133, 136, 140, 144
Britain 5–6, 8, 15–23, 26, 31–37, 39–40, 42–43,
    47–49, 53, 56–58, 61–62, 67, 70–72,
    74, 75, 80–81, 86, 88, 94, 100–102, 109,
    111–112, 116–119, 121–128, 134–135, 138, 142,
    145–146, 148, 152, 163, 165–166, 170–171,
    175–176, 179–180, 187, 193, 198
Bulgaria 35
bureaucracy (see also administration) 5
Bure, Johann 9–10
Burkino Faso 135, 140, 150
Burra Charter 46

Cameroon 135, 186
Canada 74, 99, 114, 133, 135–136, 140, 144, 146
Centrafrique 133, 140
Central America 73, 89
centralisation 14, 16, 32, 141
Chad 135, 186
characterisation 115–116, 166
Chile 136
China 32, 99, 114, 132–133, 140, 144, 146
citizen/ry/ship 5, 43, 48, 103, 141–142, 146, 168,
    170, 192
class 19–20, 47–49, 135, 175, 177–178
Classical past 6–7, 9, 11–14
codified law 59–60, 63
cognitive ownership 46, 152, 174–175, 197
Colombia 135

235